# FISHING FOR STRIPED BASS

**GARY CAPUTI**

# FISHING FOR STRIPED BASS

### GARY CAPUTI

## THE FISHERMAN LIBRARY CORP.
1620 Beaver Dam Road
Point Pleasant, New Jersey 08742

PRINTED IN THE UNITED STATES OF AMERICA
Library of Congress Cataloging-in-Publication data
ISBN 0-923155-19-8

THE FISHERMAN LIBRARY CORP.
1620 Beaver Dam Road
Point Pleasant, New Jersey 08742

Publisher . . . . . . . . . . . . . . . . . . . . . . . . . . . . . . . . Richard S. Reina
Associate Publisher . . . . . . . . . . . . . . . . . . . . . . . . . . . . Pete Barrett
Editor . . . . . . . . . . . . . . . . . . . . . . . . . . . . . . . . . . . . Linda Barrett
Design . . . . . . . . . . . . . . . . . . . . . . . . . . . . . . Allison Eagle-Rudnick
Cover Design and Illustration . . . . . . . . . . . . . . . Steve and Terri Goione
Layout . . . . . . . . . . . . . . . . . . . . . . . . . . . . . . . . . Sharon Mongan

# *INTRODUCTION*

Striped bass conjure up many memories, like pink, early-morning New England skies, the gentle swells rolling under the wooden hull of a bass boat. The skipper stands at the transom, tiller in hand, listening to the hum of the wire line as he trolls big Gibbs plugs in the rips between Cuttyhunk and the Vineyard.

There are nights spent on lone vigil at the end of the 8th Avenue jetty in Asbury Park, bass breaking under a school of frantic menhaden. The strain of the rod rebounding against the power of a trophy striper on a run for its life.

Warm mornings in May on the Delaware River under the shadow of the capitol building in Trenton, are remembered along with a shallow draft aluminum boat bobbing in "the falls". Stripers smashing into schools of hapless herring on their spawning run north, a ten pounder eagerly attacking a pencil popper is not easily forgotten.

I can recall the wind blowing over the hills at Kitty Hawk as the search for the elusive rockfish is conducted from the warm confines of a heated truck, the aroma of coffee steaming from an open thermos on the seat. Long rods jut skyward in the rack on the front bumper.

The memory of the sun rising over my shoulder while New York City slowly came to life in the early morning hours while fishing for bass next to the railroad bridge at Spyten Duyvel is still vivid. The unexpected crow of a cock pheasant can be heard from the Cloisters along the nearby East River is just as startling as the linesider attacking my yellow bucktail.

I can still feel the cold wind biting at my ears as it swirls around the windshield of the center console on a drizzly morning in late November, trolling off Island Beach State Park. Looking down at the cow bass laying on the deck at my feet, I simultaneously feel elated by the catch and guilty for killing this magnificent fish.

For people who have fished for striped bass for any number of years, these are the rewards of the sport. The memories of days spent fishing for what many regard as the finest game fish that swims. A fish of legend and beauty surrounded by a history as old as the United States, itself. A fish that has been revered since the day Henry Hudson first stumbled into New York Harbor and marveled at the majestic silver fish that "abounds in the crystal waters of this magnificent river."

For hundreds of years, fishermen have sought the striped bass as a source of food, income, recreation and enjoyment. From days of amazing abundance to more recent years of scarcity accompanied by the fear of a virtual collapse of the fishery, the striped bass remains the glory fish of anglers in our great coastal rivers, estuary systems and along the open ocean beaches of the northeast. It's the fish novice anglers dream of catching. The fish that experienced anglers chase all night, searching for the trophy that is their goal, sleep be damned.

Enough stories weave throughout the history of the East Coast about striped bass to fill a dozen volumes, but the purpose of this book is not a history lesson. It is to offer a better understanding of this great game fish and to exchange knowledge to vital to the successful pursuit of this often illusive quarry. Along the way, I hope to impart some of the respect and affection I have gained for the striped bass. The future of this fish is in the hands of sport fishermen, just like you and me.

Probably the most noticeable theme you will encounter when reading this book is the striped bass' remarkable diversity. They are found in a wide variety of habitats, both marine and fresh water. Their diet is as varied as the strategies the fish utilize to capture prey or scavenge an easy meal. Some are highly migratory, while stripers found in more southern waters don't migrate at all.

This diversity is even more evident in the wide variety of methods and techniques used to catch striped bass by sport fishermen. There are so many methods, in fact, that no one angler can claim to be an expert, or even knowledgeable, in all of them. For that reason, there will be times when I will defer to local experts to help expand on the specific techniques they use in their home waters. The list of those fishermen who have taken of their time to help with this book can be found on the acknowledgement page, but I would like to thank each and every one for their contribution at the beginning of this work. It adds immensely to the depth and breadth of the information this book offers.

Finally, there is no greater teacher than experience. This book will, hopefully, provide you with the information to help you get started catching striped bass, or provide veterans with a new tip or two. It will move through the basics of tackle and techniques, and offer insights into the fish itself. It is up to you, the angler, to put this information to use and hone it into the skills necessary to become proficient at finding and tempting striped bass into striking your offerings.

Happily, gaining experience is the most enjoyable part of the learning process, because it takes place on the water, in search of your quarry. To me, the greatest joy of bass fishing is not always the catching. It is also found in the days spent on the water, simply being there and sharing God's greatest creation, the oceans and inland waters of the earth, and the many creatures placed there for all to appreciate.

**Gary Caputi**

# *DEDICATION*

To my wife, Jeannette, who so generously allows me the freedom to pursue striped bass. To my parents, Alfred and Josephine, who never really understood my fascination with fishing but supported me in my madness. And lastly, to my little girl, Samantha, who sits on daddy's knee at the local pond to "catch a fish."

# ACKNOWLEDGEMENTS

As with any work of non-fiction, the author often finds himself indebted to many people. Some direct contributors to the book and others simply helpful in their support and friendship.

This work is a completion of knowledge gained over years of fishing in many places with many people under the tutelage of several excellent fishermen. Some are people who I've grown to love and respect. I would like to thank them for their help and support.

Foremost Pete Barrett, whose confidence in my ability as a writer and fisherman has been a driving force. My dear friend oftentimes mentor and valued fishing companion, Russ Wilson, whose amazing mind holds more fishing information than any library. Tom Fote, President of the Jersey Coast Anglers Association, whose untiring efforts promoting legislation to benefit the striped bass in the halls of congress and in the state house in New Jersey has placed all striped bass fishermen in his debt.

For insights into their local fishing scenes, I wish to thank Tim Coleman, one of New England's finest bass fisherman; Fred Golofaro, Long Island surf guru; Angelo and Abe Cuanang, for a look at how they do it on the West Coast; Bill Mathias for introducing me to the ways of freshwater stripers on beautiful Lake Anna those many years ago; John Chiola for his knowledge of fishing lures and techniques from the past; Joe Nunziato, just for being a great fishing partner whose mind works in only one direction, pursuit of the fish in striped pajamas; and to all those similarly stricken fishermen whose paths have crossed mine over the years while fishing for this majestic game fish.

# TABLE OF CONTENTS

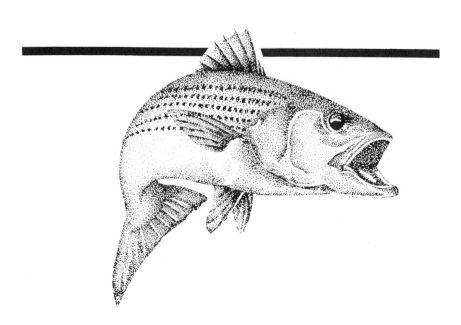

## Chapter One

# THE STRIPED BASS

From the rocky shores of Maine to the coastal rivers of the Gulf of Mexico, the striped bass is truly an all-American fish. Originally native to only the East Coast of the United States and southern Canada, a successful transplanting of fingerling stripers from the Navesink and Shrewsbury Rivers in New Jersey introduced striped bass to the Sacramento River in California in the late 1800s. The range of the striped bass now includes sections of both coasts of the United States. During the last forty years, the striped bass has been artificially introduced into major freshwater river systems and large, man-made lakes in the southeast and southwest.

There's a mystique that surrounds the striped bass. There's just something very special about this fish that makes grown men forget business, family, money and responsibilities as they seek to catch that next fish; that trophy that may be waiting at the next cast.

Through periods of abundance and decline, then renewed abundance, the striped bass has been one of the East Coast's most popular game fish. Many tackle shops exist primarily to service the ever growing numbers of bass anglers. Tackle companies specialize in building rods, lures, reels and even specialized lines that help anglers catch a few more bass. There's big business in recreational fishing for these terrific game fish.

Let's take a look at what makes them tick. The more we know about why, when and where striped bass do their daily routines, the greater will be our chances to catch them.

# Anatomy and Identification

How can the striped bass live and prosper in such diversified habitats? This is only one of the many interesting characteristics that make this fish so unique. The striped bass, once known by the scientific name *Roccus saxatilis,* is so different from most marine fish that scientists couldn't even agree on its Latin name. Some years ago, the scientific community decided *Roccus* was an incorrect terminology, so the name was changed to *Morone saxatilis,* but whatever you call it, the striped bass is unmistakable among marine fish. If its long, large head, projecting lower jaw, deep body and powerful, square tail aren't enough to give it away, the dark back, silver sides, multiple rows of dotted black lines running from the gills to the tail above its snow white belly, will surely do the trick.

It has two dorsal fins, roughly triangular in shape and of approximately equal length, but which are not connected. The back coloration may vary from olive green to black, but the silver sides and white underbelly are universal. The distinctive stripes which give this fish its name, may include seven or eight rows. The three to four rows located above the lateral line are the longest, often extending the full length of the body to the caudal fin. These lines can be straight, but in many fish they are broken and uneven. They are completely absent on young fish under 6 inches in length. The absence of stripes on small, young bass can make them easy to confuse with their closest relative, the white perch, especially since young bass and white perch are often found in the same habitat. Specimens over 10 inches are easily identifiable.

Beyond general appearance, the striped bass has perfectly evolved for its predatory life style. Its deep, powerful, highly-flexible body is built for maneuverability and short bursts of speed, rather than the sustained speed used by such open ocean predators as the tunas or sharks. The wide, square caudal fin is rooted in a tail section that is thick with muscles enabling the fish to accelerate quickly to pounce on unwary prey. The flexibility of its body allows it to make quick changes in direction, a great advantage when prowling inshore structure in search of a meal. If you've ever seen a striper toying with a live baitfish, slapping at it with its tail, you would be able to attest to the fish's amazing flexibility and its propensity for quick maneuvers.

The striped bass has highly developed senses of hearing, sight, smell and mechanoreception, the ability to detect movement in the water around its body. These acute senses are used to benefit its search for food. Knowledgeable fishermen, aware of how a bass uses its senses, can increase his chances of attracting and catching striped bass.

# Striped Bass Anatomy

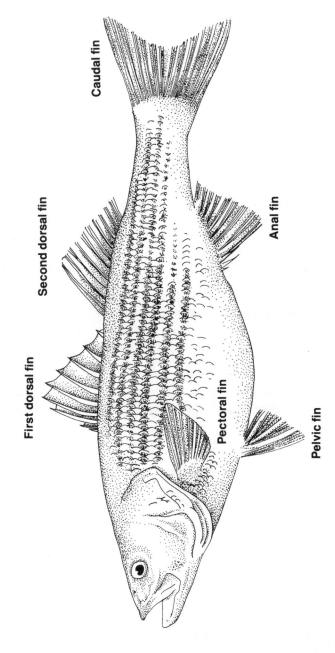

Caudal fin

Second dorsal fin

Anal fin

First dorsal fin

Pectoral fin

Pelvic fin

Probably the most interesting characteristic of the striped bass is its ability to live in both salt or freshwater, and in places where salt and freshwater mix. Like salmon, shad and some species of herring, the striped bass is anadromous, spending time in the open ocean, but returning to freshwater to spawn. We will cover this remarkable ability in another section, but it helps explain why striped bass are caught in such a wide array of habitats, and how this marine species can be hatchery raised and transplanted into rivers and lakes.

# Size and The Record Book

Legends persist of huge striped bass, over 100 pounds, that once prowled the coastal states from North Carolina to Maine. Such huge fish would be the envy of every sport fisherman who ever tried his luck at catching a trophy striper. Are they just myth, or does a 100-pound striped bass really exist today?

The question is a valid one and the possibility does exist that there are enormous stripers of these proportions swimming our coastal waters. The largest striped bass ever recorded was caught in a commercial fisherman's net off the coast of Edenton, North Carolina in the winter of 1891. That amazing specimen tipped the scales at an unbelievable 125 pounds and it was only one of many bass reported to have broken the 100-pound mark. An occasional photo surfaces from days past, showing 100-pound plus stripers being displayed by commercial fishermen, but in more recent years, those stories and chance encounters have become scarce. Even commercial fishermen targeting stripers as late as the 1950s have reported few fish over 80 pounds, and no reports of 100-pound stripers have been heard for many decades.

The mark to beat for modern day sport fishermen was set way back in 1913, when a Massachusetts angler, C. B. (Charlie) Church, caught a striped bass that shattered the imagination of the anglers of his time. The huge cow bass weighed 73 pounds and was estimated at over 6 feet in length. It was a fish that would endure in the record books for more than 60 years, until a spate of new challengers to the throne would emerge in the years between 1967 and 1982. Some call these bass the "Class of 70" because they all surpassed the magic mark of seventy pounds, a milestone in marine angling. Let's take a look at these fish of legend and the anglers who claimed, or came close to, that most coveted spot in the record books marked "Striped Bass All-Tackle World Record!"

Charlie Church's record stood unchallenged and was thought to be unbeatable by even the most dedicated striper fisherman. It wasn't until June of 1967 that the waters of Cuttyhunk, Massachusetts saw fit

# STRIPED BASS
# AGE TO WEIGHT & LENGTH CHART

| AGE | SEX | LENGTH | WEIGHT |
|---|---|---|---|
| 1 | F | 6 inches | — — |
| 1 | M | 6 inches | — — |
| 2 | F | 12 inches | 13 oz. |
| 2 | M | 12 inches | 11 oz. |
| 3 | F | 16 inches | 2 lb. |
| 3 | M | 15 inches | 1 lb., 10 oz. |
| 4 | F | 19 inches | 3 lb., 10 oz. |
| 4 | M | 17 inches | 2 lb., 8 oz. |
| 5 | F | 23 inches | 6 lb., 7 oz. |
| 5 | M | 20 inches | 3 lb., 9 oz. |
| 6 | F | 26 inches | 9 lb., 15 oz. |
| 6 | M | 23 inches | 6 lb., 3 oz. |
| 7 | F | 30 inches | 14 lb., 3 oz. |
| 7 | M | 27 inches | 10 lb., 13 oz. |
| 8 | F | 32 inches | 18 lb. |
| 8 | M | 29 inches | 13 lb., 10 oz. |
| 9 | F | 34 inches | 23 lb., 15 oz. |
| 9 | M | 32 inches | 18 lb., 7 oz. |
| 10 | F | 36 inches | 28 lb., 2 oz. |
| 10 | M | 34 inches | 22 lb., 3 oz. |
| 11 | F | 37 inches | 31 lb., 4 oz. |
| 11 | M | 35 inches | 25 lb., 4 oz. |
| 12 | F | 40 inches | 37 lb., 8 oz. |
| 13 | F | 42 inches | 41 lb., 4 oz. |
| 14 | F | 44 inches | 49 lb., 6 oz. |

* Note two interesting factors concerning age to length and weight in this chart. Starting at 3 years, female bass are larger and heavier than male bass the same age; males do not live as long as females (few males over 8 years were recorded during this survey and none over 11 years). These averages were derived from the examination of annual reings of scales taken from striped bass caught in the Chesapeake Bay by the Natural Resources Institute, University of Maryland during 1957 and 1958.

to give up another huge striped bass, this one falling to angler Charles (Charlie) Clinto. Fishing with his friend, Russ Keane, Clinto had booked a charter aboard skipper Frank Sabatowski's Cuttyhunk bass boat. They trolled big wooden plugs on wire line in the rips between Cuttyhunk and Martha's Vineyard and the catch included quite a few bass in the 30 and 40-pound range. The conditions were perfect for the night's fishing, with just the right combination of tide, moon and weather. That night, Charlie was to be rewarded with the largest striped bass caught on rod and reel in more than a half century.

The fish was brought to the International Game Fish Association (I.G.F.A.) weighmaster at Cuttyhunk and it pulled his registered scales to the exact mark Church's fish did 50 years earlier. It was 73 pounds, good enough to tie the record, but the fish was not recognized as a record catch, as wire line is not an accepted method of sport angling in the I.G.F.A. rule book. Even so, the fish sent shock waves through the angling community of the day, simply because it proved that Church's record could, indeed, be broken. New interest in beating Church's record was spawned and it didn't take long before another entry in the "Class of 70" would make its entrance.

Just two years later, Edward Kirker followed Charlie Clinto's lead when he landed a 72-pound striper from the same fishing grounds in the Elizabeth Island Chain, again from around Cuttyhunk. It was caught during the October full moon, a time when huge cow bass are starting their migration southward to winter. No more 70-pound bass were recorded until early in the decade of the 1980s when the record books would see names change, not once, but twice.

It started with a 71-pounder taken in Long Island Sound by John Baldino on July 14, 1980. The huge fish ate a bunker chunk meant for a bluefish! Once again, interest in breaking the striped bass world record was rekindled. It didn't take long before the unbelievable happened, the record fell!

It was the night of July 17, 1981 and well-known charter captain, Bob Rocchetta, was drifting the rips off Montauk Point at the eastern most end of Long Island. The night was made all the more eerie due to the lunar eclipse that was scheduled for that evening. Rocchetta, a respected striper fisherman, was swimming a large, live eel when it was inhaled by an enormous striper that taxed his tackle and fishing experience. The fish blew Church's all-tackle record right out of the record book, beating the old mark by over three pounds. This amazing 76-pound fish was expected to last the test of time and many expected it would take another 64 years before it could be beat, but the decade of the 70-pound striper was just getting rolling.

Montauk's Great Eastern Rock gave up another class member that very same year, this one, a 72-pound fish that ate a live eel fished by charter captain John Alberda. Tony Stetzko amazed beach fishermen

**The current IGFA all-tackle striped bass was caught by Al McReynolds and weighed a hefty 78-pounds, 8-ounces.**

that fall, by coaxing a 73-pound bass onto the beach, catching it on nothing more than a simple feathered teaser meant for school fish. This big striper was taken on the Cape, in Massachusetts and bolstered hopes that surf fishermen had as much of a chance at taking a record bass as boat fishermen.

Rocchetta's 76-pound mark was still standing firm when surf fisherman Al McReynolds walked out onto a jetty in Atlantic City, New Jersey, on the evening of September 21, 1982. The new record was barely one year old and was destined to last no longer. McReynolds was casting a Rebel Windcheater plug into the boiling surf at the base of the jetty, weather and wind conditions hampering his efforts. He had already beached several smaller bass when, on that eventful cast, the plastic plug was inhaled by a mouth large enough to eat the display rack the lure was purchased from a few days earlier.

The battle that ensued was one that will forever remain in the annals of surf fishing history. McReynolds fought the huge cow bass to a standstill on the unlikely combination of 12-pound test line, a diminutive Penn 710 spinning reel and a light jetty rod. When the fish was finally beached, no one could believe the feat that was accomplished. The fish was brought to a local tackle shop and placed on the registered scale. It dropped the needle to over 78 pounds, shooting Rocchetta's new mark from the pages of the I.G.F.A. Record Book.

Since McReynolds' amazing fish, no 70-pounders have been logged in. Many fish in the 50 and 60-pound class have been caught, but there have been no new entries into the record book next to the heading "Striped Bass All-Tackle World Record." Will another dominant year class of striped bass again send forth a host of big fish to challenge McReynolds' record like those caught early in the decade of the 1980s? Only time will tell.

# Life History

A striped bass begins life as one of hundreds of thousands of eggs expelled from its mother's anal vent during spawning, to be fertilized by one of several smaller males that surround her during the spawning ritual. Female striped bass can attain sexual maturity by their fourth year, but most do not become mature until they are at least 6-years-old. There is still much debate in the scientific community about the timing of sexual maturity of female striped bass, frequency of spawning and variations among different regional populations, but more on this later.

Females will continue to reproduce well into their teen years, becoming more prodigious spawners with each successive spawning season. Smaller, sexually mature females can produce as many as 65,000 eggs, while large cows in their teens can produce well over 5,000,000 eggs in a single reproductive cycle. This variation in prodigiousness among larger female bass is at the heart of some management tactics being used to determine size restrictions and catch limits in an effort to protect more of the larger females which produce the greatest volume of eggs at each spawning.

Spawning for coastal striped bass begins in the fish's southern Atlantic range as early as March or early April. This includes fish in North Carolina, Virginia and into the Chesapeake Bay region. Further north, spawning takes place later in the spring in relation to water temperature. For example, the striped bass population of the Hudson River usually spawns in April or May, while the population of the St. Lawrence River does not begin spawning until June or July. Spawning will begin when water temperature climbs into the mid 50 to low 60-degree temperature range and peak spawning activity takes place in water temperatures between 60 and 67 degrees.

Coastal striped bass spawn in freshwater rivers and streams, with some fish running upstream 100 miles or more. The spawners search for areas of strong current where there is also gravel, rock or sand bottom. Current flow is of critical importance to egg survival and hatching, since striped bass eggs must remain in suspension, prior to hatching. If insufficient current is present to keep the eggs moving, suspended in the water, they will settle to the bottom and die as the delicate membrane surrounding the egg fractures.

Eggs are a greenish color and extremely small, usually just over 1 millimeter in diameter. After being expelled from the female's body, and upon completion of the fertilization process, the egg will absorb water to create a protective space within the egg, causing it to swell to three times its original size. The eggs are semi-buoyant due to a natural oil globule found within the outer membrane. They will drift downstream with the current for 2 to 4 days before hatching. Hatching time is dictated by water temperature, the warmer the water the faster the development and hatching of the larval bass.

Once the egg hatches, it will have a small yolk sack attached to its abdomen by an umbilical cord. It takes 5 to 7 days for the small fish to completely absorb all the nutrients in the sack, at which time it disappears. The fry is on its own from the time it hatches. No parental care is exhibited by either the male or female after the spawning ritual is completed. This accounts for the large number of eggs produced by the female, since some eggs will not be fertilized and many more will not survive the first few weeks of life. Biologists estimate that as few as 5% of the eggs produced will survive to reach their first birthday.

As a note, fresh water striped bass populations living in landlocked environments, like the many TVA reservoirs of the south, do not reproduce naturally. This is due to the lack of acceptable spawning areas and insufficient current necessary to keep the eggs in solution. Stocks of landlocked striped bass are artificially maintained through hatchery rearing and stocking. There are a few notable exceptions like the fish of Santee-Cooper, which were trapped in a developing fresh water environment by the construction of dams in South Carolina. They are known to spawn in the races of hydroelectric dams, which generate sufficient current flow to enable some of the fish to spawn successfully.

During the first two years of the striped bass, it will stay within the estuary/river environment, feeding on small aquatic animals. It can attain sizes of 6 to 7 inches during its first year and grow to 12 or more and weight nearly a pound by the end of its second year.

Most coastal striped bass will begin moving out of their estuary habitat into bays and open ocean waters by the end of their second year. They usually will not join larger, migratory members of the species in their travels for another year or two. Growth continues at a relatively rapid rate. At 3 years, young fish will weigh up to 3 pounds and be 18 to 20-inches long. Fish of 24 inches average 5 pounds; fish of 30 inches weigh 10 to 15 pounds; fish of 33 to 36 inches weigh 16 to 20 pounds. A 7-year-old bass will average 36 inches in length and can weigh in at over 20 pounds. A 50-pound striped bass will be about 50 inches long and is about 16 to 17-years-old.

There are noticeable weight differences between male and female bass. Beginning at about 3 years of age, the female of the species is larger than the male of similar age and a female of any given length will always weigh more than a male. This difference becomes more pronounced the longer the fish, and is made more interesting by the fact that male bass do not live as long as females.

A study done in the Chesapeake Bay in the late 1950s determined that striped bass males rarely live to attain an age greater than 8 or 9-years-old. No males were found among samples of striped bass over 11 years, yet females regularly attain ages of 17 to 18 years. The oldest striper on record, as determined by scale samples, was a 23-year-old female. This anomaly is illustrated in the accompanying length to weight table, which depicts males in black and females in white. Notice that there are no males on the table above 35 inches in length and 25 pounds in weight.

The age of a striped bass is easily determined by scientists and laymen alike, since the fish's scales have annular rings similar to those found in the cross section of tree trunks. If you want to determine the age of a striped bass, remove a large scale from the fish's side, dye it with a water soluble ink and place it under a strong magnifying glass or a low-power microscope. You can determine the age by counting the rings on the scale at the rate of one ring for each year of life. A 6-year-old bass will have, obviously, 6 annular rings on its scales.

# Range

The natural range of the striped bass was once considerably smaller than it is today, having been expanded to new areas by the efforts of man. At the same time, some of its original ranges have been decimated by the adverse impacts of human advancement. Expanding human population with its accompanying alterations of the natural landscape to suit its needs, has taken a toll on the striped bass populations in some areas, especially those stocks located in ecologically fragile areas like Florida and coastal rivers of the Gulf of Mexico. Human tampering has also played a large part in the destruction of prime breeding habitat in some regions of the fish's range, most notably the great estuary known as the Chesapeake Bay. Add to this the burden of years of overfishing and pollution from hundreds of

# Striped Bass Distribution

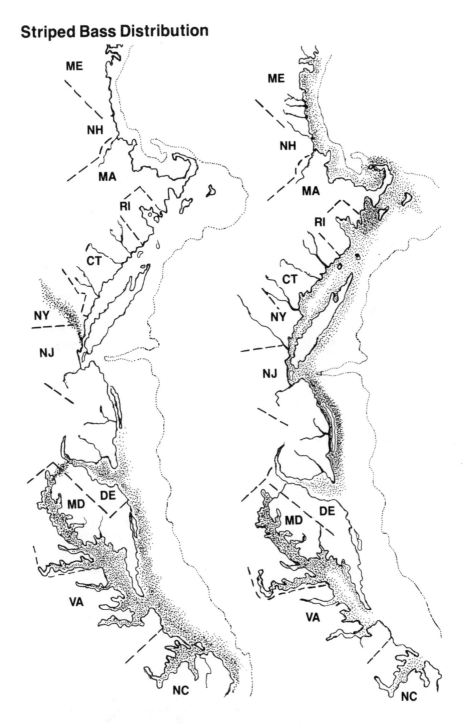

**Distribution of striped bass in winter (left) and summer (right).**

sources and it is a wonder that the striped bass population remains as strong as it does today.

In colonial times, striped bass were known to inhabit most of the beaches, estuaries and coastal rivers of the East Coast from the Gulf of St. Lawrence in Canada to the St. Johns River area of Florida. Smaller, non-migratory populations were also found in the coastal rivers of the Gulf states of Florida, Alabama, Mississippi and Louisiana. The Gulf populations, being the most fragile, were easily exploited to a state of collapse. It took generations to seriously damage the major coastal stocks from North Carolina through New England, which were the most abundant stocks and also the most migratory. Stocks in Canada have remained relatively stable, although they have experienced fluctuations in population strength and constitute only a small portion of the total Atlantic biomass of striped bass.

Striped bass were introduced into the Sacramento/San Joaquin River system and San Francisco Bay in California in the 1880s. Bringing captured striped bass taken from the natural population of the Navesink and Shrewsbury Rivers in New Jersey, the fish flourished in this environment for almost 100 years. The California striped bass stock is now experiencing similar problems as their Atlantic ancestors, but they don't stem from commercial over-harvesting pressure. Their dwindling population numbers seem to be caused more from habitat destruction and pollution than from overfishing.

While California striped bass don't migrate much outside of the two primary river systems that empty into San Francisco Bay, some did leave the area and found their way up the coast into the Coos Bay estuary of Oregon, where a confined, but strong breeding population exists today giving rise to a small, but fanatical fraternity of striper fishermen in this state, also.

Today, through experimentation by man, striped bass are also found in such diverse places as the Colorado River system and Lake Mead in the Nevada desert. Many of the larger reservoirs found in Virginia, West Virginia, North Carolina, South Carolina, Georgia, Kentucky, Tennessee, Texas and Arizona hold striped bass while smaller, less successful stockings of stripers take place in many smaller impoundments in other states. Add to this one of man's achievements in artificial fish propagation, a hybrid striped bass, also known as a sunshine bass, and the fish's freshwater range increases dramatically.

Hybrid striped bass are the man-made product of cross breeding the striped bass and its close relative, the white bass, which produces a non-fertile hybrid that mimics characteristics of both of its parental blood lines. It grows faster than a striped bass and is similar in appearance, but it has some striking differences, too. The hybrid's body is shorter and much deeper than a striper, sporting a proportionately smaller head, mouth and tail.

The hybrid is a voracious feeder that exhibits a strong schooling tendency like its white bass parents. They are well adapted to life in lakes and river systems, preying on almost any forage fish. They attain a respectable size, usually up to 15 pounds, and they are exceptional fish to catch on light to medium-weight tackle.

Hybrids are incapable of reproducing within their species. Two hybrids cannot produce offspring through natural fertilization similar to the way mules cannot reproduce by mating with other mules. For this reason, biologists felt sure that hybrids could not damage impoundments they were stocked in through over-population. Also, for just this reason, hybrid striped bass are strictly a put and take fishery, since populations can be maintained only through hatchery propagation and stocking of these fish.

My home state of New Jersey experimented with hybrids in a few smaller lakes with less than overwhelming success. As a result of one such stocking in Union Lake in the states southern region, these fish were inadvertently introduced into Delaware Bay and the Delaware River, through a series of blunders. Union Lake experienced problems with its retaining dam, and when the dam was under reconstruction, hybrids escaped the confines of the lake and migrated down the Maurice River and into Delaware Bay. Since this occurred in the early 1980s, hybrids have been intermingling with natural striped bass populations in this estuary system and they are caught regularly by recreational anglers. Biologists are unsure of the impact this mixing of species will have, if any at all, since it is not known whether hybrids can reproduce with natural striped bass.

## Seasonal and Regional Migrations

Coastal striped bass are migratory fish, but not all stripers migrate the same distance as specific regional stocks. These regional stocks or races are not different enough to be termed subspecies of the striped bass, but do have some characteristics that differ from one stock to another. The differences are minor and almost unnoticeable to fishermen, but scientists who have studied this phenomenon can distinguish certain stocks by fin-ray count and the number of scales along the fish's lateral line.

There is evidence of specific regional stocks or races in the Nova Scotia/New Brunswick areas of Canada, the Hudson River, the Chesapeake Bay, Albemarle Sound in North Carolina, Santee-Cooper in South Carolina and the St. Johns River area of Florida. These races seem to avoid intermingling with members of other races of striped bass, although this avoidance is not complete. As many as 25 percent of the Hudson River stock will intermingle, migrate and reproduce with

# Seasonal Migration Patterns

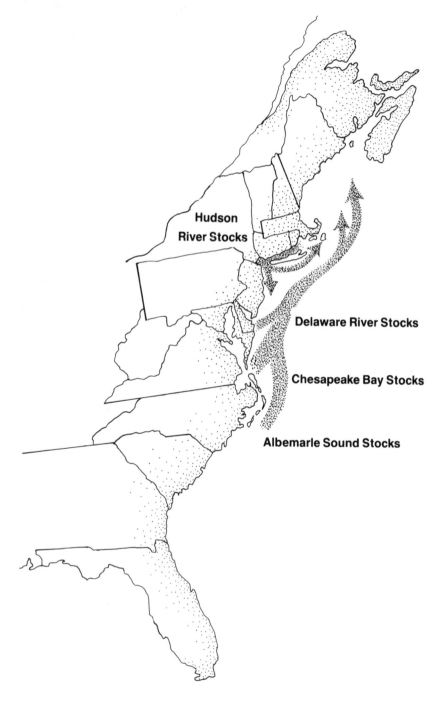

Hudson
River Stocks

Delaware River Stocks

Chesapeake Bay Stocks

Albemarle Sound Stocks

Chesapeake Bay fish. This intermingling seems to be greatest when a highly migratory stock comes into contact with less migratory stocks.

To add to the confusion, striped bass don't take part in just one type of migration, but two. Stripers migrate up rivers and streams into fresh water to spawn, just like salmon, except they do not die after reproducing. In addition to spawning migrations, striped bass from North Carolina, Chesapeake and Delaware Bays undertake another more ambitious wintering migration for reasons that are largely unknown. This migration is embarked upon by a portion of the natural populations of these areas and usually includes only fish over 3-years-old.

This migration will usually begin after spawning season when large bodies of mature fish will leave the confines of their estuary systems and head out into the open ocean. There, the fish will head northward, skirting the beaches and inshore areas of New Jersey, New York, Connecticut, Rhode Island, Massachusetts on up into Maine and even southern Canadian waters. There, the fish will intermingle with local striped bass populations feeding on abundant marine life only to begin their southerly migration back to their home waters in September and October. This migration of striped bass is an arduous journey and tagged fish have been recorded as making a round trip encompassing a distance of over 1,000 miles in each direction.

For reasons unknown to scientists and fishermen alike, not all stripers within these races migrate every year. Even more interesting is that this great migration seems dominated by only two or three regional stocks. Striped bass of the Hudson River stock migrate, but not nearly as extensively as other races. Tag return studies have shown Hudson River fish are usually most prominent in the waters off New Jersey and Long Island, with many fish found in the waters of Long Island Sound and off southern New England during the summer months, but few have been recorded further north.

No major migratory travels are undertaken by the remaining populations in southern waters and in the tributary rivers of the Gulf of Mexico. It is believed that these races are, with the exception of short spawning migrations, completely non-migratory.

## Feeding Habits

Discussing the diet of a mature striped bass, it almost becomes easier to list the marine creatures it doesn't eat rather than the ones it does. Striped bass are prolific hunters and voracious feeders. At some time during their life cycle they will consume just about any type of fish encountered that is small enough to fit into its gaping maw. Add to that its inexhaustible appetite for shellfish, crabs and worms and you have a living, breathing Hoover vacuum cleaner of the ocean.

Some of the fish stripers regularly feed upon include menhaden, sea herring, mullet, mackerel, summer and winter flounder and eels. The list grows longer when you include less commonly known prey such as shad, blackfish, sea bass, hake, ling, immature striped bass and bluefish. Keep in mind that any target of opportunity flashes an "open for lunch" sign to a hungry striped bass. I've heard stories about bass taking hooked kingfish or tomcod being reeled in by an unsuspecting angler and one friend found four blowfish in a freshly caught striper's belly.

The list gets even longer when we include non-fish dinners. Bass will gobble up crabs (pick a species, they're not very choosy), clams, lobsters, shrimps, squid, sandworms, blood worms, tape worms and mussels. With a diet as varied as this, it isn't hard to understand why fishermen use so many different kinds of bait to fish for bass and they employ an even greater variety of artificial lures in an attempt to match this wide array of food when fishing for stripers.

For the fisherman, it is equally important to know when striped bass feed as it is to know what they feed upon and this is a subject of much debate by anglers. During the winter months, striped bass feed very little in more northern climates where water temperatures can place

**Striped bass have voracious appetites and can inhale a whole bait, like this 1-pound bunker, with ease.**

them in a comatose state of near hibernation. In southern waters, they will stay relatively active year-round, but they will feed most actively in morning or evening hours, with reduced feeding activity taking place during daylight hours.

After spawning, from spring through early fall, stripers will do the majority of their feeding during the hours of darkness, with feeding activity starting around sunset and ending around sunrise the next morning. This is not a hard and fast rule, as bass will venture into shallow water to feed in daylight at times, but daylight feeding forays during these months are usually accomplished in deeper water or made on overcast days and are relatively short in duration.

This propensity toward nocturnal feeding is a direct result of their large eyes and excellent vision. Just as you would not spend much time in the sun if you had no eyelids to help shield your eyes against excessive and damaging amounts of light, bass are similarly affected. They do not have the benefit of eyelids and therefore must adjust their behavioral patterns to take this problem into account. During times of the year when the sun is high in the sky, causing increased brightness and light penetration into the water, striped bass must move away from the shallows where they do their heaviest feeding, into the shadowy deeper waters that afford protection for their eyes.

During the summer months, when light penetration has its greatest influence, bass become nocturnal feeders, doing almost all of their shallow water feeding under the cover of darkness. The same large, highly efficient eyes that force them to avoid bright light becomes a great ally during night feeding because they offer excellent vision under low-light conditions. Bass have the ability to silhouette prey against the lightness of the evening sky from great distances. Combine their excellent eyesight with an acute sense of smell, hearing and mechanoreception and you have a fish that is perfectly suited for night feeding.

As the sun arcs lower in the sky in the later months of fall, bass will start to change their feeding habits and, once again, feed more heavily during daylight. At this time of year, daylight might be nearly as bright as it was during the summer months, but due to the sun's lower angle in the sky, light penetration into the water is greatly decreased and far less bothersome to the striper. Bass can often be found in very shallow water in morning and evening, but dependent upon the degree of cloud cover, they will usually move off into somewhat deeper water as daylight grows brighter.

This behavioral pattern dictated by the brightness of the sun and light penetration into the water is one that serious fishermen take into account each and every time they go after striped bass. Paying attention to the light can increase your catch and save you many fishless hours on the water.

Freshwater striped bass exhibit a more defined menu of prey, with most lake and impoundment fish feeding almost exclusively on forage fish. The most prominent prey is the gizzard shad, a freshwater baitfish that can attain sizes to over a pound in weight. In many southern impoundments, gizzard shad overpopulate waters because upon attaining the upper reaches of their size range, there are few, if any, predators occurring naturally to thin the population. The stocking of striped bass into many of these impoundments was aimed at introducing a larger predator into the food chain capable of decreasing these out of control stocks of oversized gizzard shad.

The experiment worked well in most waters, with striped bass naturally preying on these large baitfish, just as marine striped bass feed on large sea herring and menhaden. Since striped bass do not reproduce naturally in most impoundments, the population of stripers could be controlled through hatchery stocking to meet the needs of an individual impoundment without over-taxing the lakes food supply. But stripers, being the diverse predator that they are, expanded their menu to include such delights as crayfish when small, sunfish, bream, immature bass and even catfish as they grow to larger sizes.

# Management

Without question, the striped bass is the most regulated species of fish found along our coasts. From the early days of the Plymouth colonies to present times, striped bass have been recognized as a valuable resource and efforts to prevent over-harvesting, whether successful or not, have been imposed.

As early as 1623, Massachusetts settlers recognized the importance of the striped bass as a food source and economic commodity. Even though stripers were abundant in the early years of the settling of the New World, our forefathers also realized that they were a finite resource and took steps to protect them. An act passed by the General Court of Massachusetts Bay Colony in 1639 declared that "neither cod nor bass should be used as fertilizer for farm crops," due to the wastefulness of the practice and the importance of the species as food fish. This simple declaration was the first law on this continent that served to protect an animal species from wasteful practices and over-harvesting. Little did our forefathers realize that 250 years later, the fishery they sought to protect would be exploited to the point of near collapse.

It wasn't until the late 1970s and early 1980s that it became woefully evident that the striped bass population of the East Coast was in serious decline and, if it was to survive, drastic measures had to be taken. The Atlantic States Marine Fisheries Commission, composed of directors of each coastal state's fish and game division, began a progression of emergency regulations and measures to help stop the inevitable collapse of the fishery.

Groups of concerned recreational fishermen from New York, New Jersey, Delaware and Maryland began banding together to form larger, more politically active associations, and began fielding lobbyists with the goal of generating pressure on government bodies to act on behalf of protecting the striped bass. Things began to happen as the fishery continued its decline and more interested sport fishermen and even some isolated commercial fishing interests realized that they were killing the "goose that lays the golden eggs."

Today, through the efforts of these groups, great strides have been made. While legal game fish status prohibiting the commercial slaughter and sale of these fish still alludes these groups on a federal level, there have been important victories won at the state level. Four states on the eastern seaboard today have made the striped bass a game fish within their waters, prohibiting all commercial capture and sale, with the exception of hatchery-raised fish. Hopefully, the commercial sector will realize that the future of striped bass as a commercially available food fish is in aquiculture (hatchery farming) and not through the netting of the fish in the wild. Pilot programs have proven that striped bass can be raised for market successfully and cost effectively, providing the market place with the size fish (often referred to as plate size), most desirable for sale to fish markets and restaurants.

With all the regulations in place today at both the state and federal level, it becomes extremely important for recreational fishermen to know the laws governing the fishery in the states they fish. Then, take into consideration that any striped bass caught in federal waters, more than 3 miles offshore, fall under the regulatory powers of the federal government and federal law presently imposes a moratorium on striped bass fishing. That means you cannot keep any stripers caught in waters under federal jurisdiction, whether caught by sport fishermen or commercials.

With this wide array of laws and regulations to be followed, it becomes extremely important to stay current with the law. This can be accomplished by contacting the Division of Fish and Game in your home state, questioning knowledgeable people at local tackle shops, or by reading publications which carry frequent updates on the latest rules and regulations in the states it serves.

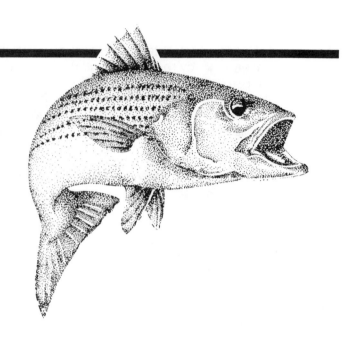

## Chapter Two

# TACKLE AND EQUIPMENT

When looking at tackle for striped bass fishing, the list of applicable equipment is long and extremely varied, dictated by the variety of methods employed to catch bass and also by the wide range of environments they are found in. The spinning outfit with 10-pound test line that caught schoolies in the Delaware River in May just doesn't cut it for casting 4-ounce swimming plugs into a raging surf at Montauk on the October full moon. That light, 7-foot trigger stick with the wide-spool baitcasting reel and 15-pound test you used for diamond jigging school bass from a boat during the November run would be useless trolling bunker spoons for trophy fish during the same time of year.

You can narrow the list of tackle you need by defining the type of fishing you will be participating in most, and then look only at the tackle you need to best accomplish it. If you plan on doing the majority of your striper fishing from the beach, then spend your time looking over tackle applicable to beach fishing. Same goes for jetty fishermen, river fishermen, back bay fly rodders or boat fishermen who like to troll. This chapter on tackle and equipment will be broken down into sections by types of fishing, rather than classifications of tackle to make your needs easier to define and fill.

Here is something to consider before you purchase any tackle for striped bass fishing. These are a powerful fish that will tax your tackle to its maximum capabilities. In addition, some of the techniques used to fish for bass can be punishing to your tackle. For just these reasons, it is important to purchase the highest quality equipment your budget allows when plunking down your hard-earned money for a new outfit. Do not settle for the bargain outfit featured in the local department store's ad in the Sunday circular just because the price is attractive. Stick with rods and reels made by recognized names in the industry who take pride in building quality tackle and who back it with a strong warranty and service policy. If you are new to fishing or unsure of yourself, ask more knowledgeable fishermen which products they use and why. Talk to tackle shop personnel and ask their opinion of the quality of the products from different manufacturers before discussing your specific tackle needs.

You will find that a few manufacturers dominate the quality tackle market and they have earned their reputations by offering products that perform exceptionally well over the long haul. Seek them out and you will be sure of purchasing tackle that will provide reliable service for many years. Buy bargain basement tackle and you will, no doubt, suffer the disappointment of losing fish to tackle failures and the realization that the "cheap stuff" needs to be replaced far more frequently than high-quality gear.

# Surf Fishing Gear

Fishing the surf for stripers requires specialized tackle, and those requirements can differ from one locale to another as surf fishing techniques and methods vary along the striper coast from New England's rocky shoreline to the sandy beaches of North Carolina's Outer Banks.

Several factors will determine the rods and reels used in your area, but prime considerations for this purpose are the weight of the lures or baits to be used, casting distance necessary for your area to reach the available structure, and the style of tackle you prefer, spinning or conventional. Let's take a look at several basic rod and reel outfits that will work for the majority of conditions you will encounter regardless of the areas you fish. We'll break them into classifications by the terminal tackle they are meant to handle, with further choices influenced by the casting distance needed to fish your home waters.

Much surf fishing for striped bass today utilizes a family of relatively light artificial lures in the 3/4 to 1 1/2-ounce range. A rod and reel to handle such popular lures as Bomber plugs, Redfins, needlefish, small metals and medium-size bucktails will, undoubtedly, be one of the most heavily used outfits in your arsenal. Both newcomers and veteran surf anglers alike, have proven the effectiveness of these lures and a whole new generation of tackle has been developed to make using them even more effective. Starting with the rod, let's put together a surf outfit for fishing the light stuff.

Casting lighter, wind-resistant plugs requires rods with special actions from 8 to 9½ feet long. Blank material of preference for this outfit is graphite, which has the ability to load and unload more rapidly and

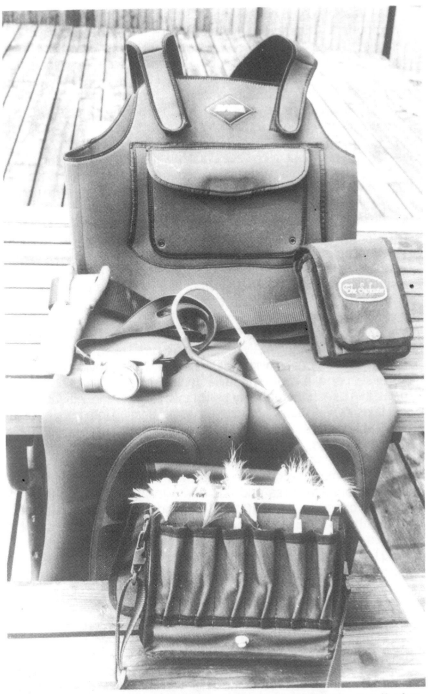

The well-equipped surf angler uses waders, head lamp, short gaff, plug bag and belt with pliers, fish stringer and accessory gear.

with far greater velocity, providing increased casting distance, while offering the added benefit of increased sensitivity, making it easier to detect a soft strike.

Surprisingly, there are few off-the-shelf rods offered by major tackle companies that fit this niche, but a recently introduced line of graphite rods from St. Croix is a notable exception. Designed by a well-known Hatteras surf guide and marketed as the Ben Dorr Surf System Series, the line includes the SS86M, and at 8½ feet it works well with lures that weigh 5/8 to 1½-ounces. While few manufacturers offer rods of this type, most shore-area tackle shops build custom models from blanks by Lamiglas, Fenwick, G. Loomis and Fisher that accomplish throwing light lures long distances with relative ease. Most custom rods in this range are between 8 and 9 feet in length.

Match the rod with a medium-size spinning reel, preferably one that incorporates the latest in long spool, long cast technology to help you get the most casting distance from lighter lures. A super-smooth drag system is a must in any reel used for stripers and the reel should have at least 200 yards of line capacity when loaded with a premium 12 or 15-pound test monofilament. You now have a highly versatile outfit that will quickly become your favorite for light to medium surf duty and it is capable of handling surprisingly large fish from the beach in the hands of a skilled angler. My light outfit has taken bass over 30 pounds from the beach with relative ease while providing me with more thrills per minute than heavier tackle ever could. As time goes by, I find it in use more than any outfit I own for surf and jetty use, plus it now finds service fishing from open boats, casting into bars or other shore-line structure.

For bigger lures, and baits that require heavy sinkers to get them out and keep them on the bottom, a longer, heavier action outfit is necessary. It must be capable of throwing big plugs in the 2 to 4-ounce range, metal lures and bait rigs with up to 5 or 6-ounces of lead. It will consist of a rod 10 to 12-foot rod, matched to a reel rated for line in the 15 to 25-pound range. This outfit will handle lures of 2 to 5-ounces.

Most long surf rods are either fiberglass, or a composite of glass and graphite. Rods constructed of 100% graphite in this size are quite expensive and the advantages of graphite in big surf sticks is not as important as in lighter action rods. Big surf rods are available from most tackle companies that offer saltwater rods including Penn, Fenwick, St. Croix, Lamiglas, Berkley, Daiwa and others. It's not a bad idea to search out a few anglers who know this type of fishing in your area and ask their advice before purchasing a big surf stick, since some regional differences in length and action do exist. You will also find a wide range of custom surf rods at many shore-area tackle shops which may fit your price range and needs.

Long rods will need a considerably larger reel, capable of holding 250 yards of 20-pound test line, with a smooth drag system. Most larger surf reels leave off the extra whistles and bells found on smaller spinning reels in favor of keeping them simple with fewer parts to break. Some of the standards are the Penn SS650, SS750 and their older 704Z; the Crack 300, still a cult reel in many areas of the striper coast; Daiwa's excellent long cast SS9000, Shimano's 4500 and 5500 Baitrunner reels; Mitchell's 406 and a few others. Since extremely large spinning reels make up a very small portion of the total fishing reel market, not all manufacturers address this segment of the market within their product lines, so there are fewer choices than in the lighter spinning reel categories.

While not many surf anglers use conventional reels for striped bass today, there is still a small, highly-skilled group of fishermen who prefer revolving spool reels for their heavier outfits. In the hands of a skilled caster, a revolving spool outfit will cast consistently farther than a surf spinning outfit. Anglers who prefer conventional tackle will tell you they get greater control of lures like big, heavy swimming plugs and with bait rigs when using revolving spool reels. They also believe that revolving spool reels have superior drag systems for fighting big fish. Finally, conventional surf outfits allow an angler to use heavier line, up to 40-pound test for special situations, and still get adequate casting distance.

Conventional outfits have their downside, too. Learning to surf cast

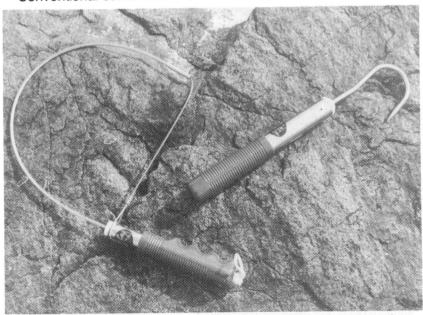

**So-Lo Marine's short-handled trailer allows fish to be released unharmed. Gaff is for trophy fish.**

with revolving spool reels is an arduous task and will, no doubt, cause serious frustration problems for beginners, not to mention a burnt thumb and the cost of the line ruined with monstrous backlashes. Take it from someone who has learned to cast conventional tackle the hard way; even after considerable practice, the occasional backlash will still occur, which subtracts from your fishing time. When fishing in the dark, a backlash in a conventional reel is a nightmare. I still prefer conventional tackle when fishing the Hatteras surf for channel bass, for soaking chunk baits for big bluefish in daylight hours or even for dunking clam baits in the surf for bass, but I opt for spinning gear for the vast majority of the surf fishing situations where striped bass are involved.

Most conventional surf sticks are custom built. An extra-heavy eleven footer (SS 11H) is available as part of the St. Croix Surf System series and Penn Fishing Tackle offers a killer 10-foot stick (SLC-2910MH) as part of their Slammer Rod series. Conventional reels for surf casting include Abu-Garcia's Ambassaduer 7000, 9000 and 10,000C, Penn's Mag Power 980 and 990, the old standby Penn Squidder, Surfmaster and Beachmaster reels, and probably the longest casting of any of the conventional surf reels, the Newell 220, a West Coast reel designed by a medical equipment genius turned tackle manufacturer, Carl Newell.

The pound-test line needed for your big stick is another topic debated by surf fishermen and it varies from one area to another, depending upon fishing conditions. Along rocky beaches like those found in New England or Long Island's north shore, the preference is toward heavier mono, 25-pound test, or heavier. Surf rats fishing in more sandy areas will prefer 15-pound test on their long sticks in the belief that lighter, thinner lines spook fewer fish and cast lures a greater distance. The decision is ultimately yours, but keep in mind that when using spinning tackle, the heavier the line, the greater the loss in casting distance, so try to stick with the lightest line your regional conditions will allow.

Many surf regulars carry one additional outfit for very light lures, such as bucktails, 5-inch swimming plugs, small poppers and spoons. It is usually employed when school bass are in the wash of the surf, or when fishing inside rivers, inlets and bays. It consists of a 7 to 7½-foot, medium action rods and a small spinning reel filled with 8 or 10-pound test mono and it fills a niche for the beach fishermen seeking light tackle action, usually in a calm surf or on the back side of the beach in bay waters.

The outfits we've just assembled will cover the majority of the situations you will encounter when fishing for striped bass from the beach. There will always be regional differences in preferred rod length, action and line test used, but these can be taken into consideration as your knowledge increases and your tastes in tackle become more discerning and personalized. As your proficiency increases with experience, you will find yourself adding outfits to your tackle arsenal to fit a variety of needs that less knowledgeable anglers would never consider.

# More Gear

The list of equipment an angler needs for surf fishing doesn't stop with a rod and reel. Let's start with your feet. A good pair of waders are a necessity for beach fishing, since much of the best beach fishing takes place in the spring and fall months when the water is cool and air temperatures can be chilly. Striped bass are notorious nocturnal feeders, so much of your fishing is done at night, further adding to the discomfort factor. Quality waders are available in a variety of materials, but most surf fishermen prefer one of the three newer generation of waders; PVC, neoprene or insulated Cordura.

Neoprene waders are similar to the scuba diver's wet suit and are made from the same material. They are lined with a nylon cloth to make them easier to put on and take off and they provide an incredible amount of warmth in cold weather. Some have boots permanently attached, but most are made with stocking type feet, requiring a pair of wader boots to go over them for traction. Neoprene waders are available from Red Ball, Hodgeman, Parkway/Imperial and other manufacturers and are preferred by many surfmen.

Neoprene waders have a few disadvantages. During the summer months when water temperatures are high, neoprene will get pretty hot inside because they fit so tightly and are made from relatively thick material with excellent insulating properties. Neoprene is a soft, flexible type of rubber that can be punctured or torn, but most damage to them can be repaired easily with special glue or by bringing them to a dive shop that repairs wet suits.

Waders made of insulated Cordura, a product of the DuPont Corporation, have also become popular with surf rats. They are tough, hard to tear and somewhat cooler for warm weather use. When used over pants and long underwear, they offer enough warmth for use in the surf almost year-round. I have a pair from Red Ball that are going into their sixth year with little sign of wear.

PVC waders were popularized under the Gra-Lite name by the Standard Safety Equipment Company of Palentine, Illinois. Many a serious surf fisherman who has complained about waders being ruined after a single season's use have found that these sturdy waders go through a number of years of hard fishing and they still keep going strong. The PVC is not only tough to rip, but easy to repair and Gra-Lite's are backed by the longest warranty offered by a wader company.

The socks you wear in the waders are as important to your comfort as the waders themselves. A good pair of cotton or wool socks will go a long way toward keeping your feet dry and warm. Socks should be selected for warmth and also for their ability to wick moisture away from your skin. No matter how cold the water, your feet should remain warm, and warm feet sweat. A good pair of hiking style socks will usually do the job, but I prefer to layer my socks in cold weather with a pair of light 100% cotton socks against the skin and wool socks over for added warmth. One of the best places to shop for specialized cold weather socks is in a ski shop, where the selection is wide. When trying on new waders, be sure to bring along the heavy socks you plan to wear for size so their bulk can be taken into consideration before the purchase.One last item of importance for your waders is a good wader belt. Whether you use suspenders with your waders or not, a wader belt is a must item. When you're standing in the surf, you never know when a large wave might catch you by surprise and knock you off your feet. A wader belt, snugged up around your waist, is your insurance that if you fall, your waders will not fill with water and drag you under or make it extremely difficult to stand and get out of the surf.

There are different types of wader belts. I presently use one made of a stretch material with a plastic, fast release buckle that works fine. Several friends purchased heavy web belts at army-navy stores and added rings or snaps as carrying straps for gaffs or tackle bags. A wading belt can serve a variety of uses, but safety is its primary purpose.

Always dress comfortably for the weather when surf fishing. Smart anglers dress in layers, usually including a bit more clothes than they think they'll need for the night's fishing. It's always easier to take off a layer if you're too warm than it is to try to add a layer if you've already allowed yourself to get cold. The top layer of clothing should be waterproof in the form of a jacket or foul weather top. Hats are optional, but you will find that a good, wool pull-over hat is an important piece of clothing on a cold night in the surf.

Since so much surf fishing is done at night, some type of light for changing lures, re-rigging or finding your way on and off a jetty in the dark is important equipment. A few companies offer headlights, which some anglers find preferable. Fuji-Toki makes several plastic, corrosion-proof headlights that operate on batteries and that are easy to wear for long periods of time. For fishermen who don't like straps around their foreheads, headlights can be hung around the neck, or try a Mini-Maglight in the size that takes two AA batteries. Attach it to a short length of cord so it can be hung around your neck. You can pop one end in your mouth if you need to use it with both hands free for tying knots or checking rigs and it is always handy. Maglights also come with amber and red lenses for night use.

A surf or jetty bag is needed to carry additional terminal tackle, lures and rigs so you don't have to walk back to a tackle box every time you want to change lures. The most popular variety is made of canvas and has plastic or aluminum compartments inside to separate the lures. It has a shoulder strap and a flap that covers the top of the bag to keep the contents somewhat dry. The largest selection and the finest quality bags I've seen are available from a specialty catalog house in Darien, Connecticut, called, aptly enough, The Surfcaster. This outfit also offers waders, wader belts and a variety of hard-to-find products dedicated exclusively to surf fishing.

I make a slight addition to my surf bag to help carry small items like snaps, swivels or additional leader material. Using a plastic 35mm film container, I poke a hole through the bottom just big enough to pass some 30-pound monofilament through. Then I tie a knot in the line and pull it tight against the bottom of the canister until it jams in the hole, inside the container. I tie a snap to the other end. A few drops of epoxy glue seals the small hole and the container's pop-on top will keep anything inside dry. I have two of them hanging from the bag at all times to keep small items needed for rigging. They hold extra snaps, snap swivels, hooks, split rings and leader material.

One last bit of equipment is a short handled gaff of about two feet or less armed with a 3-inch hook. Some are made with coiled phone cord attached to the handle so all the angler need do is stretch it out and gaff the fish. I've found that these cords get in my way when fishing, sometimes even getting tangled with line when wading in deeper water, so I use a simpler approach. With electrical tape, I attach a piece of surgical tubing on the shaft of the gaff hook that is then placed over the hook point when the gaff is not in use to keep it from sticking me. A gaff ring is installed on my wader belt and the gaff point is inserted into the ring and the surgical tube hook protector is then put in place over the hook point. The gaff is held in place in the ring by the surgical tube.

In place of a gaff, a few surf fishermen interested in releasing the majority of their catch have begun using a "tailer." This piece of equipment came from Atlantic Salmon fishermen in Canada, England and Scotland. A tailer is similar to a gaff, from the handle shaft to the grip, but in place of the gaff hook there is a nylon-coated cable that forms a loop. The loop is held open by placing the ring at the end of the cable over a special grommet. When a fish is brought near, the loop is placed around the fish's tail and a quick snap of the handle pulls the loop closed, snaring the fish's tail. It doesn't hurt the fish and allows the angler to get the fish out of the water, unhook it and, in many cases, tag it, with ease prior to release.

# Jetty Gear

Jetty fishing, while still a form of beach or surf fishing, requires some specialized tackle and equipment. Having spent many of my early years jumping jetties in the northern coastal areas of New Jersey, I appreciate the subtle differences present when fishing from these man-made rock piles.

A jetty, or groin, as it is also called, is a rock structure that extends at an angle from the beach to stop beach erosion from wave action. Most fishermen who have been around an inlet or breachway have seen the jetties constructed on either side to keep sand from filling in the entrance, but in areas like northern New Jersey's coastline, jetties are built every few hundred yards, on open beaches, to preserve the sand and retard the normal southward flow of coastal erosion. Whether they accomplish this goal or not is debatable, but one thing they do accomplish is to provide a magnet for bait and game fish. They are an excellent place for fishermen to seek striped bass.

From Manasquan Inlet north to Sandy Hook in New Jersey, there are over a hundred jetties that beach-bound anglers have used for decades as platforms to cast for striped bass. Jetties can be found in almost every state along the East Coast in varying numbers and, in almost all cases, they offer a haven for baitfish, crabs, clams and eels, all the things striped bass like to eat.

Jetties are excellent fishable structure in themselves and, since they usually prevent the formation of inshore sand bars which are important structure when fishing open beaches, the angler's needs are different when fishing from them. Stripers are usually attracted close to the jetty and casting distance becomes far less critical, since the fish are often almost at your feet at any given time. Jetties also offer an excellent platform for live-lining baits like herring, menhaden and eels, so tackle requirements are not the same as those needed by open beach surf fishermen.

For years, my favorite jetty stick was constructed by shortening a Fenwick LB966, an 8-foot fiberglass blank. I cut it to 7½ feet by trimming 6 inches off the butt. The resulting stick was a fast taper, very powerful rod with a soft enough tip to cast the lighter lures we discussed in the surf gear section. It can throw Bombers, needlefish and smaller metals quite well, and it has all the power necessary to turn a substantial bass when it begins a powerful run. Fitted with a Shakespeare spinning reel loaded with 15-pound test line, this was my ultimate jetty stick from the late 1960s through the early 1980s, when it was replaced by a graphite rod of 7½ feet. Even today, I keep two LB966 rods in the basement and they still go fishing with me when it's time to jump the jetties.

**Rock jetties attract striped bass and are great places to fish along the coast, especially at inlets.**

There are many rods available for jetty fishing from most manufacturers. Since casting distance is a secondary consideration here, rods of 7 to 8 feet with a medium action capable of throwing lures from 5/8 to 2½ ounces are all the jetty jockey needs. When matched with a medium-size spinning reel loaded with 15-pound test line, the result is a good, all-round outfit capable of handling plugs, metals, rigged eels or just about any of the artificials that might be used. Since jetties extend out, livelining big baitfish and eels becomes a practical way to catch large bass here. A livelining outfit can be put together using either spinning or conventional reels. Most proficient jetty fishermen use conventional tackle, since casting distance is not a major concern and because many of the herring or menhaden used for bait can weigh well over a pound. A livelining rod should be over seven feet in length and offer a lot of backbone with a lure rating of at least 3 ounces. Line that tests in the 25 to 40-pound range is used and conventional reels with a line capacity of 250 yards or better are recommended. If spinning is your preference, the Shimano 4500 or 5500 Baitrunner series reels are the only way to go. Match them with a stout 7 or 7½-foot stick and that's all you need.

For safety purposes, jetty fishing requires spikes on the soles of your waders. Walking on wet, slippery rocks can be treacherous enough in itself, but trying to accomplish it without spikes is foolhardy at best. Several companies offer jetty spikes and they should be considered standard wader equipment for this environment. A longer

**Jetty rocks can be slippery. Boots, Korker sandals or slip-on golfers rubbers with cleats are essential for sure footing.**

gaff will also be needed to bring your fish in from the base of the rock pile. Serious jetty fishermen usually carry a long handled gaff built on a fiberglass rod blank for this purpose, but if a fish is very large, it's usually necessary to walk the fish toward the beach while it's still in the water, then gaff it when the angler is off the jetty.

# Boat Trolling Gear

Trolling striped bass from a boat is an entirely different ball game from shoreline fishing and the tackle it requires is very different, too. There are three types of trolling gear used and each offers the fisherman different properties to accomplish different tasks. Let's look at trolling outfits that are used with monofilament or Dacron line, wire line and with downriggers.

**Monofilament/Dacron Trolling Gear:** Typically, monofilament or Dacron line trolling outfits are the most common trolling outfits used in saltwater. They are best used for trolling a variety of lures near the surface. This is a favorite trolling technique in the Chesapeake Bay, where much bass fishing is done in relatively shallow water.

A 30-pound class trolling rod of 6½ to 7½ feet in length and matched to a 3/0 or 4/0 conventional reel is the ideal outfit. The reel is usually loaded with 30 or 40-pound test monofilament or braided Dacron line and it's ready to go. If deeper trolling is needed with this outfit, drail weights or dropper sinkers of 2, 4 or 6 ounces, even up to a pound, can be used to achieve extra depth.

An outfit like this can be used to troll large spoons, tube lures, big bucktails, nylons and a variety of live or dead baits effectively.

**Wire Line Trolling Gear:** Wire line trolling has been a popular way to fish for stripers for decades. While it may not sound all that sporting to the uninitiated, until you've felt a bragging-size striped bass fight on wire, you cannot imagine how vibrantly a fish fights with the direct connection that wire affords. You feel every pulse of the fish's tail, every shake of its head and you learn to appreciate just how strong a big bass really is. There is no stretch in the wire to deaden the feeling between fish and angler.

Wire line is used not for strength (wire line rated at 40-pound test breaks the same as 40-pound mono) but because it offers an angler the option of trolling larger lures down deep. Wire doesn't stretch and it has the ability to cut through water, unlike mono which actually rides higher in the water the more line is let out. When drail weights are added to wire, the depth capabilities are further increased.

Rods for trolling wire can vary from 6 feet to special rods of 9 feet for trolling bunker spoons. Standard rods in the 6 to 7-foot range are available from Penn and Daiwa and are capable of fishing most

**Levelwind and lever drag reels are fine for trolling with monofilament lines, but wire line requires a reel with a chromed or stainless spool to avoid corrosion.**

**Wire line can wear grooves into hard-chromed guides quickly. Carboloy guide (left) or Fuji heavy duty ceramic guide are best choices.**

artificials like big plugs, umbrella rigs and tube lures effectively. Regardless of length, a wire line rod should have a relatively soft, parabolic action that bends and then rebounds to set the hook when a fish strikes. This soft action is absolutely essential when fishing bunker spoons, since the flex of the rod is an important factor in imparting the correct action to these big spoons, but more on that in a later chapter.

Whatever wire line rod you select, be sure it is fitted with carboloy guides, or at least, extra heavy duty, braced Fuji aluminum oxide guides. Do not use stainless, chrome over brass or ceramic guides for wire line as they will become grooved in short order and ruined. Roller tips are fine on wire line rods, but they should be of the special hardened type manufactured by AFTCO for this purpose, or they will eventually groove like soft ring guides.

Reels that will accommodate wire include the Penn 113H or 114H and the Daiwa Sealine 400H reels. Both have proven to be strong enough to handle the rigors of wire line fishing, which put an amazing amount of strain on rods and reels. Stay away from reels with anything faster than a 4.5 to 1 gear ratio since higher gear ratios make reeling in large lures more difficult in the winching style retrieve necessary with wire.

The reel should be loaded with 200 to 300 yards of 40 or 50-pound test backing. Some fishermen prefer mono backing, but I've found that Dacron holds up better and chafes less than mono when spooled under wire line. Trolling wire should always be single strand and is available in stainless steel or in a softer, nickel alloy variety called Monel. Stainless is less expensive and quite serviceable, but has a considerable amount of spring to it and can create problems if pressure is not maintained on the spool when letting out line. Monel, on the other hand, is more expensive and somewhat more apt to kink, but spools easier and has less spring. Either line will do the job. Most experienced wire line trollers use either 40-pound test stainless or 45-pound test monel.

Attaching the wire to the backing is accomplished in two ways, depending upon the type of tip on your trolling rod. If the rod has a ring type tip, tie a small, 125-pound test barrel swivel to the wire with a haywire twist, then use an improved clinch or Uni-Knot to attach the backing line to the swivels other side. If the rod has a roller style tip, a barrel swivel will not pass through it, so tie a haywire twist in the wire and then use an Albright Special to attach the backing directly to the wire.

When loading the reel with new wire, it is important to mark it at regular intervals, since the amount of wire you have in the water will determine the depth of your lure. There are several methods of marking wire line, but the simplest is to use 3M colored vinyl tape, cross winding it into a four-inch swatch every 25 or 50 feet. How much wire to load on the reel is also debatable and skippers from different locales will offer varying opinions. A minimum of 150 feet of wire is needed almost anywhere, but you can use as much as 300 feet if you anticipate fishing in areas requiring deeper running lures. For the areas I fish regularly in New Jersey, I load my reels with 300 feet and if additional depth is needed, trolling drails of varying weights can be added at the bitter end of the wire, before the final monofilament leader.

The leader between the wire line and lure should be at least 10 feet long and some fishermen will run them 15 feet and longer. I prefer 50-pound test, heavy duty mono, which is attached to the wire with an Albright Special or Uni-Knot. This system allows the leader to be reeled down the rod onto the reel when bringing fish close to the boat.

One final useful piece of equipment for wire line trolling is a pair of offset rod holders that place the trolling rods out to the side of the boat and horizontal to the water. These holders add a wider spread on the lures in the trolling pattern and when using large bunker spoons, adds considerably to their action. Rod holders of this type are available from Reliable Gaff, Seabrite Stainless and Climax Blue Water and are indispensable. They can be used with mono or Dacron trolling outfits also.

**Downrigger Trolling Gear:** Downriggers are becoming an important tool for trolling in saltwater. These devices are a transplant from the Pacific and Great Lakes salmon fisheries, where they have been used for years to catch fish in deep water on relatively light tackle without the need for excessive weight. They perform well under a variety of circumstances when trolling striped bass, but their entry into this fishery is relatively recent and techniques are still being developed by enterprising fishermen.

One downrigger is okay, but a pair is better. They can be mounted permanently to the boat's gunwales or set up with removable bases so they can be stowed when not in use. Several manufacturers address the saltwater market with downriggers that are rugged, corrosion resistant and made to take the abuse of fishing in a saltwater environment. Penn Fishing Tackle and Cannon have lead the way in this market, but other companies, like Big Jon, Walker and Scotty, also offer highly serviceable, saltwater units.

If cost is a primary consideration, then manual units are the way to go. My first downriggers were manuals, but the drudgery of cranking up the downrigger weights by hand did more to discourage their use than anything else. It wasn't until I sprung for a pair of electrically driven units that I began to enjoy the benefits downriggers can provide.

You'll need a heavy trolling ball for saltwater use, one of 12 pounds and preferably streamlined to prevent excessive drag, or blow back at faster trolling speeds. I've found that the Water Slicer model from Cannon is as good as they get.

The release clip is another important consideration, since lures used in saltwater place more pressure on the clip. Be sure that the release you choose is capable of exerting enough pressure to keep the line from popping out of the clip while trolling large lures.

Beginners with downriggers have a tendency to use rods that are too light in action and line class. I know that when I first began using riggers, I opted for 12-pound test rated trigger sticks that cost me more fish than they put in the boat. After a lot of trial and error, I've settled on a fast taper, 6-foot conventional rod mounted with a 20-pound class reel with a level wind. The best rod I've found for this chore is the Shimano Beastmaster BL1653. It has a soft enough tip to allow the rod to be loaded downward toward the water without pulling the line from the release clip, which provides good hook setting ability when set in this manner. Yet, even more important, if a large bass is hooked, it has the backbone to give you a fighting chance at boating the fish.

**Downriggers can be readily mounted in existing rod holders with a simple adapter. Latest models are corrosion resistant and durable for long life and hard use.**

# Boat Jigging and Casting Gear

Some of my favorite striped bass fishing is done from boats without the use of trolling tackle. Working shoreline structure from the decks of a center console boat casting bucktails, plugs, rigged eels and live baits is great fun and allows a fisherman to cover far more territory than a shore-bound angler can in the course of a day or evening's fishing.

For lighter lures or rigged baits, a 7-foot, medium action graphite spinning rod with a reel loaded with 12 or 15-pound test line is fine. If larger fish are about or bigger baits are being used, opt for a 7 to 7 1/2-foot heavy action graphite rod and a reel with 20 or 25-pound test line. These outfits will handle most all of the boat fisherman's shore casting needs. When fishing into a wind that keeps your boat moving off shoreline structure, a longer rod of 8 to 8½-feet will help gain extra casting distance.

Using diamond jigs will also account for striped bass on inshore structure, lumps, rock piles and even wrecks, especially during the fall months when the fish are schooled tightly and competition for bait is heavy. For lighter diamond jigs, up to 4 ounces, a trigger style graphite rod rated for 12 to 20-pound test is excellent when mounted with a

**Conventional reels capable of holding 15 to 30-pound mono are ideal for casting or jigging for striped bass.**

wide spool baitcasting reel. Many rod builders offer rods called "Musky Specials", which fit this type of fishing quite well. Just be sure that the rod you select has enough backbone to set the hook when a fish hits your jig on the bottom in 50 or 60 feet of water. Too wimpy a tip and you will not get a solid hook set.

## River and Bay Gear

Tackle for fishing in rivers, bays or other estuary environments will vary with the area and size of fish available. The outfit used for casting small lures to schoolie bass in the upper Hudson, along stretches of the Delaware and in the James River of Virginia can be light spinning to medium baitcasting tackle. If big fish are there during their run upriver in the spring, then tackle must be balanced accordingly.

Excellent fishing exists in the Delaware River in May and June when large bodies of stripers work upstream. Larger fish come to spawn while smaller, immature fish, harass the massive schools of herring also on their spawning run during that same time. Tackle used from boats would typical be 6 to 7-foot spinning gear with 10 to 15-pound test line. Fish size will vary from as small as 12 inches to as large as 25 pounds, so going too light can cost you a fine fish.

This type of tackle can be utilized in many river situations from boats. Shore-bound river anglers have to contend with gaining extra casting distance and may also be using heavy terminal tackle. When choosing rods, a longer and somewhat heavier rod will do the job better than a short, light rod. Bay fishing tackle will vary in the same manner, with the outfits just described more than adequate for most bay fishing forays.

## Fresh Water Striper Tackle

Since lake-bound stripers are caught by a variety of methods, rods and reels will also vary. My experience in Virginia's Lake Anna to the Carolina's Santee-Cooper reservoir, shows we've caught stripers on everything from pistol grip baitcasting tackle meant for largemouth bass to surf rods, for throwing large chunk baits from the shoreline.

Impoundment stripers are most frequently caught casting to breaking schools of fish chasing shad. Lures will usually be under 1 ounce in weight and can be handled with medium action spinning rods of 6½ feet and 10 to 15-pound test line. Many southern fishermen prefer baitcasting tackle for this purpose with conventional reels loaded with 12 to 15-pound test and trigger stick rods up to 7½ feet in length.

**Fly fishing for stripers is gaining popularity. A 10-weight outfit and a selection of streamers will provide the ultimate in light tackle action.**

In winter, lake stripers are caught deep on vertical jigged bucktails. The fish are suspended or holding over deep river channels or points. A stout baitcasting outfit, usually with a straight butt and trigger grip for extra leverage rather than the popular pistol grips used for large-mouths, will do the trick. So will a relatively heavy spinning outfit.

# Fly Fishing Gear

The use of fly tackle for stripers is gaining in popularity in recent years. For fishing from boats, a 9 foot, 9-weight outfit will usually provide the power to cast large, wind-resistant flies and popping bugs. Reels can be simple, direct drive models, but should be large enough to hold 200 yards of 20-pound test backing behind the fly line. Whatever style reel you choose, be sure it has a smooth drag for fighting large fish.

Line selections will vary with the flies to be used. A floating line will be necessary for popping bugs and shallow water flies. An intermediate sink line will usually handle flies that are meant to be fished deeper. Leader materials of at least 12-pound test are preferred and should be at least 10 to 12 feet in length.

Even surf fishermen can be seen carrying a fly outfit in their buggies to take advantage of the times when bass move into the wash chasing small offerings like spearing and sand eels. To catch a striper on a fly is an experience unlike anything you've tried in salt water. When fly fishing from the surf, an additional bit of equipment is a necessity, a basket worn around the waist, commonly called a stripping basket. It holds the line being stripped in while working the fly. It's a convenient place to store line without having it floating around your feet in the water and it keeps the line ready for the next cast.

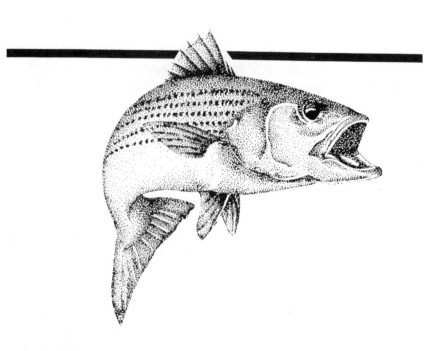

**Chapter Three**

# OF BOATS AND BUGGIES

Fishing for striped bass, whether from the shore or on the water, has lead to the development of vehicles and boats to aid a fisherman's mobility. Not satisfied to park himself in one place and hope that the fish are there, or will arrive soon, today's striped bass fisherman wants the freedom of movement that can increase his chances of finding and catching fish.

The desire to cover more territory, in a shorter period of time has lead to the development of more dependable and seaworthy fishing boats in a much wider range of sizes than at any time in the past. And, don't count out the shoreline fisherman. His pursuit of game fish along the open beach has led to a generation of specialized trucks that, with some custom touches, can move him and his increasingly large collection of tackle over great distances in search of the elusive striped bass.

There's also the fun of customizing your buggy. We'll cover the basics here in this chapter, but there's an infinite number of ways to personalize a beach buggy to ideally suit your fishing needs. From the fanciest campers to the simplest pickup truck, you'll see every imaginable modification on today's beach buggies.

# The Well-Equipped Beach Buggy

Many shore-based anglers who ply the beaches from Cape Hatteras to Cape Cod use a variety of four-wheel-drive trucks, loosely termed beach buggies. These curious vehicles began appearing on the beaches in the 1930s in the form of Model T Fords. Since those early beginnings, they have evolved into highly specialized fishing companions for thousands of hard core "beach rats." They can be simple as an old Jeep or as sophisticated as a large pickup truck sporting special suspensions, rod and cooler racks, live-well systems and camper tops. A really loaded beach buggy can also carry quite a price tag. One angler seen along north Jersey beaches lately was driving a fire engine red Lamborgini four-wheel-drive truck with huge tires. It was rumored to cost upwards of $100,000!

It isn't necessary to spend a ton of money on a beach buggy, but your dedication to beach fishing will, no doubt, influence your financial investment if a buggy is in your future. Almost any 4X4 can run the sand with just a few minor modifications and with the addition of some safety equipment. Whatever your choice in a buggy, it will increase your ability to catch striped bass by virtue of the increased mobility it will afford. When bass are breaking on schools of sand eels in the wash a mile or so down the beach from where you are fishing, nothing beats a buggy for getting you there before the action stops. When fishing the many state-run beaches from Massachusetts to Cape Hatteras, it is often impossible to get to remote, off-road areas without a buggy.

Beach buggy fishermen are engaged in an increasingly more difficult struggle for the privilege of continuing to use their vehicles on many public and municipal beachfronts. To date, their successes have been few and far between when it comes to reopening areas closed to buggies once the closure goes into effect. Some closures fall under the banner of protecting "endangered species" from intrusion by motor vehicles, others are due to complaints from beachfront property owners and still others are simply government's way of saying "we just don't want to deal with fishermen on public beaches all hours of the day and night."

Organizations like the United Mobile Surf Fishermen are fighting for access to beaches for fishermen with these specialized vehicles. Several hard-earned court victories with various government agencies, plus the work of the organization in sponsoring beach cleanups, dune reclamation and protection of shore-bird nesting sites, has begun to change some minds about fishermen and the funny looking buggies they drive on the sand. So, if a buggy sounds good to you, let's take a look at the basics plus a few upscale pieces of equipment that go into making it a fishable motor vehicle.

**Four-wheel-drive beach buggies provide mobility for the surf angler. Front-mounted rack holds rods and cooler while tool kits, safety equipment and extra tackle is stowed inside of vehicle.**

Probably the most important consideration necessary for a beach buggy is tire selection. Hard side wall truck tires will get you into trouble on soft sand. Oversized radial tires have become the standard for beach use in recent years because the soft side wall construction and the strength of the radial ply design lend themselves to repeated use at very low tire pressures. Tires of this type are available from almost any tire company and a good rule of thumb is to always purchase quality tires. A quality tire will show less side wall wear and deterioration when run on the sand at low pressure and will offer considerably longer service than a set of low end retreads. Buggy tires are usually run at pressures as low as 10 pounds per square inch so the tires float over soft sand, rather than sink into it. The softer the beach composition, the lower the pressure necessary to drive on the beach.

If you plan on fishing the beach a lot, you will want to look into a portable air tank or auxiliary air pump system for the truck so you can re-inflate tires upon leaving the beach. Radials, or any tire, will over-heat when run on road surfaces in an under-inflated condition. Tanks are capable of holding enough air at high pressure to re-inflate all four tires, but they must be recharged after each use. Also good are the latest generation of mini tire pumps that are always ready to go when

**Portable, hand-held LORAN units allow beach anglers to "remember" exact locations of bars, shoals and deep holes discovered at low tide.**

needed. They have dropped in price to the point of making an air tank a more expensive investment than a pump. A few new vehicles that boast self leveling rear air suspension systems come with a hose and gauge set up already built in for just that purpose or they can be adapted to use the suspension pump with a simple modification.

Now that you are ready to hit the beach with a basic four-wheel-drive buggy, let's make it safe. A complete safety kit should be carried on a buggy whenever you go beach fishing. Many state operated recreational areas require specific equipment and will check period-ically to be sure you have it on board before they allow entry to the beach. Here's a list of basic equipment required by the State of New Jersey at Island Beach State Park, the most heavily used beach in the mid-Atlantic region by buggy fishermen. Frequently, a ranger will check vehicles at the park entrance gate before permitting access in to the park. The ranger may ask to see the following equipment:

Tire gauge
Tow chain or rope
Tire jack
Boards to support the jack
Spare tire
Shovel
Flashlight

Not required, but highly recommended:

Fire extinguisher
First-aid kit
Litter bags
Tide Chart
Water jug
Spare radiator hoses

Some recreational areas in other states also require buggy fisher-men to carry a portable toilet and ask that you use it, rather than the dunes, when nature calls.

The reason for much of this equipment is to help extricate your vehicle in case of a breakdown, should it get stuck in the sand, or to keep the beaches clean. A basic buggy kit is available packed neatly in a camo nylon bag from The Surfcaster's catalog in Darien, Connecticut.

A couple of additional items serious beach runners wouldn't be caught without are boards as wide as the truck's tires and at least three to four feet long to help extricate a truck stuck in the sand. A set of emergency flares is also a good idea. Some buggies are also equipped with CB or VHF radios to call for assistance if needed. If you are really safety conscious, you will probably want to look into a bumper mounted winch, not only for pulling your truck out of danger, but also to help the other guy who might be in trouble.

A smart buggy driver, like a good fisherman, knows the tides for the area he is driving and takes them into consideration when parking his vehicle to fish. Buggies have been left during a hot bite only to have the driver return to find the truck up to the floorboards on an incoming tide. Once the water is lapping at the tires, they dig deeper into the sand and it becomes nearly impossible to get loose without the help of several other vehicles. Don't let yourself get caught in that situation because it is no laughing matter. Know your tides and learn where the high tide line is on any beach you happen to fish.

Buggy rod storage can be accomplished in a variety of ways, from roof-mounted horizontal rod racks to just tossing them in the back of a pickup, but if you plan on spending more time fishing and less time chasing and untangling your tackle, a bumper mounted rod rack makes real sense. A bumper rack will hold a number of outfits rigged and ready, vertically across the front of the buggy out of harms way and ready to fish at a moment's notice. You can construct them yourself from a few sections of PVC tubing cut to size and attached to the bumper with clamps, or you can purchase factory-made rack

**Live bait can be kept frisky for long periods of time in a 40 gallon tank equipped with a circulating pump. Many tackle shops sell additives that keep the oxygen level comfortable, or add fresh, cool water each hour.**

systems from a variety of regional manufacturers. Built from stainless steel, aluminum or PVC, they are available as rod holders or they can be elaborate affairs that accommodate up to eight outfits and a large marine cooler.

Among the best I've seen are built by Hamberger's Racing Systems of Toms River, New Jersey, a company that started out specializing in making aluminum racing parts for automobiles. Several of their welders are avid beach fishermen and they began experimenting with different rack designs, which became extremely popular. They now offer a complete line, all crafted from marine grade aluminum for years of long life.

If live-bait fishing is a consideration aboard your buggy, a live well will have to be installed. One capable of handling a few large baitfish like herring or menhaden, can be made by jury rigging a 100-quart (or larger) cooler combined with an aerator system. Larger tanks and sophisticated aeration systems are available from a number of small companies. A complete system based on an Igloo 94-quart marine cooler is available and ready to go from G-LOX Products Company of Houston, Texas. It includes the cooler and the aeration system. All you have to do is attach a couple of wires to the truck battery for power and you're set to go.

# *Boats, Boats and More Boats*

Stripers and boats go together like peanut butter and jelly. After years of fishing the beaches and heaping abuse on my body jumping jetties in search of stripers, it was time for a change. That change came in the form of a 23-foot Mako center console boat, rigged specifically for the many ways I fish for bass.

If you have to choose one style of craft to handle all the methods of striper fishing that can be done from a boat in the ocean, bays and coastal rivers, from casting shoreline structure to jigging bass on inshore lumps; from trolling with wire and downriggers in the fall, to fly fishing for schoolies in the back bays, it would have to be the venerable center console. The center console design has been with us since 1961 when Boston Whaler built the very first stand-alone console boat and introduced it to the American market. It was not an overnight success, but it began a revolution in fishing boat design. Today there are dozens of center consoles being built today by many boat companies.

The versatility of this style of boat is unmatched by anything else afloat and successful striper fishing requires every bit of versatility you can find. The center console might be cold in the early spring and late fall, but its wide open design more than makes up for any discomfort.

After all, isn't cold-weather fishing what they invented snowmobile suits for?

You don't necessarily need a whole lot of fancy equipment to make a good bass boat. Consider my Mako. Many people would call it sparsely equipped, but I think it's perfect, although I may be somewhat biased. Let's take a look at it and you will get an idea of the equipment needed aboard most boats for casting, jigging and trolling tactics that work on striped bass. You will probably find that the list of necessary equipment isn't as extensive as you thought.

This 23-foot, deep-vee, center console is similar to those offered by almost every fiberglass fishing boat builder in the country. I took pains to purchase mine from a builder with a long history with the center console design, and that had a record of building boats that can take a terrific amount of abuse, year in and year out and keep on fishing. A quality-built boat will also hold its resale value, making it as much an investment as an expense.

It is kept wide open, without the addition of the popular T-top many center consoles are equipped with. No T-top means no wrestling hooks out of it when casting plugs or rigged eels from the boat at night. No diamond jigs are left dangling from it when the fishing is fast and furious in the fall and the jigs are flying. In other words, a T-top is an obstruction I can live without when so much of my favorite fishing is done casting from the boat.

It sports a pair of removable electric downriggers for trolling and also a removable set of horizontal rod holders for trolling wire line. A built-in, below-deck 38-gallon live well is mounted in the stern with a pump system that circulates fresh sea water into the well rather than an aerator, which is ineffective for keeping large baitfish alive for long periods of time. A larger, auxiliary bait tank is brought on board when livelining gets really serious or when we go out hunting baitfish with cast nets and we have to keep a lot of baits to bring back to the bait pen. This tank receives a constant supply of fresh sea water from a saltwater wash down pump located in the bilge.

Electronics consist of a combination LCD fish finder/LORAN/plotter, a paper graph recorder, a sea surface temperature gauge, a trolling speed indicator, a VHF radio and, a stereo tape player system for use when fishing gets too slow (a little music never hurts). Antennas are mounted high on the console, out of the way, rather than along the gunwales, where they can interfere when casting, drifting or trolling. No outriggers are kept on the boat for the same reason and also because outriggers are rarely if ever used when striper fishing. A large fish box is located forward, but it's proven to be a bit small when we've tried to stuff a couple of 40-pound bass in it. Unfortunately, the problem doesn't arise often enough.

Plenty of storage for additional gear, clothing, tackle and beverages

**Author's center console is typical of the great fishing boats available to striped bass anglers.**

is found throughout the boat. A small rocket launcher replaces the helm and passenger seats. It is capable of holding four rods and is mounted on a frame that also holds a 94-quart cooler and several tackle boxes. With the rocket launcher, the boat has out-of-the-way storage for 18 rods, not counting the four flush-mounted rod holders in the gunwales. A collapsible canvas spray boot for the bow comes in handy when the wind blows in the fall.

That's my ideal saltwater striper boat, and it has served me admirably for the past several seasons seeing action from March through the end of December, before winter forces a short layover on dry land in January and February. Similar center console rigs are available in sizes from 17 to over 26 feet, but boats larger than 26 feet becomes difficult to handle when fishing around tight structure in rivers, in shallow bay areas and for holding in tight off the end of a jetty.

Center consoles aren't the only way to go and if you have another type of boat, you can still chase bass. One type or another of striper fishing can be accomplished from just about any boat and if you stop to look at the amazing variety of craft used by the occasional fisherman right on up to professional charter captains, you would be astounded. River bass can be pursued in anything from an aluminum jon boat to a canoe. Bay anglers can catch bass from any boat large enough to handle bay waters. Offshore trollers fish with center consoles, cuddy cabins, cruisers and even big, million dollar sport fishermen.

There have been days during the fall, when the bass are making their run south, that you can see everything from small aluminum skiffs to huge offshore sport fishermen trolling or jigging alongside one another. Believe me, the bass don't care what kind of boat you're in when they are hungry and the small boater has just as much chance of catching as "Joe Gotrocks" on his yacht. In fact, the small boat probably has a better chance than the big boat because it is more maneuverable and capable of fishing shallower water with better speed control and has the ability to hold position in tight places.

Freshwater lake striper fishermen use a wide a variety of fishing boats just as their saltwater brethren. High speed bass boats, aluminum jon boats, dad's borrowed ski boat and even pontoon craft can catch stripers when livelining or trolling is the method to be used. Today, a few boat companies offer specialized fresh water striper boats that are catching on fast with lake guides and pro striper fishermen. They feature oversized live wells that keep baits and the catch alive for eventual release after fishing. They are powerful, fast and sleek, with lots of open deck space for 360 degree casting ease. Almost sounds like a saltwater center console, doesn't it?

Whatever you decide upon in the way of a boat for chasing stripers, rest assured that it will make catching bass easier and more fun. Diehard beach fishermen may sneer at boat fishermen for taking the easy way out, but when the fish are breaking and the catching is hot just out of casting range of the beach-bound fishermen, it's tough to be on the beach.

## Boat Electronics

Striped bass fishing does not require a huge investment in marine electronics. While big boat, offshore fishermen have enough electronic instrumentation on their boats to rival the Space Shuttle, it just isn't necessary for the average bass fisherman who will spend the majority of his time pursuing fish on the inshore grounds.

**Depthfinders:** Probably the most important piece of fishing electronics needed aboard a boat for stripers, the depthfinder/fish finder is indispensable. It isn't necessary to spend several thousand dollars on a commercial quality color scope or an 8-inch paper machine, since the average depth you will find bass in rarely exceeds 100 feet. A unit with a 3,000-foot depth capability is a waste of money if striped bass are your main quarry.

Today, boat fishermen have three major types of depth finders to choose from and your decision will be influenced by the type of boat you use and your personal display preference. The venerable, paper graph recorder is still one of the most accurate depthfinders available to serious fishermen when it comes to accurately displaying bottom contours, structure and fish. The difference between the average high-quality LCD screen, a video screen and a top quality paper graph recorder, like the Lowrance X-16, is in the number of lines of resolution from the top of the screen to the bottom.

The best LCD's offered today have 200 lines of vertical resolution on a 4-inch screen. Top of the line 4-inch video depthfinders offer 240, but the venerable X-16 paper graph recorder from Lowrance Electronics provides 1000 lines of resolution in that same 4-inch screen format. The difference becomes obvious and that's why so many serious saltwater fishermen wouldn't structure fish without a high quality paper machine on board. An additional advantage of a quality paper machine like the X-16 is its ability to alter the transducer pulse width, which is the length of the sound wave being emitted by the transducer that rebound off the bottom or any targets in between. By lowering the pulse width to 50, the unit will discriminate between the bottom and a target sitting only one inch off the bottom. No other type of depthfinder has this capability. If fishing in extremely deep water, which is rarely done when searching for striped bass, the pulse width can be peaked to as high as 1,750 and the signal will penetrate the

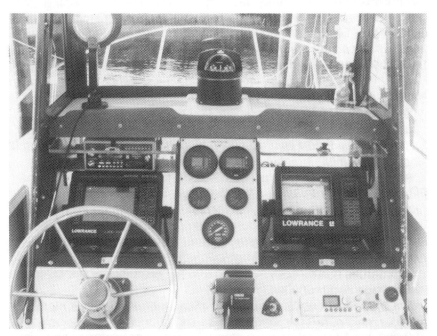

**"Must have" electronics include a graph recorder or LCD fish finder, VHF radio, LORAN and temperature gauge.**

deepest waters and provide a solid bottom reading, but will sacrifice clarity of fish targets close to the bottom.

The downside of paper graphs are the expense of paper, which can cost as much as $9.00 per roll. When you use a graph to its greatest advantage, which requires cranking up the paper speed, the investment in graph paper can become considerable, if you fish frequently.

I like graph recorders, but there are other good recorders available. Today's sophisticated LCD and video depthfinders have come a long way and offer excellent screen definition and clarity and many fishermen have found that they can do the job well enough to make the additional expense of graph paper a bit hard to swallow. I added a high quality LCD to my boat several seasons ago and have been pleased with its performance for most fishing applications. And, it never runs out of paper!

For open boats, center consoles or any boat that does not have a top of some type to shield a depthfinder from direct sunlight, an LCD type unit is the answer because the screen is easily seen in very bright sunlight. Video depthfinders suffer from screen washout on bright, sunny days. If your boat has a place to keep the depthfinder out of the direct sunlight, then you have the choice of video or LCD technology. Either will do the job well.

Older style, flasher depthfinders, have no use for serious fishing. Twenty-five years ago, they were the state of the art in fishing electronics technology, but in today's highly competitive electronics market where a basic LCD unit can be purchased for about $200, they just don't cut it any more.

**LORANS and Plotters:** While originally designed as a navigational device, LORAN is equally effective as a fishing tool. This simple electronic box with numbers can tell you where you are, how to get to where you are going, and when you find fish or a likely area of structure away from shore, it has the capability of bringing you right back to that spot next time you go fishing. It is simple and remarkable at the same time.

As with depthfinders, it isn't necessary to buy the most expensive LORAN made. The differential between top-rated units and more moderately-priced models can be $1,000 or more. You may be spending more for added performance and increased capabilities that are not needed by the average boat fisherman seeking stripers. Reception of distant signals from far offshore fishing grounds won't be a consideration and fancy features and huge memory capacities are of little use for most inshore situations.

It is always recommended that you purchase a fish finder manufactured by a reputable company with a strong background in electronics and one that stands behind its products with a strong service network.

While LORAN is most widely used by boat fishermen, don't discount its use in conjunction with beach buggy fishing. Many savvy surf fishermen have spent the money for a hand-held LORAN for use in locating productive sand bars, discovered at low tide. Later at high water, when bass and bait are most likely to be holding on beach structure, but when the bar is not so visible, they simply drive back to the bar's location using the numbers they recorded or saved in the units memory bank. Hand-held units are presently offered by Micrologic, Inc. and Ray Jefferson Electronics and can be purchased for under $300.

If you are not familiar with the basic operation and technology behind LORAN operations, you can purchase one of the many fine books or video cassettes available on the subject. While the concept is simple, it would take up far too much space for this book to cover.

For the boat fisherman who trolls extensively, a plotter is a terrific aid, especially for getting back on fish once you've had a knockdown in a specific location. A plotter is simply a circular screen with compass rose that tracks the course you've run by leaving a trail across its face using a dotted line or similar marking system. It is electronically coupled into the LORAN, and better units have the ability to mark a spot chosen by the operator where a fish has been caught, or a particularly interesting piece of bottom structure was located, by depressing an event key on the key pad. It becomes simple to retrack a course and get back to an exact spot time after time.

Since it is tied into the LORAN, when a knockdown occurs and the event key is pressed, that location can be saved as a LORAN waypoint and marked with a "t" on the face of the plotter. There's no worrying about losing the position of the hook-up spot as the boat runs or drifts away during the fight. A plotter has put many additional fish in my boat when trolling, since schooled bass will often be holding on a specific piece of bottom and getting back on that spot is essential to catching more fish from the school.

**Combination LORAN/Depthfinder/Plotter Units:** Several manufacturers offer combination units that incorporate all three of the above mentioned functions into a single LCD or video screen unit. Combination LCD's are available from Lowrance, Eagle, Raytheon, Apelco and Impulse, while Interphase Technologies offers separate LORAN and depthfinder that interface and read out on the all three functions on the depthfinders LCD screen. A video screen unit is offered by Si-Tex Marine Electronics and is a unique product in the electronics market.

I've had three years experience with the Lowrance LMS300 and have been extremely pleased with its performance. The split-screen capability allows the use of both the plotter and depthfinder simultaneously, an excellent feature. Its large, extremely fine resolution screen made it the first LCD depthfinder to get me to turn off my paper graph machine, although I still keep the paper graph on the boat to use when hunting fish on inshore and offshore structure, wrecks and rock piles, or any time I need very high resolution.

**VHF Radios:** While a VHF radio might not be considered a fishing tool by most fishermen, it has put me on fish many times. Keeping an ear tuned to the frequently used fishing channels can help you get in on action that you might otherwise miss. When fishing an area with friends in nearby boats, it becomes possible to fish a wider variety of areas by spreading the boats over a wide area and keeping each other informed as to any action found.

While listening to other fishermen can be a help when they talk about what's happening, it can also be a hindrance when you get on fish in a particular spot and you don't want everyone else to know about it when you call your friends in. To prevent that from happening, it's always a good idea to arrange an alternate channel with your fishing friends before you hit the water. When it comes time to communicate something important like fish locations, instead of using the common fishing channel for your area, simply tell your buddy to go to the "other channel."

A VHF radio can also save your life. It is an indispensable piece of safety equipment on any bay or ocean-going boat no matter how close to shore you fish. Get to know the procedures for contacting the Coast Guard, should an emergency occur that requires assistance.

**Surface Temperature Gauges and Trolling Speed Indicators:** While water surface temperature is an interesting factor in finding many types of fish, its importance in striped bass fishing is less critical than when fishing for certain species of sharks, tuna or other pelagic fish. Striped bass can tolerate a wide range of water temperatures and when they are in the open ocean, they most often hug the bottom where temperatures can vary greatly from surface water.

While I would hesitate to spend the money on a separate temperature gauge specifically for striped bass fishing, most depthfinders offer a surface temperature/boat speed indicator option that is inexpensive enough to make the addition worthwhile.

A trolling speed indicator is extremely important when bass fishing, since controlling boat speed can often mean the difference between getting strikes and pulling your lures past disinterested fish. With most bass trolling lures, trolling speeds are usually quite slow. Tube lures, umbrella rigs and big spoons produce best when trolled at speeds from 2 to 3 knots. When the range of speed is that narrow, being able to control your boat speed becomes all the more critical.

For example, when trolling the rips at Montauk for bass, optimum speed for a specific lure might be 2 knots. That speed might be easily controlled when trolling in one direction, but when the course is reversed into the current, the engine rpms will probably be very different to maintain the same speed. I get a kick out of fishermen that claim to be able to control lure speed by watching nothing more than their engine rpms because engine rpms will vary to maintain the same speed under different wind and current conditions. A trolling speed indicator is much more accurate for this purpose than guessing about lure action by using engine rpms. You can also use your LORAN in the navigation mode to check speed.

**Stereo Music and Fishing:** Some of my friends say I'm crazy, in fact a lot of them know I'm crazy, but I feel that certain types of music played on the stereo in my boat can stimulate feeding or at least curiosity in certain types of fish. Shark fishermen have known for years that low frequency vibrations can attract sharks from long distances. Some tournament shark fishermen have gone to considerable lengths to mount stereo speakers in the bilges of their boats to make the hull resonate into the water around it. They play music with strong bass tracks and heavy use of percussion instruments and it gets results.

While my theory on sound waves is only a hunch, I have had nights when playing music with high frequency sounds like flutes, keyboards and string instruments seemed to have an effect on fishing action. These high frequency sounds can mimic small baitfish splashing on the surface in the same way a spray of water from a wash down hose can attract and hold dolphin on the offshore grounds as it mimics the sounds of bait on the surface.

I don't play music most of the time while fishing, although on several occasions when fishing was slow, I turned on the stereo in the boat, which resonates the hull mildly, and suddenly had fishing action pick up. The times that this little experiment seemed to work were all on quiet nights when not much wave action was about.

Who knows, maybe I am crazy like my friends say, but stranger things have been found to work to a fisherman's advantage. And if the fishing is slow anyway, the music helps break up the monotony and soothes the savage beast, which some anglers have been known to turn into when the bass aren't cooperating.

# Miscellaneous Boat Equipment

Besides a compliment of electronics, boat fishermen will need a few other basic items for the wide variety of fishing techniques employed to catch striped bass. Let's run down these items, their uses and the types of fishing that require them.

Starting with the very basics, your boat should be rigged with an anchor with an adequate amount of chain to make it grab bottom and set quickly. Anchoring chores for bass are often employed in rivers, bays and along shallow stretches of beach. Anchoring off a jetty is tricky enough without an improper anchor making it even more difficult, so be sure yours is large enough to set and hold your boat under any sea or wind conditions.

An interesting devise for trollers who have trouble getting their boats to idle down to speeds under 3 knots is a sea anchor. This umbrella-like device is constructed of canvas or heavy nylon and acts in the same manner as a parachute, except that is deployed into the water behind your boat to slow down your drift or trolling speed. Many fishing boats have problems trolling down to striper speeds and the sea anchor is an inexpensive solution. In an emergency, you can substitute a five-gallon bucket on a length of rope for a sea anchor with acceptable results.

Your boat should be equipped with an adequate fish box for the keepers you decide to bring home for dinner and if you're serious about your bass fishing, a large, circulating live well is a necessity for keeping menhaden, herring or eels healthy for livelining.

A cooler, either molded into the boat or as an add on item, will also

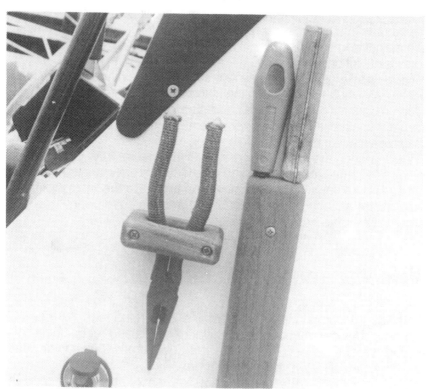

**Author's handy teak holders for knife, hook file and pliers keeps these tools ready for instant use.**

# Sea Anchor

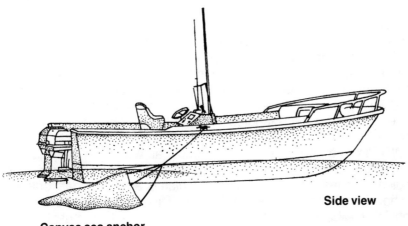

**Canvas sea anchor**

**Side view**

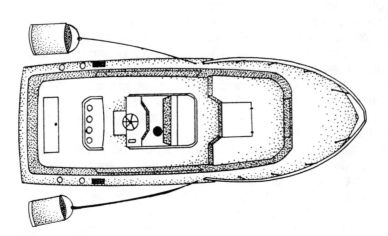

**5-gallon bucket**

**Top view**

be handy for more than just keeping a few drinks and lunch fresh and cold. It will come in handy when livelining eels or for keeping dead baits firm and ready for use. A couple of 5-gallon buckets always seem to come in handy when striper fishing, too, so find a place to stash one or two on board.

For smaller stripers in bays, rivers and lakes, a landing net is all that's needed for getting your catch into the boat. Even in these inland waters, bass can be encountered in the 20-pound range, and larger, so you need more than your old trout net. A net with an opening of at least 30 inches is preferred. For ocean fishing or when larger fish are to be expected, a long-handled gaff with a 3 or 4-inch hook is the tool of choice for fish to be killed for consumption.

With limits found on stripers in almost all waters, another landing device that doesn't injure the fish is also necessary. There are a few choices, the least recommended of which is a release gaff, one with a short handle that has a small hook. This type of gaff is used by hooking the bass under the jaw and out the mouth. It must be used carefully or it can injure the fish badly enough to make survival highly questionable.

A less damaging device is a tailer, a snare that encircles the fish's tail and tightens around it when activated. It will work reasonably well on medium to large stripers. Small fish can be boated by inserting your thumb into its mouth and grabbing the fish by the lower jaw. Be careful of hooks if the fish was caught on a plug with several trebles. Stripers have no teeth, just sandpaper-like rough areas on the jaw to help them hold their prey. When picked up by the lower jaw, they will usually relax and become relatively easy to handle. We've "lipped" bass as large as 20 pounds on my boat, but when they are bigger than this, you just can't hold them in this manner.

Rigging tools to keep on board include a good set of pliers. I like a pair of stainless steel 8-inch needle nose style for everything from removing easily accessible hooks to cutting leader material when tying rigs. I keep a pair in a special teak holder on the side of my console at all times. The holder also fits a knife and hook sharpening file in one easy-to-reach location. Sharp hooks are a must for all fishing, so the file is an important tool. A fine-mill bastard file found in any tool or hardware store does wonders for most bait hooks and is inexpensive to replace once it eventually rusts, as most files do. If you want a hook sharpening file that will stand up to years of use without corrosion problems, Braid Products offers one that is impregnated with diamond chips and has no metal to rust.

A hook disgorger is also a good item to have aboard for dislodging deeply set hooks. Keep in mind that if a hook is embedded in a bass' gills or gullet, the fish is probably better off if you cut your leader close to the hook and leave it in place. If you further damage these vital

**Side rod holders mount in existing gun'l rod holders and angle rods at 90 degrees from boat. This additional spread helps prevent lines from tangling and aids maneuverability while trolling.**

areas during hook removal, the chances of survival are minimal and most fish have the ability to reject a hook in a short period of time, barb and all.

One last item of importance for trolling is a pair of offset rod holders, as described in Chapter Two under wire line trolling. Don't leave the dock without them if wire line is to be employed. They add width to the trolling pattern so the lines of the side rods don't come close together and tangle on a turn, and they enhance the action of some lures, like bunker spoons.

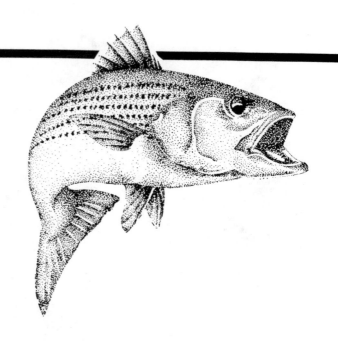

Chapter Four

# BASIC TERMINAL TACKLE

Using the right rig for different styles of fishing and to match daily fishing conditions can be the edge you need to catch stripers consistently. Impale a delicate sand bug on an oversize tuna hook and you can be sure it isn't going to attract much attention from a feeding bass. Not knowing the correct rigs to use, or how to tie them, puts you at a disadvantage to anglers who do know their terminal gear and when to use it. Let's take a look at the terminal tackle, knots and a few of the basic rigs that are used for striped bass. You can pick out the ones that will apply to fishing in your area.

Keep in mind that rigs will have regional variations and alternate hook selections. Bait rigs have always been a subject open to experimentation and adaptation. As your knowledge of the fishing conditions in your favorite haunts increase, the desire to try things your way will grow. The terminal tackle suggested here will serve as a starting point and should cover almost any situation you will encounter. Most are tried and true rigs used by experienced striped bass anglers.

The rigs, and the knots to tie them, that follow in this chapter have been proven by the test of time and they are all easy to prepare with minimal practice. You'll find your favorites and will come to depend on them to catch more fish.

# Know Your Hooks

The most misunderstood and least appreciated piece of tackle sport fishermen use is the fish hook. Its simple appearance belies the fact that it is the culmination of thousands of years of evolution. The ancestor of the hook was nothing more than an oddly shaped bone that, when attached to a length of string made from animal skin or twisted vines, would get caught in the mouth of a fish enticed into swallowing it. It was a discovery akin to the invention of the wheel because it allowed men to catch fish for food. Today, the hook is too often taken for granted. Such a simple device almost doesn't seem to deserve much thought in such a high tech world. Nonsense!

A hook is the ultimate connection between fisherman and fish. Consider that there are literally hundreds of hook styles and sizes to choose from, with designs offered for just about any type of bait or artificial lure application and you can see that the subject bears investigation. Hooks haven't been left behind as tackle technology swept ahead into the 1990s. Hooks are more sophisticated today than ever and the manufacturing process more finely tuned. Some models are ground mechanically, sharpened chemically and hardened cryogenically to provide points sharper out of the box than you can get after careful hand sharpening with a good file.

Let's look at some of the choices that have become popular through trial and error for specific types of striped bass fishing. We'll look at hooks for baitfishing and then replacement hook applications for a variety of artificial lures.

Bait fishing hooks: Striped bass are caught throughout their many ranges on a variety of live or dead baits. These can include, among other regionally preferred baits, clams, crabs, sea worms, cut bait, squid and sand bugs. For the majority of these baits, the beak hook is ideal. It is offered by most hook companies in gold, bronze or nickel plating, but most anglers prefer the gold or bronze finishes. The baitholder style has two reverse barbs or slices on the back portion of the shank and they are forged from a relatively light, yet strong wire. Their one drawback is they are relatively brittle and conceivably can be broken, although I can't ever remember breaking one fighting a fish. I have broken them when removing a hook from a fish with pliers.

Models are available with straight, downturned or upturned eyes for different uses, but each has the distinctive, hollow-ground beak point. It is quite sharp out of the box, but most larger sizes require a couple of quick passes with a good hook sharpening file for quick penetration into a striper's mouth.

These hooks are found regularly on pre-tied rigs in tackle shops, listed as Striped Bass Rigs or Surf Rigs and they are used for a wide

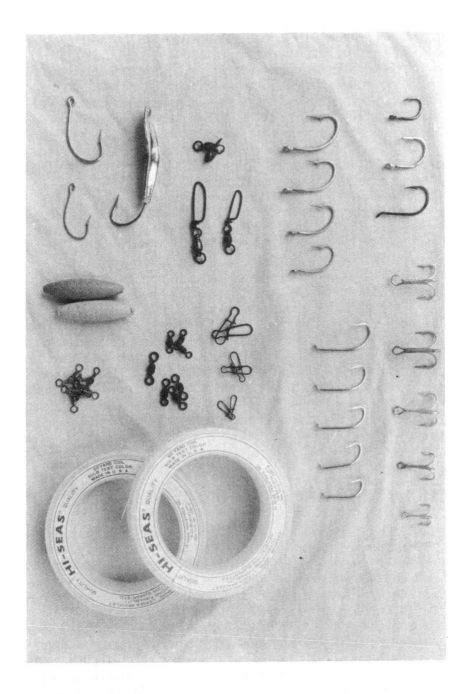

A selection of hooks, squid heads, floats, swivels, snaps and leader wheels necessary for striped bass fishing.

variety of fish. The downturned eye version works best when used snelled to the leader line, while the straight eye is better suited to other connecting knots, which we'll cover shortly.

The baitholder style is employed for soft baits to prevent them from sliding down the hook's shank and balling up on the bend. Sea worms, crabs and clams are prime examples. The smooth shank model is employed with baits like sand bugs or cut baits. Since beak hooks are so versatile, you can cover a wide variety of fishing situations by keeping a small plastic box with an assortment of a few sizes on your boat or in your tackle box and you'll be ready no matter what situation arises. My assortment consists of size 1, 1/0, 2/0, 3/0 and 6/0, and I usually use the baitholder style.

Two hooks are popular when fishing live bait, such as bunker, herring or eels. For livelining big baitfish and eels, I've experienced good results with a tinned, short-shank O'Shaughnessy in 2/0 through 6/0 sizes. Some tackle shops call them short-shank tuna hooks, but they work well with baitfish like menhaden, herring and eels and do an admirable job when used as tail hooks in rigged eels.

Some anglers prefer to use treble hooks on large live baits, especially when bass are being picky and not hitting a bait aggressively. This occurs regularly in the spring when bass are feeding on large blueback herring. The baitfish numbers are so great that bass often play with a hook bait even though they aren't feeding. Using a treble can generate hook-ups at these times when you could go fishless using single-hook rigs. A tinned, extra-strong, treble hook in sizes 2/0 or 3/0 will increase your chances dramatically. They will also be useful when slow trolling live baits of this size either as a nose hook or a stinger at the fish's tail.

# *Replacement Hooks for Artificials*

While lures come with a nice, shiny new set of hooks already installed, in some cases, the hooks are woefully inadequate for serious striper fishing. This is particularly true of treble hooks found on some plugs. Few fish can mangle a set of treble hooks like a striped bass, so for insurance purposes, many new plugs receive a hook change before I cast them for the first time.

This is particularly true of plugs originally designed for fresh water use that are adapted to saltwater. Lures like the original Rebel minnow, the Redfin and the old Hellcat, which probably had the weakest hooks ever placed on 5-inch long plug, can use sturdier hooks. A stout bass can do considerable damage to 2X strong trebles without even working up a sweat, so you can imagine how long the freshwater treble hooks lasted on these plugs once they were inhaled by a

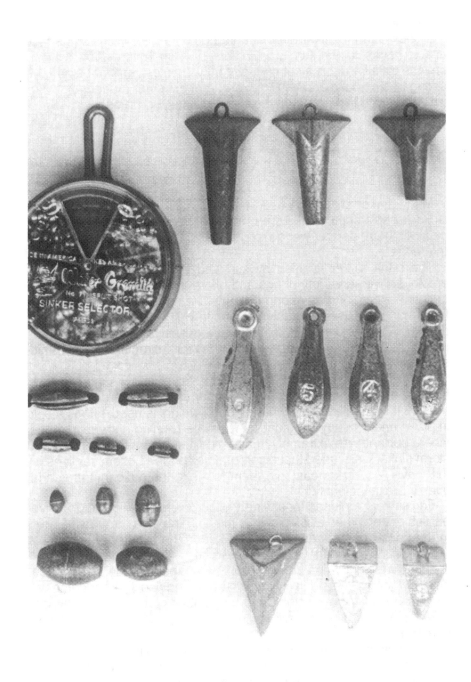

**The bass angler will use a wide variety of weights such as egg, rubber core, crimp-on, storm, bank and pyramid sinkers.**

30-pound striper, hell bent on getting rid of that plug at all costs.

If you have plugs with inadequate hooks, or flimsy split rings that attach hooks to the lure body, replace them before they have a chance to fail. Put on a set of heavy duty stainless split rings and 3X strong treble hooks and you'll never regret the small, added expense. It will save you fish and keep the lures in usable condition.

# Sinkers

Many sinker styles are used for bass fishing. From the old bank sinker to split shots, sinkers are a bait fisherman's best friend. Let's catalog them before we go on to basic bait rigs to serve as a reference.

The bank sinker is used by surf and boat fishermen alike. It is employed with a variety of rigs and offers adequate contact with the bottom, just as long as strong currents are not present. For the boat fisherman, it is used in conjunction with drift rigs or to bring a bait deeper, when holding bottom is not a necessity. Its smooth, rounded shape keeps it from hanging up in bottom structure as pyramid sinkers will do.

The pyramid sinker is preferred by surf fishermen when keeping a bait stationary in strong currents is important. Its squared-off edges prevent it from rolling and, when enough weight is used, keeps a bait in place under heavy tide conditions or in a running current. In areas where currents are extremely heavy, modified pyramid sinkers, called storm sinkers, are used that incorporate extended bottom sections or that have wire forms cast into them to make them dig into the sand even more tenaciously.

Egg sinkers are used for a variety of purposes, often to weight a live baitfish or eel. When a fish picks up the bait, line slips through the hole in the center of the lead weight and keeps the fish from feeling any pull or resistance on the line as it moves off.

Crimp-on sinkers in varying sizes and shapes can help add a little weight when needed, quickly and without re-rigging. If larger crimp-on sinkers are to be used, look into the rubber core, re-usable types. They don't damage monofilament as easily because they aren't crimped onto the line.

Drail weights are used by trollers to increase the trolling depths and for some drift rigs when fishing live baits or chunk baits. The more weight, the greater the depth, within reason. Drails much over 12 ounces become a hindrance rather than a benefit, which is why bass fishermen will resort to wire line or downriggers to attain greater depth, rather than by adding extreme weight to the line.

# Floats

In the opposite direction from sinkers are floats, which can also be used with baits. Cork floats are commonly used to make worms, sand bugs or cut bait rise off the bottom, out of reach of perky crabs.

Other types of floats are used occasionally. Some bass fishermen will use a balloon to buoy a live eel fished in shallow water to prevent it from running into rocks or other structure and hanging up. Some use cork floats for similar reasons, and school bass fishermen may use Styrofoam popping style floats in shallow waters. Floats do have a place in your bait rigging tackle box.

# Snaps, Swivels, Leader Material and Other Goodies

A few other items are used regularly when rigging up for striper fishing. As with other tackle we've looked at, it is recommended that you spend the extra change to purchase quality rigging products. Snaps and swivels from recognized names like Rosco, Sampo and Berkley assure you that the products will test out consistently and will not become the weak link in the chain of tackle connecting you to a trophy bass.

Consider shock leader material as a separate entity from the line on your reel. True shock leader material is heavier and far more abrasion resistant than running line. It is also a little stiffer, which can be helpful when tying rigs. Quality leader can be purchased on wheel-type spools from a host of line companies, with some of the notables being Ande, Hi-Seas, Maxima, Triple Fish and Jinkai.

Many artificial lures require nothing more than a shock leader and a snap at the bitter end to make changing lures easier. A snap will also allow many types of lures to swim more enticingly than a direct connection to the line with a knot. A snap is an absolute necessity when using rigged eels or specific types of squids. The Duolock style is preferred because its widely curved shape allows lures to swing smoothly from side to side. Just a few sizes will cover your needs, since it is best to match the size of the snap to the relative size of the lure. I keep Duolock RDS-53s, 54s, and 55s in my rigging box and go through them rather quickly in a season's fishing. I strongly prefer the black ones, which carry the suffix BL after the model number. You can save money by buying them in bags of 100.

Barrel swivels will be used for making rigs for trolling, baitfishing and with some types of lures. Standard barrels are fine for bait rigs, for making leaders for certain types of lures used while casting and for light trolling duties with monofilament and wire. For trolling with down-riggers or with tube lures that spin, a ball bearing swivel is a must to prevent line twist. Ball bearing swivels are highly recommended for downrigger use in particular, since line twist can be excessive between the lure or bait and the release clip holding the line to the downrigger weight. This can cause line to curl up into an unsalvageable mess in no time, ruining 50 to 100 feet of line.

Ball bearing swivels rated for 125-pound test will work well with downriggers. Wire line trolling with lures like umbrella rigs and bunker spoons requires heavy-duty ball bearing swivels, preferably with a rating of at least 200-pound test. Ball bearing swivels are worth their weight in gold and cost about that much too, but they have their place in the troller's tackle box. As was the preference with snaps, black is most often used with all terminal hardware since it doesn't reflect light underwater.

Three-way swivels are an interesting connector for attaching the line, a leader and a sinker to a rig. They are used in bait rigs and occasionally in specialty rigs for jigging two lures at once. Connecting links are used on some rigs to attach an appropriate sinker weight. The fishfinder rig employs a hollow plastic tube through which the running line is passed. A leader and bait hook is attached to the plastic slide and the sinker is attached to the end of the running line, which allows the bait to be picked up by a fish without undue pressure. A standard barrel swivel serves as a stopper.

## *Practical Knots*

Any good fisherman should have a few knots he knows well and can tie under almost any fishing conditions, during daylight or in the dark. It's best to learn a few knots well, rather than learn to tie a lot of knots in a mediocre fashion. For tying rigs, which is usually done away from the water under ideal conditions in your workshop, some slightly more difficult specialty knots will come into use, but they are usually tied in an unhurried atmosphere which helps keep mistakes to a minimum.

The most common knots are used for tying your line to a lure, hook or a connector like a snap swivel. A variety of knots apply here, but pick one that you can tie consistently well, rather than the most fancy or the ones you find more difficult. After years of trial and error, most of it on the water, but some spent testing knots with special meters to gauge relative strength, I've settled on a knot system that can do it all for the striped bass fishermen. From simple connections in light or heavy mono to joining two unequal diameter lines, as is the case when adding a shock leader to your main line. It's called the Uni-Knot system. It is simple to tie, day or night, and after you use it for a while, it becomes second nature. Its breaking strength tests out comparable with other terminal knots and it works well in line from 2 to 100-pound test, but most of all, it is a snap to learn and tie well under almost any conditions.

It can be used when a loop knot is called for by simply pulling the tag line snug, but not all the way tight before cinching up the knot. You can use it to join equal or greatly different diameters of line. I've used it to connect 60-pound test leader to 6-pound test running line with excellent results. You can even use a version of the Uni-Knot to snell a hook. Probably the greatest benefit of the Uni-Knot is its versatility. Once you learn the basic knot, you can do just about anything needed without fumbling or trying to remember a wide variety of different knot patterns.

Other basic connector knots include the improved clinch, the palomar and the snell. The snell is used extensively when tying beak style hooks on bait rigs and is usually used with down-turned eye hooks only.

Many surf and boat anglers like to have a length of double line tied at the terminal end of their running line. I do this in addition to a shock leader when surf fishing and always when light tackle fishing from a boat, even if no shock leader is employed. A double line can be accomplished with either of two knots, the Bimini Twist or the infinitely easier to tie Spider Hitch.

Offshore fishermen scorn the use of the Spider Hitch because it doesn't have quite the impact strength of the Bimini. While this is true to a certain extent, for striper fishing, the Spider Hitch is fine. A striper can blast a lure pretty hard, but we're not talking about a marlin striking a lure being trolled at 10 knots on 80-pound test line. A Bimini is a nightmare to tie in lighter lines, especially line under 20-pound test, and a poorly tied Bimini is far worse than a correctly tied Spider Hitch. Diagrams for both knots are included, but the secret to tying a good Spider is in the final drawing up of the knot. Be sure it is wet and then cinched up smoothly and with even pressure on both the tag and standing line. If the knot isn't even, or if either the tag or running line leaves an open loop at the bottom of the knot, cut it and re-tie.

For adding a teaser or making double hook bait rigs, the dropper loop is commonly used. The Albright knot comes into play for joining lines of drastically unequal diameters or for joining a monofilament leader to a wire line.

The Haywire Twist is the accepted standard for making a knot or loop in wire trolling line or for wire leaders used in rigs. All are pictured with directions for tying them.

# Clinch Knot

An old standby, this is a basic knot for attaching hooks, lures and swivels. It works best with monofilament lines up to 20-pound test.

1. **Pass the line through the eye of the hook, lure or swivel. Double and make five turns around the standing line. Hold the coils and pass the tag end through the loop formed at the eye of the hook.**

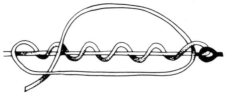

2. **Pass the tag end through the large loop as shown. This extra step makes this the "improved" clinch knot and brings the strength of the knot up to 98% of the main fishing line.**

3. **Hold the standing line and the free end, then pull the coils tight. Make sure they lie next to each other, not criss-crossed.**

# Surgeon's End Loop

Use this knot to tie a loop in the end of a line for attaching leaders, sinkers or other terminal gear quickly.

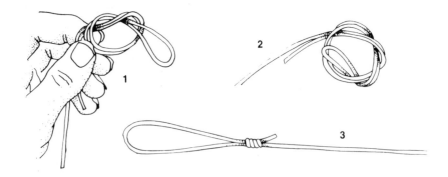

1. **Double back a few inches of line and make an overhand knot.**

2. **Pass the end of the loop through the overhand knot a second time.**

3. **Hold the standing leg of the line and the tag end and pull the loop to draw the knot tight.**

# Snelling A Hook

Years ago factory-snelled hooks were common. Today, fishermen prefer to buy loose hooks and leader material of their own choice and tie the snells themselves to suit a variety of bait fishing needs.

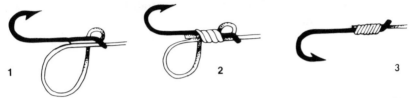

1. Pass one end of the leader through the hook eye and past the bend. Pass the other end through the hook eye in the opposite direction. A large loop is now formed below the hook.

2. Hold both lines along the hook shank. Use the line on the eye side of the hook and make five tight coils around the shank and both legs of the leader.

3. Hold the coils and pull on the long end of the leader until the coils come tight, leaving no loop.

# Surgeon's Knot

This is a handy knot which can be used to join two lines of different diameters, such as when adding a leader to a reel filled with light line.

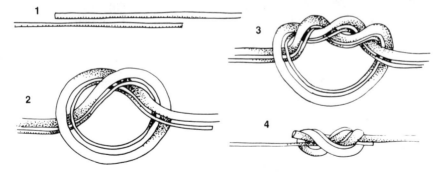

1. Lay the line and leader next to one another for about 12 inches.

2. Treat the two lines as if they were one line and make an overhand knot.

3. Pass the tag end of the line through the loop a second time.

4. Hold both sides of the lines and draw tight. Give a final pull by grasping the fishing line and the leader to set the knot.

# Palomar Knot

The palomar knot is a favorite of light tackle anglers because it is easy to tie, yet is exceptionally strong and resistant to breaking under the rapid strain caused from sudden runs of hefty fish. Freshwater bass anglers depend on this knot for tournament winning fish so you know it is a strong knot capable of handling trophy fluke.

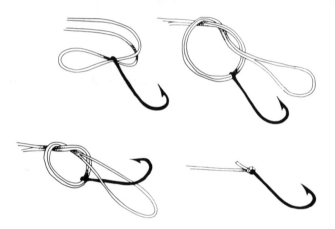

# Dropper Loop

The dropper loop is an old-time knot that is still popular today. It is used to tie a loop(s) in the leader for adding hooks, short leaders and even sinkers. Many fishermen prefer using a three way swivel, but for a simple rig with minimal hardware, the dropper loop is indispensable.

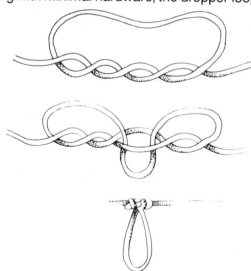

# Uni-Knot

This is an excellent, strong knot for tying on hooks, swivels and lures. For complete instructions on all the variations of the Uni-Knot, including ways to snell a hook and join two lines, write to Stren Line, c/o DuPont, Fishing Products Group, Wilmington, DE 19898 and ask for their "Powerlines to Better Fishing, Choosing and Using Lines and Knots" booklet. It's free!

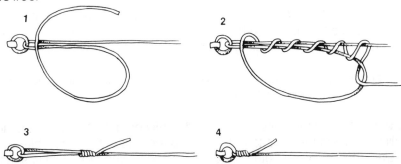

1. **Run the tag end of the line through the eye at least 12 inches and fold it back against the standing line. Bring the tag end back as shown to form a loop.**
2. **Make six turns with the tag end around the two side by side lines and through the loop. Pull on the tag end and the standing line to snug up the coils.**
3. **Pull on the hook and the main line to draw the knot close to the hook eye.**
4. **Continue pulling until the knot is good and tight.**

# Trilene Knot

The Trilene knot is an all-purpose connection to join mono to swivels, snaps, hooks and artificial lures. The knot's unique design and ease of tying yield consistently strong, dependable connections while retaining 95% of the original line strength.

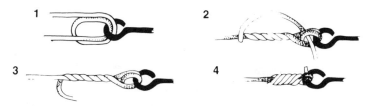

1. **Run the end of the line through the eye of the hook and double back to pass the line through a second time.**
2. **Make five turns around the standing part of the line.**
3. **Thread tag end back through the small loop formed between the twists and the hook eye.**
4. **Moisten the knot with saliva and draw tight.**

## ALBRIGHT KNOT

An excellent knot for tying a leader to heavy line, or vice-versa, or tying a line to a wire leader.

1. Double back a few inches of the heavy line (or wire) and pass about ten inches of the lighter line through the loop.

2. Wrap the light line back over itself and both strands of the heavy line. This is a bit easier if you hold the light line and both leader strands with your left thumb and forefinger, and wind with your right hand.

3. Make ten snug, neat wraps then pass the end of the line back through the original big loop, as shown.

4. While holding the coils in place, pull gently on both strands of the heavy line, causing the coils to move toward the end of the loop. Take out the slack by pulling on both strands of light line. When the knot is snug pull hard on the main light line and main heavy line. Pull as hard as you can for a good solid knot. Clip both excess tag ends close.

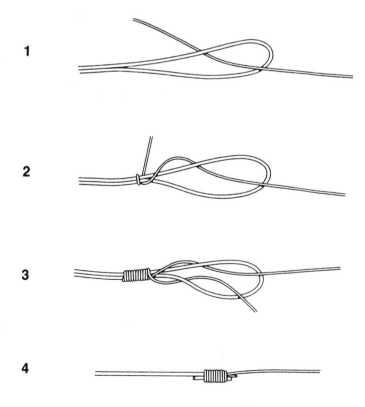

## SPIDER HITCH

This is a fast, easy knot for creating a double line. Under steady pressure it is as strong as the Bimini twist but does not have the same resiliency under sharp impact. Because of the manner in which it is tied, the spider hitch is not practical with lines above 30 pound test.

1. Form a desired double line-length loop. Near the tag end, twist the strands into a small reverse loop.

2. Hold the small loop between your left thumb and forefinger, with the thumb extended well above the finger.

3. Wind the double line strands around your thumb and loop strands, taking five parallel turns. Pass the end of the original big loop through the small loop, pull the slack out, and pull the five turns off your thumb. Pull the tag end and standing line strands against the loop strands to tighten the knot. Then pull the standing line only against the loop for final tightening. Clip off the tag end.

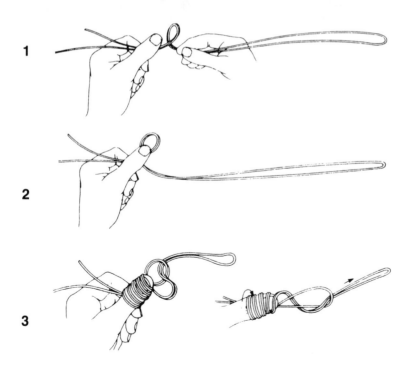

1

2

3

## HAYWIRE TWIST

This is the strongest connection for attaching a swivel, hook or lure to solid wire.

1. Pass several inches of the tag end of the wire through the hook eye. Bend the tag back and crossing the standing wire to form a small loop.

2. Hold the loop firmly with the thumb and forefinger of your left hand. Form a wide V between the two wire strands. Both sections of wire must be twisted simultaneously, or else the tag will simply wrap around the standing wire, producing a much weaker connection.

3. Make at least 3 1/2 twists in the two wires. Next, bend the tag end so it is 90 degrees to the standing wire.

4. Hold the already twisted section and wrap the tag end around the standing wire in several neat, tight, parallel coils.

5. Bend the last inch or so of the tag to a right angle, bending away from the standing line, not over it, to form a "handle."

6. Hold the twist steady and rock the tag end back and forth. It should break quickly, leaving a smooth end at the twist. If the wire is cut at this stage of the twist, it will leave a sharp burr that can cut your hand.

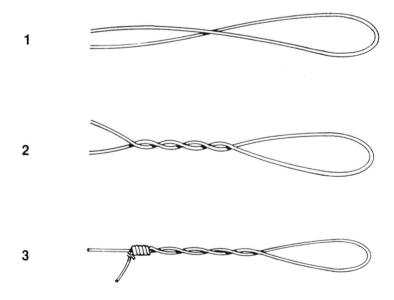

# Common Bait Rigs

There are more different regionally popular bait rigs available up and down the coast than any writer would dare attempt to catalog. Many are nothing more than variations of rigs that have been with us for decades, while others are quite unique. We'll try to keep the rigs needed for baitfishing for stripers to a simple few and you can add modifications to these to meet regional conditions. It never hurts to discuss rigs with fellow fishermen or with a knowledgeable tackle shop owner. They can offer their experience on the rigs that produce the best in your corner of the striper coast.

Most soft baits, like clams, crabs, sea worms, sand bugs and chunk baits are fished with the simplest of rigs known as the fishfinder rig. It is employed in the surf, in bays and tidal rivers and from anchored boats. The fishfinder rig is tied on sturdy leader material using a barrel swivel at the top of the rig, a sinker at the bottom. A fish-finder style sliding hook attachment that allows the baited hook to ride up and down the running line, is threaded on the line with a beak style bait holder hook. A small cork float is attached. It works well when baits are to be kept off the bottom and the sinker slide allows a fish to pick up your offering and run with it without dragging the full weight of the sinker, which can often spook a wary striper into dropping the bait before you can set the hook.

Another common bait rig for surf, bay or river that most often sees use with sea worms, is the Carolina Rig or High-Low-Rig. It consists of a barrel swivel at the top, leader with two dropper loops or three-way swivels that lead to snelled bait hooks and a sinker at the bottom. This rig works well in areas where current flow keeps the baits out from the main line and corks are not usually used. Early season fishing with worms in places like the Mullica River in New Jersey, the Croton River in New York and the Connecticut River are ideal territory for using this rig early in the season.

A drift or slow trolling rig for worms or eels can be put together in two ways. One uses a three-way swivel and a leader dropped to a bank or dipsy style sinker, and the other uses a leader and a rubber core sinker attached directly to the line or an egg sinker attached above a swivel to prevent it from sliding down onto the bait.

Live eels, bunker and herring are best fished on a short, heavy leader of 50 to 80-pound test with a barrel swivel at the top and a short-shank, O'Shaughnessy hook in 3/0 to 6/0, to match the size of the bait. The same rig can substitute a 1/0 to 3/0, 2X treble hook when bass are not hitting aggressively. Leaders for wire line and downrigger trolling serve different purposes. With wire trolling line, a leader of at least 10 to 12 feet is needed between the wire and the lure. It acts as a shock absorber since the wire line has no stretch and prevents fish from breaking off with a sudden dash at boatside. The leader also gives the angler or mate something to hang on to while leadering the fish to net or gaff.

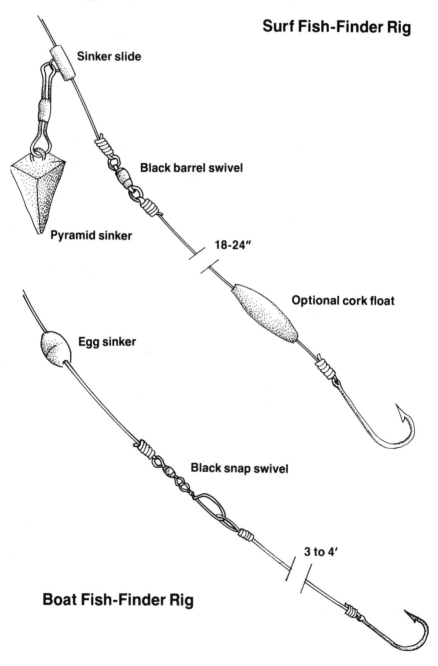

**Surf Fish-Finder Rig**

Sinker slide

Black barrel swivel

Pyramid sinker

18-24″

Optional cork float

Egg sinker

Black snap swivel

3 to 4′

**Boat Fish-Finder Rig**

# Carolina High-Low Rig

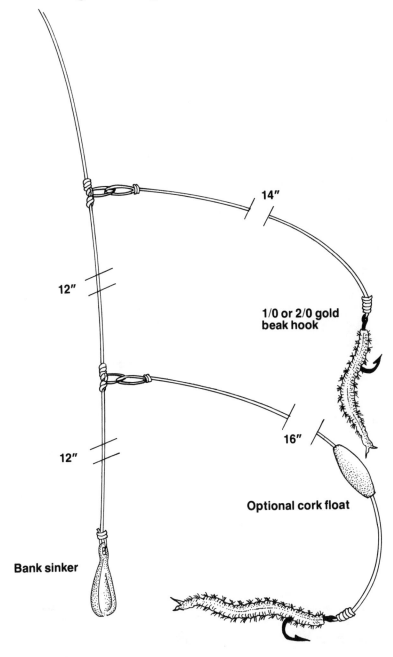

14"

12"

1/0 or 2/0 gold
beak hook

12"

16"

Optional cork float

Bank sinker

# Worm Drift Rigs

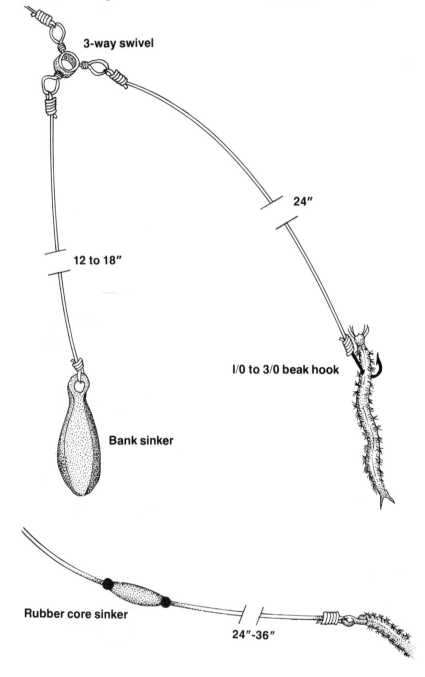

**3-way swivel**

**24″**

**12 to 18″**

**Bank sinker**

**I/0 to 3/0 beak hook**

**Rubber core sinker**

**24″-36″**

# Live Herring/Bunker Rig

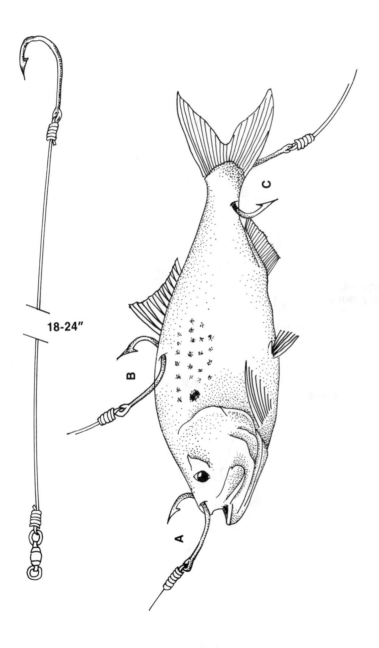

18-24"

On a fast drift, place hook in nose of bait (A), at dorsal on a slow drift (B) and at (C) near anal vent to make bait swim naturally towards a jetty.

# Liver Bunker Stinger Rig

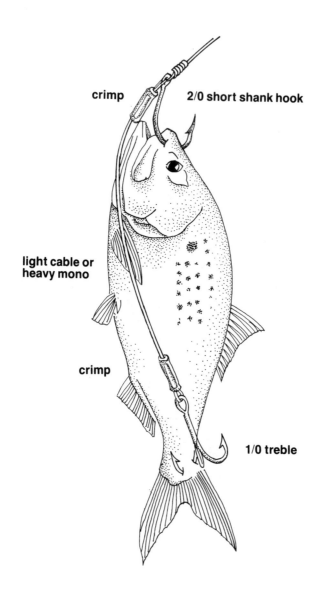

crimp

2/0 short shank hook

**light cable or
heavy mono**

crimp

1/0 treble

# Mono Trolling Rigs

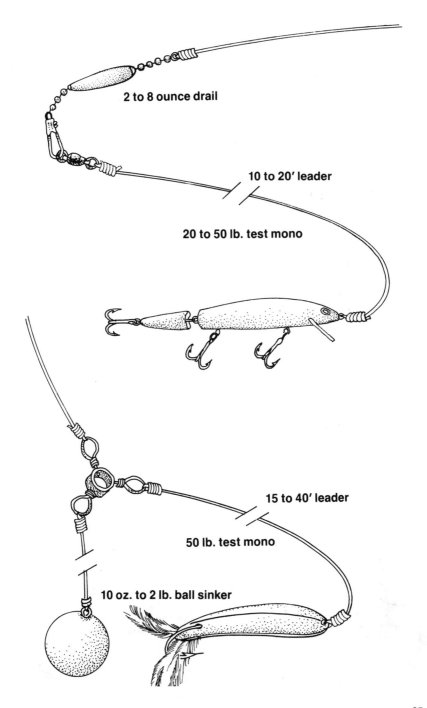

2 to 8 ounce drail

10 to 20' leader

20 to 50 lb. test mono

15 to 40' leader

50 lb. test mono

10 oz. to 2 lb. ball sinker

# Live Eel Casting Rig

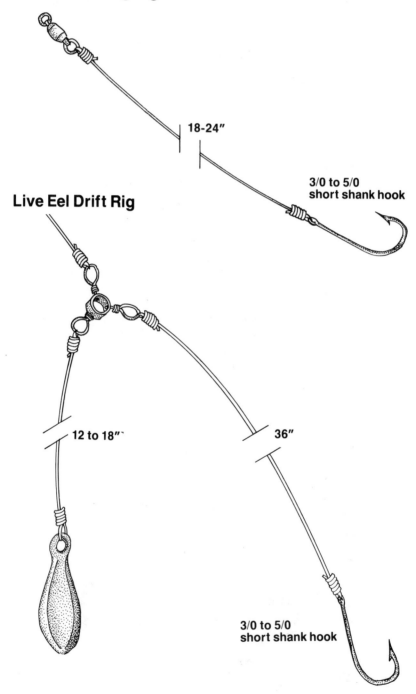

**18-24"**

**3/0 to 5/0
short shank hook**

# Live Eel Drift Rig

**12 to 18"**

**36"**

**3/0 to 5/0
short shank hook**

# Rigging Wire Line

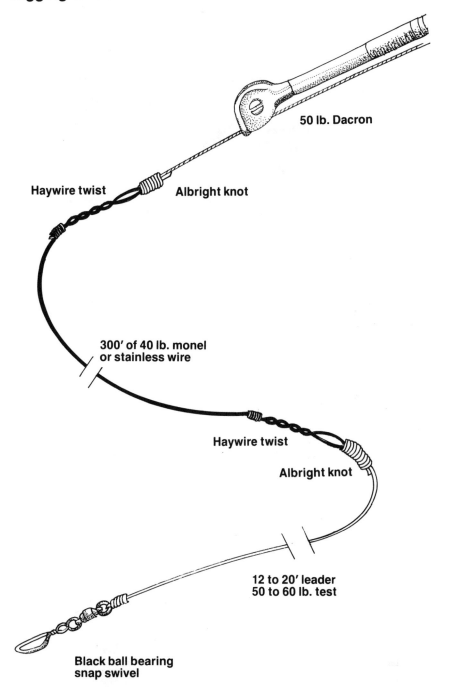

**50 lb. Dacron**

**Haywire twist**     **Albright knot**

**300' of 40 lb. monel
or stainless wire**

**Haywire twist**

**Albright knot**

**12 to 20' leader
50 to 60 lb. test**

**Black ball bearing
snap swivel**

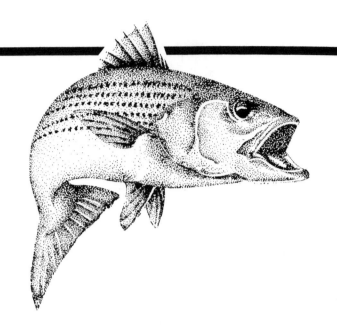

Chapter Five

# THE MENU

Striped bass are highly adapted predators capable of feeding on a wide variety of live prey. Their agile bodies are capable of quick bursts of speed making them able hunters as they search around bottom structure and in areas with strong currents. Structure that bass find of interest can include sand bars, inlets, jetties, areas of hard bottom, rips and even inshore wrecks. Structure attracts bait and bass use it to their advantage.

The list of baitfish a striped bass will eat is comprehensive and at times you might think there are few fish a bass won't eat if given the opportunity. When small, bass will prey upon any smaller fish in an estuary environment. As they grow larger, their preferences turn to larger baitfish like menhaden, mullet, mackerel and herring, but they are still not above feeding on small baitfish when a school is concentrated in a tight area. Scenes of large bass rushing through schools of sand eels, their mouths agape, are common during the northeast's fall migration run.

Baitfish aren't the only food to fall prey to stripers. Many popular sport species such as ling, whiting, blackfish (tog), winter and summer flounder, find themselves in the wrong place at the wrong time. And let's not forget eels. They rank high on the gourmet food's list of any self-respecting striped bass from New England's rocky shores to Florida's St. Johns River.

Freshwater stripers are equally adaptable to the forage fish found in lakes and reservoirs, with gizzard and threadfin shad making up the majority of their diet, but they don't stick with these baitfish exclusively. They will not pass up a nice trout dinner, bluegill or even a small catfish. Near some southern reservoirs, there are thriving bait businesses that specialize in selling 10-inch trout for use as striper baits!

While the mighty striped bass is an efficient predator, it is also an accomplished scavenger, rarely passing up crabs, clams, sand bugs and pieces of fresh fish commonly referred to as chunk or cut baits. They will happily accept a chunk of fresh herring or bunker, and in the fall, a small, dead mullet often rings a bass' dinner bell. Let's look at the menu that makes up the striped bass' dietary delights, those appetizer size morsels or oversized entrees that are accessible to fishermen as bait by catching them yourself or by purchasing them in bait shops.

# *Eels*

In my stretch of the striper coast, few baits equal the response generated from striped bass, whether smaller school fish or cow-size bruisers, like an eel. Sometimes they prefer them alive and at other times, they will wallop a rigged dead eel so hard you better be holding onto the rod tight or it will be yanked overboard. Bass will often hit an eel with a vengeance other baits just don't seem to illicit. You might say I'm partial to fishing eels and I'd have to agree, but so are thousands of other striper fanatics from Maine to Florida. Surprisingly enough, I recently found out that West Coast striper fishermen haven't a clue what eel fishing is all about because there isn't an equivalent to the American Eel (Anguilla rostrata) found in the Pacific Ocean.

For striped bass fishing purposes, eels from 6 inches to as large as 18 inches are most desirable. For rigging purposes, eels from 6 to 12 inches are best, while the larger l3 to 16-inch eels are best fished live when bigger bass are about. Eels have become a popular enough bait in some areas that live eels can be purchased at local bait stores. Prices will vary with the demand in your area and the availability. The free market system is alive and well in the bait business.

In areas where bait dealers don't handle eels, you will have to trap your own. An eel trap looks much like a killie trap with a longer center section, but it sports adjustable entry holes, so you can keep huge eels from squeezing in. It is usually deployed close to, or on, the bottom of a river or bay area. Best baits include crushed clams or crabs, but dead fish will work when nothing else is available.

It is surmised by biologists that brackish water areas are home only to male eels and that the females migrate further inland, up into freshwater rivers and streams. That means eels, like the striped bass, are capable of living in fresh or saltwater. As an interesting aside, American eels no matter where along the East Coast they are found, spawn in one remote area of the northern Atlantic Ocean referred to as the Sargasso Sea. There they mingle with spawning European eels (Anguilla vulgaris), and after breeding, the spawned-out adult eels die. The larval European eels head east and the immature American eels head west, and never do they meet again until it is their turn to spawn, 10 to 20 years down the line. The transparent larvae of the colonial member of the eel family reaches our shores about one year after hatching while the European stock takes almost three years to reach their home on the far side of the Atlantic.

Livelining eels is an exciting way to fish for striped bass, but keep in mind that eels are most productive when fished at night. They can catch fish drifted or trolled during the day under low light conditions, but after dark, there isn't a better bait in the warm summer months. Eels are not as productive when waters are cold early in the spring or later in the fall. At these times, other more prevalent baits will produce better results. But, from late spring through early fall, eels are deadly baits; fished live or rigged.

There are several methods of fishing live eels that will catch bass around structure like jetties, inlets, over inshore hard bottom areas and around prominent geographical features that create rips.

## Hooking Live Eels

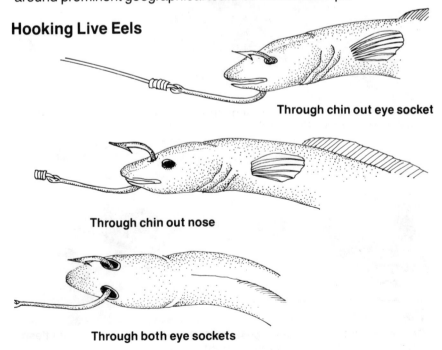

**Through chin out eye socket**

**Through chin out nose**

**Through both eye sockets**

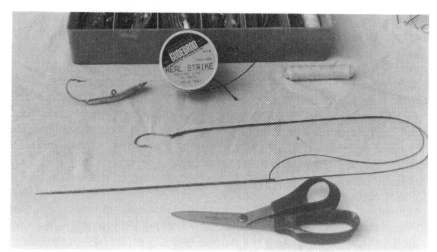

Eel rigging items: squid head, short shank hook, Dacron line, rigging needle, cotton thread and scissors.

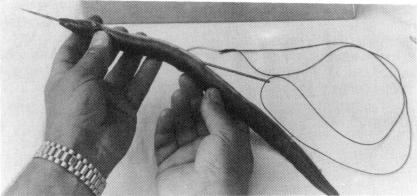

Tie hook to a 24″ length of 80-pound Dacron, attach to end of rigging needle, pass needle through anal vent and out mouth.

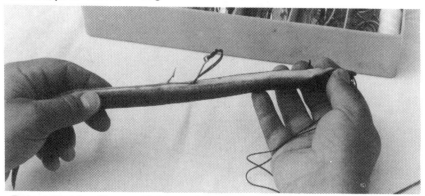

Before drawing Dacron tight, push hook through vent and through flesh about 1″ behind vent. Draw Dacron tight.

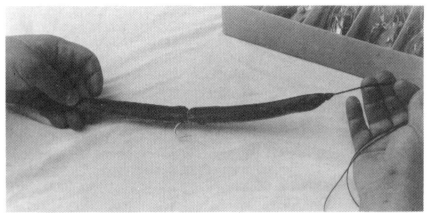

Use cotton bait thread to tie vent hook securely into place and then tie nose of eel tightly against the Dacron line.

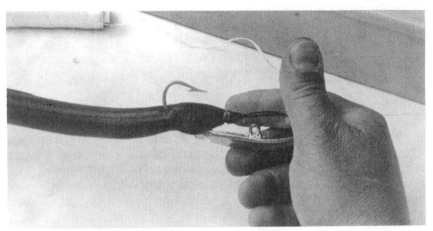

Insert swimming head hook just behind gills.

Tie nose of eel tight against squid head, then tie Dacron line into the center eye of the squid head. Eel is ready to fish.

When casting eels, a simple shock leader with a barrel swivel tied to a 24-inch length of 40 or 60-pound test leader material with a short-shank hook is all that is required. Use hooks from 2/0 to 5/0 to match the size of the eel. This rig can employ an egg sinker or rubber core sinker if extra depth is needed. Anglers in some areas will use a partially inflated balloon to control the depth eels are swimming at and to prevent them from diving into rocks around jetties. Personally, I've had the best success using live eels unweighted and without a float.

A live eel is hooked from the bottom of the jaw up through the top of the jaw, with the hook exiting just forward of the eyes, or out through an eye socket. The eye socket method is preferred if you'll be doing a lot of casting, since it will keep the hook from pulling through the eel's jaws from the extra strain.

Eels are easy to handle if you keep a bucket in the boat with a couple of inches of water in the bottom and add a few handfuls of ice, enough to get the water really cold and keep it that way. Put a few eels in the ice water and let them stay there until you're ready to bait up. They will be completely docile when you pick them up. Use a rag, and you can hook them without the struggle and without getting your hands slick with their natural slime coating. They will come back to life within seconds of hitting the water, as frisky as they were before they were chilled.

When casting live eels, it's a good idea to keep the line between your rod tip and the bait slightly taut to keep the eel from rolling up in the line. This will also make the eel swim more naturally and allow you to cover some real estate with each cast. Bass hit a live eel in different ways depending upon tide stage, current and how aggressively they are feeding. Sometimes they will pick it up and play with it or even swat at it with their tail, like they do with larger baitfish when they aren't feeding aggressively. When they are hitting tentatively, it is wise to give the fish a few seconds to take the offering before setting the hook. At other times, bass will smash an eel and gulp it down, requiring nothing more than a momentary drop of the rod tip and a solid hook set by the angler.

When using live eels for drift fishing from a boat, a different rig is employed. The eel is usually weighted, either with an egg sinker, a rubber core sinker, or by using a rig tied with a three-way swivel between the leader and hook and another short leader that leads to a drop sinker. Eels can be slow trolled using this type of rig, also. In some areas, particularly the Chesapeake Bay, eels are drift fished from head boats in this manner, but they employ a dead eel, rather than a live one.

The rigged eel is a fantastic cross between an artificial and a natural bait that has been catching stripers for close to 100 years. It is still one of the most deadly lures I know of for bass. It is made by marrying a fresh, dead eel to a tin squid swimming head that can make the eel swim more enticingly than a live one. This lure has accounted for more striped bass for me than any other.

There are a variety of ways to set up a rigged eel, all of which work. Pure tin squid swimming heads are available from J & J Tackle Manufacturing Company. The rest of the necessary rigging materials include waxed rigging thread, 50-pound test black Dacron line, a short shank tinned O'Shaughnessy hook (3/0 to 5/0), a 12-inch bait-rigging needle, a pair of scissors and some patience.

Don't discard the live eels that die on the hook or that get killed by bass. Save them and rig them later. They serve double duty for one low price. If you have to kill live eels for rigging, place them in a plastic zip lock bag and put them in the freezer for a few hours. They will be dead and undamaged when you remove them to thaw.

Rigged eels must be "tuned" before fishing. I do it in my swimming pool, much to my wife's consternation, but I don't have to play with the eels once I get down to the boat or jetty. Here's the technique; take a completed rig and grab the eel by the head and tail and stretch it firmly. You'll feel the body loosen up the way your back does when the chiropractor twists it just right. Now, attach the rigged eel to the line using a Sampo Duolock snap and, with about 4 feet of line between the rod tip and the eel, slap it hard on the water to loosen its muscles. With the eel hanging by a few feet of line from the rod tip, pull the eel and watch how it swims. It should have a pronounced "S" shaped pattern to the body at a s-l-o-w retrieve rate. If it does not, adjust the tin squid by bending the front portion upward slightly and then bending the brass eye out straight again. Try the eel again, adjusting the squid until the desired action is achieved.

Rigged eels work best when fished s-l-o-w, the slower the better under most conditions. Most fishermen who don't catch stripers well with rigged eels, or with a variety of artificials for that matter, are simply retrieving them too fast, a problem compounded by today's high-speed retrieve reels. To attain the best action at slow retrieves, position the rod tip relatively low to the water, just slightly above horizontal. Fishing with the rod tip held high can cause the tin squid head to ride up in the water rather than dig in and roll enticingly from side to side, imparting that amazingly lifelike motion to the eel.

Allow the eel to sink to a desired depth and then retrieve it. How deep a rigged eel runs depends on the shape of the squid it's mounted on. A squid with wide wings and a shallow keel on the bottom will cause the eel to ride up and run shallow, whereas a squid with a deep keel and narrow wings will stay deeper at the desired slow retrieve speed. Weight of the squid is a secondary factor to its shape when depth is your main consideration.

Other combination eel-lure offerings are the eel skin plug and the eel skin trolling jig. They both utilize salt-preserved eel skins, rather than a complete dead eel. An eel skin plug is made by sewing the skin of an eel over a large, wooden swimming plug. These plugs can be cast from the beach or boat and also effectively used as trolling lures when pulled with wire line in rips and around bars or rock structure. They have been around for a lot longer than I have, but due to the time-consuming process necessary to make them, they are not used as frequently today.

The same goes for eel skin trolling jigs, which are made from a special metal trolling jig head which is hollow down the middle. A preserved eel skin is tied to the head, which looks rather flat and uninviting when you're done rigging it. But when trolled behind a boat, the water rushes through the hole in the jig head, which causes the empty eel skin to billow out seductively. Old-timers swear by eel skin rigs of this type, especially in New England waters, where they have been a tradition for generations. A savvy few still fish them to this day, but few newcomers to the sport have the desire to invest the time and effort into skinning eels, preserving the skins properly and then rigging the lures. Even after the lures are complete, they must be kept in large jars of water heaped with kosher salt so they will not decompose.

# Herring and Menhaden

There are three members of the herring family that striped bass utilize regularly as forage. They include the Atlantic herring, Atlantic menhaden and the blueback herring. All three are similar, but each is slightly different in appearances and characteristics, and they are usually available at different times of the year.

In the early spring months, the blueback herring, or alewive, is of greatest interest to striped bass fishermen. This member of the herring family is anadromous, and works its way inshore toward inlets, bays and rivers to run upstream into freshwater to spawn, just as striped bass do, and at the same time of year. Since these fish are inhabiting the same waters of most estuaries, they are easy prey for bass, both spawners and the younger fish not ready to take on the challenge of reproduction.

The blueback herring is slab-sided and silver in color with a darker blue/black coloration on the back, hence its name. It has a small mouth, large eyes and deeply forked tail and travels in large schools. They attain sizes up to 15 inches in length and may weigh over a pound. In my home waters of New Jersey, herring can be found in just about any creek, stream, river or pond that is accessible from the ocean and they are often seen numbering in the thousands. They can

**A cast net is a handy way to gather baits like bunker in creeks and rivers, or mullet along the beach.**

be gathered in areas where they congregate as they enter sheltering waters by using a heavily weighted cast net. Check the local fish and game laws in your state before you throw the net in freshwater areas. They can be fun to catch on ultralight tackle with tiny feathered herring darts or with bare, tiny gold hooks.

Live herring can be fished with a single, short shank hook, but many anglers prefer using a single, 3/0 treble hook to increase their chances for a hook-up. Stripers will often play with a live herring and may mouth the bait before swallowing it. A treble increases your chances of hooking a fish that is only toying with the bait and allows the angler to set up on a bass earlier, usually avoiding hooking the fish too deeply in the gullet. Beach, bay and river fishermen will use chunks of cut herring for stripers, especially when waters are still cool and the fish are not aggressively pursuing live baits.

The Atlantic menhaden, also called mossbunker, bunker, or pogy, is a favorite food species for stripers later in the spring and through the summer and fall months, when they usually inhabit inshore waters, schooling like herds of finny cattle near the surface. While menhaden are available in more southerly waters in the winter months and in early spring, states from Virginia north see these fish as migratory visitors as coastal water temperatures warm. They will retreat south again as temperatures dip in the fall months.

The menhaden is the largest of the three herring species we'll look at and can weight over four pounds, while not growing much longer than the blueback. Maximum length is about 18 inches, but the menhaden has a much larger head and is considerably deeper in the body. It has comb-like edges on the rear portion of its scales, unique to this species, and coloration is dark blue, green or gray above with the sides varying from silver to brown on the sides with a brassy sheen. A large, black spot adorns the menhaden's sides just behind the gill plate, high on the fish's shoulder and is followed by a number of smaller spots in the same area. Menhaden are found from Nova Scotia to northern Florida, with a subspecies present in the Gulf of Mexico.

Much of their life history remains a mystery, but it is known that they spawn in the open ocean, usually in late summer or early fall. They can be found around inlets and inside tidal rivers and bays when waters reach their optimum temperature range and they are an extremely effective bait for livelining for striped bass throughout the summer and fall months. They are also cut up as chunk baits by beach fishermen throughout the summer and fall months, but its oily flesh readily attracts bluefish during this time of year, too, so heavier leaders might be necessary to avoid being cut off by this toothy neighbor of the striper. When blues are about, an 80-pound test mono leader can be used instead of wire without deterring bass from taking the bait.

Menhaden are hardy and can easily be kept alive in a live well if not overcrowded. They can be caught from a boat with a specially designed bunker cast net that opens to more than 16 feet in diameter and can carry as much as 40 pounds of lead weights around the outer edge to make them sink quickly around the schooling fish. Cast nets are employed in sheltered waters where menhaden are found milling about just under the surface, or they can be snagged with large, weighted treble hooks known as snatch hooks, bunker snag hooks or gang hooks. Just as long as the snag hook doesn't damage the fish's vital organs, menhaden will usually survive snagging and remain alive. Both menhaden and blueback herring can be kept alive for long periods of time in a bait-pen as long as it is kept in an area of a tidal river or estuary that receives at least a mild current flow to keep water from stagnating around the pen.

Like the blueback, menhaden are fished live on simple rigs with nothing more than a black swivel to prevent line twist and a large, single, short shank O'Shaughnessy hook in 5/0 or larger size. They are usually hooked in the back, forward of the dorsal fin, but they can be hooked behind the dorsal to better control their swimming direction.

A little trick I brought back from a Long Range tuna trip on the West

Coast works well when bunker decide they don't want to go where the bass are. Hook the bunker just behind the anal vent on the underside of the fish and put it gently into the water facing in the direction you want it to go, be it toward a jetty, inlet or rock pile. To get the fish moving, simply jerk lightly on the rod tip and the twinge of the hook and the pressure of pulling the fish backwards will usually cause it to swim forward in the direction you want.

Bass will often wallop a bunker hard, inhaling it, crushing it and scaling it in the back of its mouth with powerful throat muscles. If you miss a hit, you can tell if it was a bass because the bunker will come back with nary a scale on its sides. When a bass strikes a bunker, a count of five is usually all it takes before rearing back and setting the hook, hard!

The Atlantic herring or sea herring as it is sometimes called, is the sea-going member of the herring family that spends most of its time offshore in deep waters. They are more slender than the blueback and menhaden, and they are rarely caught live for use as baits by fishermen. This is an important commercially caught species that is known to spawn at sea in waters as deep as 100 fathoms.

During the fall, sea herring will often move close to shore, especial-

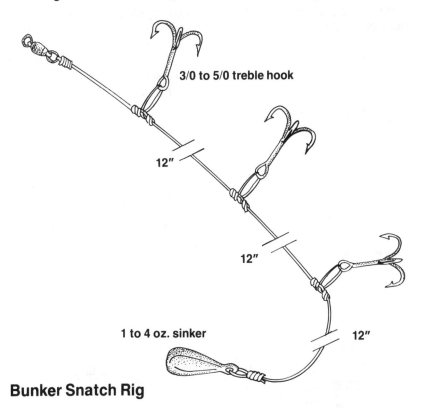

3/0 to 5/0 treble hook

12"

12"

1 to 4 oz. sinker          12"

**Bunker Snatch Rig**

ly late in the fall when water temperatures dip into the mid 50s and below, and it is then that striped bass will feast on them. Due to the difficulty in obtaining live sea herring as bait, few bass fishermen know much about them. We've foul hooked them accidentally while diamond jigging for bass. You can be sure that these unlucky herring found their way onto a hook and back into the water as live baits, only to be swallowed by a bass in short order.

# Mullet

During the fall months, the mullet, more commonly associated with Florida and Caribbean waters, can be found in great numbers along the surf in waters from New England through the Carolinas. The smaller finger mullet, are caught by surf anglers in cast nets and fished fresh, but dead, on specially designed mullet rigs. This rig incorporates a double hook that is used to impale the mullet and hold it out from the leader in a more natural way, plus a cork float to keep the bait from resting on the bottom. Ideal mullet for surf baits are less than 6 inches long.

Mullet are best fished from the beach, along sand bars. Serious surf fishermen won't go bass fishing in the fall without a cast net to take advantage of a passing school of mullet to make fresh baits. Cast nets used in the surf are usually smaller and lighter than the nets used to catch herring or bunker, since they are thrown from the beach while the angler is standing in the water. Mullet schools will usually swim within easy reach of a cast net during the fall southerly migration, so gathering them is a breeze. Keep in mind that bluefish love fresh mullet baits, too.

# Mackerel

While not a common live bait for striped bass in most waters, the Atlantic mackerel, also called a Boston mackerel, is used from late spring through the summer months from Rhode Island north through the southern Canadian provinces. I remember fishing with an old-time bass fanatic some years back off Point Judith, Rhode Island. Live mackerel were the baits. We would depart his slip in Point Judith Pond in the town of Galilee and as the boat was passing through the outer breakwaters, we would lower a large diamond jig with a five-hook teaser rig and troll up our live baits. It was explained to me that large numbers of mackerel summer in this area most years and they were easily caught in this manner.

With a live well full of mackerel, we would head out around Point Judith Light and begin drifting these strong swimming baits around the huge rocks found in this relatively shallow area of Rhode Island Sound. Big bass would rise up out of the rocks and chase the mackerel around the boat in an effort to catch these fast moving critters, often forcing them back to the protection of the boat in their bid to escape. Some were so fast and strong that it was necessary to quiet them down a bit by slapping them on the side of the boat, so the bass could catch up with them on the next cast.

Small mackerel, called tinkers, are also used for striper bait, but less frequently than the larger variety. They are more difficult to catch and keep alive and they seem to be less attracting to big stripers.

Mackerel are also used as cut bait for bass, but their oily flesh also does a good job of attracting toothy bluefish.

## Miscellaneous Baitfish

As we mentioned earlier, striped bass are not above making a meal out of just about any fish that swims too close when it is on the feed. Some of these fish that have proved effective as live baits include small winter and summer flounder, blackfish (tautog), ling and even the lowly bergall. A fishing buddy of mine recently cleaned a keeper bass and, upon examining its stomach contents, was startled to find four blowfish and a sea robin in its belly. You never know what a bass will be eating when the mood strikes it to feed.

For years, blackfish and flounders have been secret baits in Long Island's inlets and around its many bridges. These fish are deadly when livelined around structure or in strong currents. Fishing out of Freeport, New York some years back with Al Ristori, a well known outdoor writer and an excellent fisherman, our plan was to catch some small blackfish for use as bass baits, but the tog wouldn't cooperate. We did catch a bunch of medium size bergalls, so we kept a couple of dozen in the live well and headed for the inlet. It didn't take long before we were hooked into bass. These "trash fish" worked very well as we drifted the inlet at the top of the outgoing tide. Bergalls for stripers? It surprised me as much as it probably does you, but the bass weren't being picky that day.

## Killiefish

The lowly killie, whose proper name is the mummichog or Fundulus heteroclitus for you more scientifically oriented fishermen, is not your average striper bait, but for fishing in bays, estuaries and rivers for school or small bass, they can provide plenty of action. These little fish are hardy beyond belief and you can actually keep them alive for hours in nothing more than a bucket with some cool, damp sea grass. Killies fished for small bass are usually cast with light or ultralight tackle and are fished on a single, light-wire beak hook matched to the size of the killie so it can swim freely. Killies are also prime baits for the striped bass' nearest saltwater cousin, the white perch.

# Spearing, Sand Eels and Rainfish

These small, schooling baitfish can attract stripers in sheltered bay and river waters, or in open ocean waters when schooled in large numbers. Spearing are most often found inside, where immature bass will harass schools mercilessly when intent on feeding. They are easily caught in a seine net or in a fine-mesh cast net, but due to their small size, they are difficult to fish live. Most die on a hook almost immediately, but they can catch small stripers when fished as dead baits.

Sand eels, also called the sand lance (actually not eels at all but long, thin, silver baitfish), often attract school-size and larger striper

**A wide variety of metal lures resemble the sand eel and similar small, slender baits.**

when tightly concentrated. During the fall run, when sand eels are found in great abundance in inshore waters, bass will rush through a school of these hapless baitfish, their mouths agape, vacuuming in all they can in large slurps. While fishing individual sand eels as dead baits is difficult due to their size, there are times when the largest specimens can be fished on bait rigs and catch bass. When sand eels are present and bass are feeding on them heavily, artificial lures like diamond jigs will catch far more fish than trying to use a sand eel as bait. Small, artificial eels also imitate sand eels and are a favorite of surf anglers.

# Sea Worms

Worms are deadly bass baits, especially early in the year when water temperatures are cold and stripers are feeding on the easiest prey they can find. Sea worms most often used for bass are blood-worms or sandworms, and both are used in the same manner. Sand-worms are preferred, since they are tougher, stay on a hook better when cast and are usually easier to dig, or buy at a local bait shop.

Most worms are fished on either a fish finder or Carolina rig from shore, drift fished from a boat or slow trolled later in the season using a simple, single hook drift rig. They are also used to sweeten trolling tubes by New England bass fishermen.

When seeking early-season stripers in shelter waters, river winter-ing grounds, bays or along the open beach after they begin moving into the ocean, worms are a hard bait to beat. Sandworms can be dug on inland salt flats at low tide with a pitch fork and a pair of high top boots. It might take some time to find the most productive flats, but those with a muddy composition seem to hold the greatest concentra-tion of sandworms.

A relative of the sandworm, which is more green in color, can be found by digging around beach rocks, jetties or groins at low tide. These worms are not as firm as sandworms, but they also seem to hold a stronger attraction for feeding stripers. Old-timers in my neck of the woods used to pay their grandchildren to dig green sea worms for them, because they caught bass better than the "other worms."

While spring is prime worming time, sea worms can be effective throughout the spring and summer months. In spring, they are effec-tive day or night, but during the summer months, they are most effective fished at night from the beach or from an anchored or drifting boat.

When obtaining worms for striper fishing, try to get the largest, fattest specimens available. Most tackle dealers who value their strip-er clientele will make allowances and let you pick your own worms from the flats or make an effort to provide them with larger worms, saving the little ones for flounder fishermen. An old-timer showed me a trick to make sandworms tougher, firmer and easier to keep on the hook that definitely proved effective. The night before going fishing, take the worms out of the refrigerator. (Yes, always keep your sea worms in moist seaweed in the refrigerator or they will die in no time). Use newspaper or paper towels, starting with a few sheets, take the worms one at a time, and lay them on the towel stretched from side to side and roll the paper towel around it. Then lay in another worm and roll the towel until all the worms are rolled up. Put the towel in a bag and put it back in the refrigerator overnight. The dryness of the towel will cause the worm's skin to get tough and it will not break as easily on the cast or be torn off the hook by small bait stealers, either, yet it doesn't kill the worms as long as you use them the next day.

# *Clams*

Clams are responsible for catching many a striped bass from the beach and inlets, especially when they are used after a recent storm that has stirred up the surf. Beach fishermen know the effectiveness of fishing a simple lump of clam on a fish finder rig at these times and they catch many a keeper fish in this manner.

Clams can be dug, but before you go harvesting, check the laws regarding clamming in your state. A permit might be required, which is available for free in some states or for a small fee in others. Clams can be caught along the surf line with a short handled clam rake or a pitch fork. In bays, clams are raked over shallow sand bars. If digging clams isn't your cup of tea, you can buy frozen or, at times, fresh clams from your local bait dealer. Fresh are best, but frozen will produce if nothing else is available.

Fishing a clam from the beach or an anchored boat is simplicity itself. From the beach, break out the fish finder rig, being sure it is tied with a bait holder style beak hook. Thread the firmest part of the clam onto the hook and cast it into the surf. Often, bass will be looking for clams broken or stirred up during the storm right in the wash, so a long cast can actually put your bait well past the feeding fish.

Clams can be utilized in a similar manner by boat fishermen at anchor, but chumming is a more effective method, often attracting bass right up to the boat. It requires more than just hook baits, because you will need a sufficient supply of clams to grind or chop into chum. Clam chumming only works in waters with a current to carry the scent and particle of clam away from the boat to attract fish. Bass will work their way up the slick created by the chum to search out the source, feeding along the way. This method relies heavily on

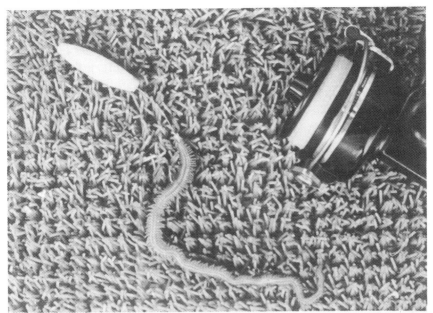

To hook a sand or blood worm, push hook through the mouth of the worm, push the bait along the hook shank until hook point exits the worm behind the mouth. Float is optional.

Calico crabs are great bass baits. Lay hook along underside of bait and tie hook to crab body. Legs are tied together along the leader.

knowing the area you are fishing and then anchoring your boat up current of a good location. Effective chumming can be done in rivers around bridges, in bays where tidal currents wash past prominent structure like bars, mussel beds, points or channels, or in the ocean around inshore rips or sand bars.

After anchoring your boat in an appropriate location, begin seeding the area with chum either in a chum pot hung from the side of the boat or by tossing a few pieces of clam over the transom of the boat at regular intervals of 15 to 30 seconds. Before tossing a small chunk of clam into the water, squeeze it in your hand and let the juice drip into the water. Keep the slick going, but don't put too much chum in the water or you feed the fish instead of attracting them closer to the boat. Hook baits are fed back into the slick on short leaders with bait holder hooks in size 3/0. They are usually fished unweighted, but if current conditions warrant, large split shot or small rubber core sinker can be utilized to get your bait a little deeper.

The most successful tides for clam chumming vary, but moving water is a prerequisite. Outgoing water is usually the most productive, with the last half of the tide stage usually offering the most action, but we have caught fish on the last half of the incoming tide, also. Most fish caught clam chumming are schoolies, but lucky fishermen get surprised from time to time, by a hungry cow that just couldn't pass up an easy meal.

# Crabs

Crabs, especially shedder or soft shell crabs, are an irresistible bait for stripers and most often used by beach fishermen. The species of crab used can vary from region to region, but the key to catching game fish with them is that they should be soft crabs. In New Jersey waters, the crab of choice is the calico, a species commonly found along ocean beaches, steeling your bait when fishing for flounder or other species. They are caught by raking the surf line, similar to the way clams or sand bugs are caught in the same area. They are not usually harvested in traps like their larger cousin, the blue claw, which is used as striper, weakfish and flounder bait in more southerly waters.

Soft crabs are fished on a fish-finder rig with a cork float to keep the bait off the bottom. Larger crabs are sectioned into two or four baits, depending on just how large they are. The bait is impaled on a large, bait holder, beak style hook and then tied in place with bait thread to prevent fish from steeling it without getting the hook and to keep it on the hook during the cast. Bait thread is difficult to find in many areas, but it comes in small, football shaped rolls, about the size of a small

**Several small sand fleas can be placed on a Beak hook. These unlikely baits are great for stripers.**

egg sinker and has elastic in the center so it can be stretched around the bait and hook to hold the bait securely. When you get done tying a piece of soft crab on a hook, the last thing in the world it resembles is a crab. For that reason and others, it is believed that soft crabs attract stripers almost exclusively through their acute sense of smell.

The theory is that when crabs shed their shell to grow, the soft, developing shell that is exposed, exudes a powerful scent into the water that can attract game fish from long distances. Crabs are at their most vulnerable right after shedding and a variety of fish, stripers included, will search them out like a gourmet will search out a fine French restaurant. During the hardening process of the new shell, the crab's body emits a substance that causes the shell to become firm and then hard and it is believed that this substance is the all-powerful scent that gets the fish's attention.

Crabs are most often used by surf fishermen who enjoy relaxing alongside several baited outfits held in surf spikes. This method of fishing is easy on the arms and can be quite productive when bass are prowling the surf line looking for an easy meal. Many of the fish caught on crabs are school size, but big fish have been taken using this method, also.

In some areas, pieces of soft crab are used to sweeten a lure, primarily bucktails or jigs. A small piece of shedder is impaled on the hook to give scent and flavor to artificials, but this technique is used more frequently for weakfish or seatrout, than it is for bass.

# Squid

A technique used successfully for catching big stripers from the inlets on Long Island incorporates the use of a large, fresh squid on a drift rig. In much of their inshore range, bass do not come in contact with large bodies of these creatures. That doesn't mean bass won't eat a squid if the opportunity arises and this seems to be the key behind this technique.

Some of Long Island's inlets have holes and pockets that bass use as feeding stations on a strong tide. They will lay in these holes, rising up to grab morsels that are carried by on the current, usually keying in on the easiest meals. Boat fishermen on the island use large squids, usually over 10 or 12 inches long and the bigger the better, to fool these wary feeders.

The rig is similar to the drift rigs used in this area with eels. A three-way-swivel is attached to the running line and a short leader is tied to a dropped sinker at one eye and a longer leader is run to the hook and squid. The size of the sinker will be dictated by the speed of the current and the depth of the water, but you want to keep the sinker bouncing bottom occasionally so the squid is riding just a few feet above the sand. As the rig passes over a hole, it will usually attract a bass that has taken up a feeding station there.

# Sand Bugs

One of the weirdest looking baits used for striped bass has to be the sand bug, also called a sand flea, sandhopper or mole crab. This tiny amphipod is found in large colonies along the water's edge on ocean beaches, moving in and out with the tide stages. They can be raked or dug with a pitchfork or shovel, but you have to be fast to catch them because they can burrow back into the sand extremely fast.

They have a heavy, curved carapace and large antennae that fold up under their bodies when withdrawn, and four pair of legs. They live in the sand, finding food with their feelers. Many species of fish will feed upon them readily. In southern Atlantic states, they are used for a variety of surf-caught game fish, and from Virginia north, they are used for seatrout, weakfish and, occasionally for stripers. For bass, they can be fished on a fish-finder rig from the beach or by casting them on lightly weighted, single-hook rigs into the running water of an inlet, drifting them back to feeding bass. Several are placed on a bait-holder, beak-style hook, by running the hook point up from the bottom and out through the carapace near the rear. When school bass are prowling the beaches, a sand bug will often out catch any other bait.

# Miscellaneous Soft Baits

Bass will eat a variety of other soft baits beside those previously mentioned. They might not be practical baits due to cost or the inability to obtain them, and in most cases, they aren't utilized by bass as forage regularly enough for fishermen to bother with. But in the interest of being complete, let's mention just a couple.

Lobsters (yes, those tasty little bugs that you'll never find me putting on a hook for bait) were a traditional striper bait in New England during the 1700s and into the grand era of striper clubs in the late 1800s, when wealthy anglers banded together. Catwalks were built out into the ocean as casting platforms to catch trophy bass. Just the tails were used which seems like an awful waste, but back then, lobsters were plentiful and to the wealthy striped bass men on the stands, money was no object.

Grass shrimp, while not widely used for stripers, will catch bass. Enterprising fishermen with time on their hands will go to the trouble of seining grass shrimp from bay grasses and use them to chum stripers in estuary waters. The gathering process is laborious, but the results can be rewarding. I'll leave it to others, since I'd rather be fishing than seining shrimp.

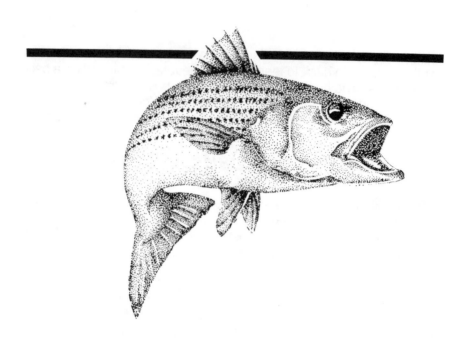

## Chapter Six

# THE LURE OF FISHING WITH LURES

Artificial lures catch striped bass! The facts are the facts, and the right lures in the hands of an accomplished fisherman will catch fish, often as well as bait and maybe even better. Some lure/bait combinations, like the rigged eel, eel-skin plugs and eel-skin jigs we mentioned in the previous chapter, are actually more lure than natural in the ways they are fished, even though they employ natural components. There is a certain lure to fishing with artificials, excuse the pun. It's the ability to fool an adversary as wary as a striped bass with a man-made lure fashioned from a hunk of metal or a piece of wood with hooks attached. It's more challenging than waiting for a fish to find a natural food source that just happens to be located on the hook at the end of your line.

Lures are especially enjoyable to anglers who prefer more active fishing methods. Casting and retrieving plugs, working trolling rods in an effort to put together the right combination of lures or presenting flies with the graceful motions of the long wand require more involvement than dunking baits. So, if casting a bait into the water and standing by quietly waiting for a fish to bite is your cup of tea, then lure fishing won't be much to your liking.

I've long preferred being an active fisherman. Even when fishing baits, my time is spent more happily with large live baits or eels which can be cast and worked around some type of visible structure. Sitting on the beach with baits washing in the surf line will probably become more inviting later in life when I'm not capable of moving quite so fast or for long periods of time, but for now, lures hold a special fascination for me and I'm certainly not alone. Artificial lure sales in this country are a billion dollar business.

Practice, patience and concentration are the keys to becoming a successful lure fisherman. With the wide variety of lures available to the striper fisherman, knowing which ones to employ at certain times of year and under specific prevailing conditions is critical, but it usually doesn't take long to learn the tricks of lure fishing.

You can spend a lot of money amassing a collection of striper lures. Simple bucktails in striped bass sizes can cost upwards of $3.50 each and large wood or plastic plugs can quickly strip your wallet of $6.00 to $10.00 a pop, so it pays to take the time to learn about the artificials that work in your area from more experienced anglers. If you're like me, badly bitten by the striper bug, it becomes almost impossible not to try new lures in that search for the ultimate imitation. It just keeps getting harder to find room in the basement for all the plugs that don't find favor anymore; the ones that have been beaten to death on jetty rocks or by bluefish teeth; the oddball colors that seemed to work so well last year but for some reason don't draw even a passing glance from the fish this season. I guess that's why they invented garage sales.

Some artificial lures are made to catch fishermen, but a surprisingly wide variety will also catch striped bass. In this section, we'll separate some of the wheat from the chaff by looking at the categories of lures that have a place in the striped bass angler's tackle collection. We'll also look at techniques and tips to make these lures effective in the quest for striped bass.

# Lure Speed

The single most important factor and probably the best kept secret to fishing most artificials for striped bass is lure speed and its ultimate affect on action. Lure speed will be mentioned a lot in this chapter, and you cannot pay too much attention to lure speed because it can make all the difference between getting hits and going fishless. Whether you troll, or cast and retrieve, learning the correct speed for specific lures is absolutely critical!

I can't tell you how many times I've had friends or fishermen I've met at clubs and on the beach remark, "I was fishing the same plug as the other guy who was catching them, but I couldn't buy a bass," or "I catch plenty of bluefish on my lures, but I just can't seem to catch a striper!" If you're fishing in the right place with the right lures and there's action going on around you, there's obviously something you are not doing right! Here's the key to the problem for 90% of the newcomers to striper fishing in the simplest terms possible. . . you are fishing your lures too fast!

Lure speed is critical with most artificials, especially rigged eels, plugs, tin squids and even diamond jigs. For trollers, presenting your lures at the proper speed is of the utmost importance and the proper speed for bass is usually as slow as you can possibly troll a lure and still generate the correct action. A bunker spoon trolled among feeding bass will rarely attract a strike if it is pulled too fast. A classic wood swimming plug should swim so as to appear alive. The same lure worked too fast looks totally unnatural coming through the water. It's the fisherman's hands and concentration that brings an artificial to life.

For trollers, the problem can be complicated by the boat. If you cannot get a boat to troll down to speeds as slow as two knots or slower, you may need a sea anchor. For lures that are cast, the problem is compounded by today's high speed retrieve reels, which is why many veteran surf casters still prefer large, old fashioned reels with 3 or 3.5 to 1 gear ratios over today's high tech, graphite spinning reels with 5 or 6 to 1 gear ratios. The faster the reel's retrieve ratio, the more it is necessary to compensate by turning the handle even more slowly.

When casting or trolling in areas of strong current, it is also necessary to compensate for the effects of water flow on the action of the lures. When fishing lures along beaches with wave action working against them, more than just a slow retrieve must be taken into consideration. It is necessary to judge the effect of the current on the lure's action. For example: when casting from a boat into shore line structure with plugs, the action of the waves intermittently pulls at the plug during the retrieve. How should you compensate for this factor and the way it effects your lure's action?

First, you must start by knowing the speed at which a lure generates its most seductive action in calm water. I usually resort to the family swimming pool for this bit of information, where the water is clear and calm. Get to know the way the lure feels when it's working right. Then, when a wave effects the lure during a cast, you can reduce speed or stop the retrieve to compensate, and in doing so, keep the lure working in its peak efficiency range throughout the retrieve. When fishing any swimming lure under these conditions, keep in mind that live baitfish are affected by current forces and it stands to reason that your lures should react in the same manner. The stronger the current action against the lure, the more you must compensate for it. When the waves are particularly strong, it is often necessary to stop your retrieve when you feel the water pulling the lure, so it is swimming in place making no forward progress. You'll be surprised how often bass will strike a lure that is swimming in place in a current like that.

If you're fishing in areas affected by tidal currents like inlets, over areas of drastically changing bottom depths where rips occur, or in rivers or streams where substantial currents are present, the same rule applies. Compensate for the current's effect on the lure by adjusting your retrieve speed accordingly. Understanding how to make a lure swim naturally under these conditions will be most important to your success as a striped bass fisherman whether you troll or cast.

# Swimming Minnow Plugs

Plugs are most often fish-shaped, with solid bodies either carved or turned from wood, or molded from some type of plastic. The debate over the virtues of one material over the other has raged for years, but stripers are caught regularly on plugs made from both materials. Each has its place, although wood has characteristics that benefit certain types of plug actions while plastic enhances other actions.

The most well-known plug is the swimming minnow, popularized by Rapala in the 1950s. The original Rapala was the first of a series of slender-bodied swimming plugs designed to imitate a wide variety of baitfish in fresh and saltwater. As the original Rapala gained favor among fishermen, other companies introduced their versions with familiar names like the Rebel minnow (the 5½-inch model of this lure holds the 78-pound All Tackle World Record striped bass as of this writing), the Bomber Long A series, the Hellcat, Cordell's Redfin, Storm's Mac Series and the Arbogast Snooker. With the exception of the Rapala Magnums and the Arbogast Snooker, most lures in this style are plastic.

These lures evolved into striper baits after years of freshwater popularity. Today's lures are sturdy and well made, but that was not the case some years ago when a middle-weight striper could straighten hooks or pull the hook hangers right out of these plugs. A striper can do more damage to treble hooks than any fish I've ever seen. It might be because so many seem to get hooked both in the mouth and outside on the cheeks, which can provide leverage to do the damage, but however they accomplish this feat of piscatorial prowess, they're capable of bending hooks and ruining hardware exceedingly well.

These failures were overcome by coastal striper fishermen, who replaced the hooks with 3X strong saltwater trebles and heavy-duty stainless split rings. Today, most manufacturers are making plugs with heavy duty hardware that will stand up to big bass.

Swimming minnow plugs are a good offering for saltwater and coastal stripers for much of the fishing season along the Atlantic coastal states when water temperatures are in the mid 50-degree range or higher. The 5½-inch versions seem the most popular size,

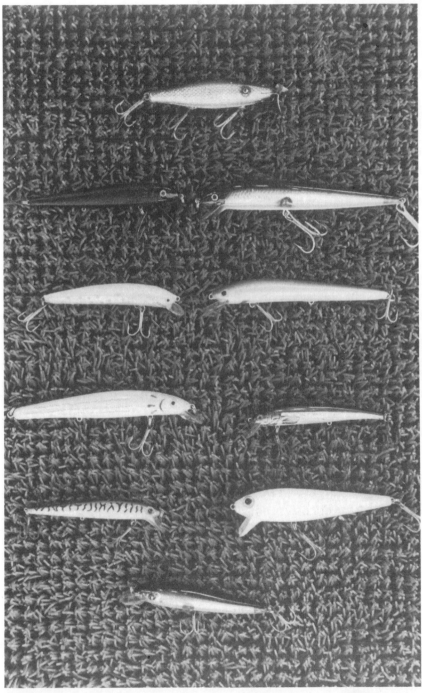

**Small swimming plugs are among the most popular lures because they are easy to fish and catch bass for novice and veteran anglers.**

although the longer and smaller sizes have their place. When school bass are feeding on small baitfish, a drop to a smaller 4½-inch lure can trigger strikes when they show no interest in the longer plugs.

Swimmers should be fished slowly. They are most effective when the angler imparts a slow, gentle, side-to-side wobble. Since they impart little or no twist to your line, they should be fished with only a Duolock snap as a connector, or simply tied direct. If one of these plugs is not swimming straight, but runs off to one side or the other, they can be tuned by bending the front eyelet slightly in the direction it is running. If it is veering off to the right, bend the eye a little to the right.

Swimming minnow plugs are particularly popular among beach fishermen and boat anglers who fish from their craft into beach or shoreline structure. They are available in hundreds of color combinations, but just a few colors will be responsible for the majority of your fish. Natural colors like silver with a variety of different back colors, mackerel imitations, yellow back, solid black or solid white are the most popular. It pays to experiment with colors when fishing, since varying light conditions and water clarity can make one color more productive than another.

The key to catching stripers with these plugs, instead of bluefish, is in the retrieve speed. Work swimming plugs as slow as possible, while maintaining the correct side-to-side wallowing motion. When I first began fishing them, the correct retrieve speed seemed agonizingly slow, until I started catching bass. Now it seems just right.

## Big Swimmers

Trophy stripers like big baits and a variety of large swimming plugs are available to imitate big baitfish. They are available from long-time lure makers with highly recognized names like Gibbs, Atom, Creek Chub and from dozens of small companies that make lures from small workshops. In my neck of the woods, there are several local plug makers building big swimmers and a variety of other bass lures with names like Beachcomber Lures, Bob Hahn Plugs, Oceanport Tackle, Shure Strike and others.

Big swimmers differ from swimming minnow lures in size, shape and action. While the swimming minnow plugs are made to imitate small baitfish like sand eels, spearing or tinker mackerel, big swimmers are usually 5 to 10 inches in length, can weigh upwards of 4 ounces and are engineered to imitate herring, bunker or larger mackerel. They are usually constructed of wood, although some very interesting new plugs are being offered in plastic by a company called MagnaStrike that are aimed at the heart of the striper market and they do catch bass.

**Large wooden plugs are legendary in their fish-catching ability and are favorite lures used by surf and boat fishermen for trophy fish.**

These plugs in their smaller versions, are popular with beach fishermen. In some regions, Montauk and the New England coastline in particular, even the biggest swimmers are cast from the beach. But most of the bigger models are more useful to boat fishermen as trolling lures pulled on wire line or mono rigs with drail weights to get them down deep. They even make excellent center lures used with umbrella rigs for a change of pace.

It should be no surprise that these lures work best when trolled or retrieved slowly. Trolling speed should be determined by watching the plug's action alongside the boat as you vary engine rpms before dropping it back into the pattern. It should have a seductive rolling motion and not a violent side-to-side shaking action. It's the roll that fools the bass. When casting them, the same rule applies. With some big plugs, it is necessary for a caster to "jump start" the lure. This is done by beginning the retrieve with a hard jerk on the rod tip to get the plug moving and then falling into a slow cadence with the reel. Keep your rod tip at a 45 degree angle toward the water, rather than keeping it high, which can cause the plug to ride up, reducing the action.

Big swimmers that incorporate metal lips to generate the swimming action can have their running depth altered by bending the eye at the front of the plug. Bend it up slightly and the lure will have a tendency to dig in a run a little deeper. Bend it down and the lure will run shallower, but avoid bending the lip, itself. These big plugs impart no twist to your line so they should be fished with a minimum of hardware. Use either a large Duolock snap or a loop knot to tie direct to the line.

For casting, most large swimmers will not run much deeper than a couple feet under the surface. Many will have a tendency to run on, or just below, the surface, creating a "V" wake behind them. Getting a big swimmer to "wake" like that will often generate considerable interest from bass, especially in relatively calm water. Bunker will often create a similar wake in calm waters, hence the resemblance.

As a trolling lure, big swimmers can be deadly, especially trolled at night. The largest of the swimmers, like the Gibbs Trolling Swimmer, the Creek Chub Giant Pikie or the Atom 40, are excellent choices for fishing in rips at night on wire. The lure offers bass a representation of a jumbo baitfish disoriented by the currents of the rip. In northern New Jersey, we fish a rip at the tip of Sandy Hook, just south of the entrance to New York Harbor. When conditions are right, the water passing through the rip moves extremely fast. So fast that when the boat is nosed into the current, it will barely move when engine rpms are set to move the boat at 2 to 3 miles per hour. The current generates the action of the plug as the skipper holds the boat in position, almost not moving at all. Big bass are caught there each season using this tactic. It also works in places like The Race, Pigeon Rip, Plum Gut and many other areas on the striper coast.

## Needlefish Plugs

These unlikely looking plugs have gained amazing popularity, especially with beach fishermen. Originally introduced by Boone Lures, their Needlefish was designed for southern waters to catch barracuda, redfish and seatrout. They were shaped to look like a needlefish, hence the name, but it didn't take long for some enterprising striper fishermen to realize they looked a great deal like a sand eel in the water. If you've ever seen a sand eel swim, there is very little side-to-side motion in their bodies. The tiny tail does all the work and the body stays pretty much straight. A needlefish plug does a remarkable job of imitating a sand eel, when retrieved at a slow, steady rate with no additional action imparted by the angler.

For just this reason, needlefish plugs are difficult to gain confidence in. When I first started fishing them, I just couldn't convince myself that any lure that just came straight through the water with no apparent action could catch bass. I was uncomfortable fishing it and I had no confidence in its ability to take fish, until that first 25-pound bass hit one so hard that I almost lost my grip on the fishing rod! It didn't take long before I changed my tune.

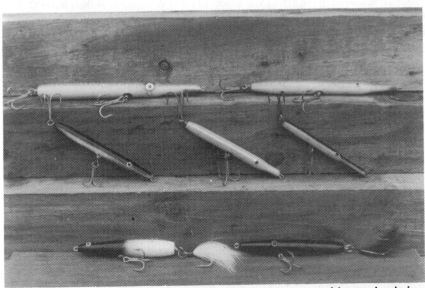

**Despite a lack of inherent action, needlefish plugs resemble sand eels in the surf and are a hot lure for many surfcasters.**

Needlefish come in sizes ranging from 4 inches to over 8 inches in length. In my area, the jumbo models are not used often, with 4 to 6 inch versions taking the majority of the fish. In fact, the needlefish that has caught the most fish for me in home waters is a skinny four-inch model not much bigger around than a pencil. In New England and on Long Island, where the larger sand lance is more prevalent, the bigger models gain more favor. I fish needles in just a few colors, which include all black, black and white, all white, yellow and white, and occasionally blue or green. The most productive sizes have been small, either four inches with two trebles or the new, stubby models with their fatter bodies and a feathered tail hook.

Needlefish are most effective fished over sandy bottom in the fall months, when the baitfish they imitate are most prevalent in the surf. I usually don't even put them in my tackle box or jetty bag until September. After the cast, allow the lure to sink to a desired depth and then simply retrieve at a slow rate of speed. Some beach fishermen work them with a little action imparted through manipulating the rod tip, but I've found that needles get the most hits when fished with the least amount of action.

# Surface Plugs

While I've never been overwhelmed by the success of poppers for bass in the ocean, they can be quite effective in bays and rivers. River stripers feeding on herring will often cream a popper. When fishing the May/June run of bass in the Delaware River, there have been mornings when the stripers were literally going crazy chasing the herring in shallows and rapids. Casting a white, 3/4-ounce pencil popper or a Creek Chub Striper Swiper in chrome imitated the bait they had been smashing on the surface in wild attempts to eat them.

In the ocean, bass working a school of baitfish near the surface will also fall to the enticement of a well-presented surface lure. Poppers that have proven their worth include two from Gibbs lures, which are probably the most famous still being made. The pencil popper is unique among surface lures and really isn't a "popper" at all. It's cigar shaped, fatter and weighted at the back and narrow at the front where the line attaches, without the scooped out, wide face that makes other poppers pop.

This lure is worked by rhythmically whipping the rod tip, which makes the lure move from side to side while almost standing in place. More knowledgeable anglers hold the rod high up the blank to whip the rod better. As the rod tip is worked, a single turn of the reel handle is added between jerks to take up slack and to keep the lure moving slowly toward you. Nothing else on the market swims like a pencil popper and for whatever reason, bass find it quite enticing. This particular lure is a striper catcher on both coasts, having found favor with San Francisco's bay area striper fishermen many years ago.

The other Gibbs offering is the Polaris popper, a bottle shaped plug that bass fishermen have sworn by for over 40 years. Its wooden body is extremely buoyant, which means it can be worked slowly on the surface and it won't sink when you stop the retrieve. This is important, since bass will often hit a popper when it is stopped momentarily during the retrieve.

Another famous popper is the venerable Creek Chub Striper Strike, which is as popular in freshwater sizes as it is in the bigger saltwater versions. This is a plastic lure that will sink when the retrieve is stopped, but it still seems to catch bass well. The larger sizes of the Rebel popper also catch bass and they are floaters, allowing the lure retrieve to be stopped for a moment. The Atom popper is also recognized as a good striper bait. It is molded from a unique foam plastic that is somewhat more buoyant than most, but that still sinks when the retrieve is stopped. Just as with other lures, poppers seem to catch better when the retrieve is kept slower than you would work it for other fish. Lures that can be worked and stopped will often draw the most interest.

# Diamond Jigs

Diamond jigs and a variety of lures similar in shape and construction are most effective on schooling bass. During the fall migration southward, bass concentrated into tight schools will fall victim to diamond jigs in large numbers. There have been days during recent fall runs when three anglers on my boat caught upwards of 60 school bass from 8 to 25 pounds on diamond jigs in a morning. When sand eels are in the wash, some surf sharpies will turn to diamond jigs dragged just off the bottom, allowed to hit the sand to create puffs from time to time.

The key to catching bass instead of bluefish with diamond jigs is, once again, in the retrieve speed. Bluefish revel in nailing a fast moving diamond jig, a method that is called speed jigging or squiding. Drop the lure to the bottom, crank like hell and hold on! It catches blues exceedingly well, but not bass. The same lure, fished among schooling bass, is worked at a slow retrieve rate or simply jigged up and down just off the bottom. Most schooling bass will hold close to the bottom, rather than up in the water column, so just lifting the lure with the rod tip, about four or five feet and dropping it back down, will often be all you need to interest bass. Remember that most hits when jigging in this manner will come when the lure is dropping, so let it drop on a tight line and watch carefully for hits on the way down. If a bass hits the jig on the drop, lift up and set the hook immediately, since it is unlikely the fish will hold the jig for more than an instant.

If the fish aren't hitting while jigging, a slow, steady retrieve will often be their undoing. Drop the jig to the bottom and just reel it in slowly and you'll probably be surprised at the attention it will get from bass.

Diamond jigs will catch bass with or without tube tails. It often pays to try a few with different color tails and others without tails altogether to see what the preference of the day, or even during that tide, will be. Tube tails that have produced the best were usually green, dark red, wine colored and occasionally yellow or white.

Unusual shaped jigs work well from time to time. Bead Tackle Company's Sand Eel Jig and Wobble Eel are two prime examples. There have been days when these two lures have caught far better than a standard diamond. Another interesting example is the Sand Eel Jig offered by J & J Tackle, a tin reproduction of a jig manufactured by a long defunct company called Tri-Fin. It has a sand eel-shaped body that flows into a colored surgical tube tail with a single hook. While it is not very effective jigged vertically, it can produce amazing results cast from the beach and retrieved so it touches bottom from time to time, puffing sand like the real thing.

More recently, fishermen have found that herring-shaped jigs will catch fall stripers when large concentrations of Atlantic herring are in residence on the inshore grounds. Two excellent examples are the Crippled Herring Jig from Luhr Jensen and the stainless steel Pirk Jig imported from Finland by Harrison-Hoge. Bass show an uncanny preference for these wide profile jigs and will often catch fish when other lures cannot illicit a strike.

## Block Tin Squids

Over 100 years ago, fishermen had no fancy plugs to use for striped bass, yet they consistently caught bass on homemade lures that imitated a wide variety of coastal baitfish. The lures were made from tin, cast in bronze molds that were closely guarded family secrets. They were called block tins or tin squids. They were popular until the outbreak of World War II, when tin was declared a strategic metal and it became difficult to obtain for anything but military use. When the sanctions on tin were finally lifted in the late 40s, tin squids were already just a memory for most surf fishermen and plugs were beginning to eclipse their popularity.

Recently, a few small tackle companies rediscovered tin as a lure material and began offering some of the old, time tested striper lures again in their original forms. J & J Tackle Manufacturing Company in

**Block tin lures, like these in the J&J Tackle collection are experiencing a resurgence in popularity because they catch stripers so well.**

Belmar, New Jersey has lead the revival, offering mass-produced tin squids molded from the original designs, some of which are over 80 years old. Guess what? They catch fish as well today as they did way back then!

Block tin squids are available in sizes and shapes to match everything from sand eels to mullet and there are models that swim at different depths and with actions so varied that there is one to match almost any baitfish and any set of fishing conditions. They have a few advantages over plugs, too. Since they are metal, they cast considerably farther than plastic or wood. They are far less wind resistant when casting into the teeth of a stiff wind. Since they sink, you can fish them at almost any depth. Due to the wide variety of shapes, there are models designed to run deep and others to run just under the surface or anywhere in between.

Tins are interesting lures both from a historical standpoint and due to the interesting characteristics they offer an angler. Their shapes, while matching the silhouette of specific baitfish, also mimic the swimming motions of these baitfish. Add a small strip of pork rind to some of the hooks and the action and attraction factor is doubled.

When looking at tin squids and trying to determine how deep particular models will run, keep in mind that the shape of the squid has more influence over depth than weight. All squids incorporate wings and keels to generate swimming action. The wings are the portion of the squid that creates lift and the keel generates the wobble. Tins with wide wings and shallow keels will ride up in the water no matter how long you let them sink. Tins with deep keels and narrow wings will have a tendency to stay deep upon retrieve. The angle of the fishing rod on retrieve will also affect running depth. Most squids work best when the rod is kept close to horizontal to the water. If you raise the rod tip, the lure will want to ride up in the water.

# Artificial Rigged Eels

We looked briefly at natural rigged eels in the previous chapter, but artificial rigged eels are also available with soft plastic eel bodies that look like the real thing. Pure tin squid heads are better than lead or tin alloy heads, which don't swim an eel as well. Old-timers would check the pureness by gently biting the squid head to confirm it was pure tin. Pure tin crackles when you put pressure on it with your teeth; alloys and lead do not.

Rigged eels are deadly, even with plastic eel bodies. I still prefer rigging my own natural eels, since I feel the scent they leave and the natural feel they offer when a bass hits them adds that much more to their catchability. When natural eels are not available, the plastic versions have caught pretty well for me, also.

Rigged eels are deadly around jetties, inlets and sand bars. Work them slowly enough to impart a natural "S" shaped swimming motion to the eel body. Be sure to keep the hooks, especially the tail hook, extremely sharp, so they will penetrate quickly when you set up on a fish. Bass will strike a rigged eel and hold on for just a few seconds, so just dip the rod tip and then lift hard to set the hook immediately.

Larger plastic rigged eels, those in the 16-inch range, make great trolling lures, especially after dark. Slow trolling them along beach fronts, over high bottom and just outside inlets on the outgoing tide change can be productive areas. They work well when fished on wire or from downriggers.

# Spoons

Spoons are hot striper lures, but are most usually employed when trolling. From gigantic models like bunker spoons or the 13/0 Crippled Alewife to smaller spoons like the Tony Accetta or the Huntington Drone, spoons can catch bass of all sizes, especially big ones.

When spoons are working properly, they can produce catches of

Big, flashy spoons like the Drone, Acetta, Crippled Alewive, and Montauk, Reliable, Graves and J&J Tackle bunker spoons are favorites of charter captains from Maryland to New England.

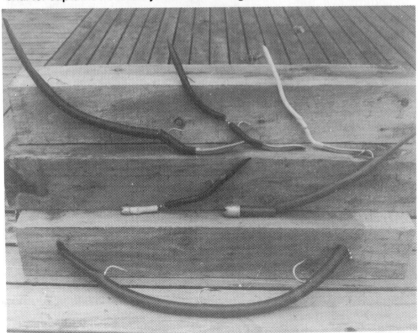

Surgical tube lures come in a variety of sizes and shapes, with and without swim heads, with and without jointed bodies to match many fishing opportunities.

huge proportions. One morning's trolling trip during late November off New Jersey's Island Beach State Park is a classic example. Although smaller bass were being caught along the beach in shallower waters to 40 feet by anglers using diamond jigs, we decided to see if bigger fish were in deeper water chasing sea herring. The hunch paid off as we matched the hatch with Reliable's jumbo size Lupo Bunker Spoon. We fished in 60 to 80 feet of water on wire line with 8-ounce drail weights for extra depth. As boats inshore of us scored on schoolies, we boated 11 bass from 28 to 44 pounds in just three hours fishing, tagging and releasing all but two fish. Critical to our success that day was the color and size of the spoon and working them at just the right trolling speed to impart the erratic action these spoons are famous for.

Spoons are not just fall offerings. We've had great success using Fred Mear's Crippled Alewife spoons in 11/0 size in the spring when blueback herring are the main baitfish. These spoons have been famous for decades in the Chesapeake Bay for catching rockfish and jumbo blues, but they are just as deadly in any area that experiences a spring run of bluebacks.

The big Tony Accetta size 21 accounts for hefty bass when trolling on wire, too. The Huntington Drone spoon, which has been manufactured since 1919, is also a hot offering for stripers in larger sizes on wire and in small sizes for downrigger use. For trolling bass, spoons can be the ticket to bigger and better fish.

Spoon color for stripers is an interesting subject. The vast majority of bass are caught on spoons that are white enameled or polished natural stainless, but enterprising fishermen play with spoon colors and can often achieve success on unusual combinations. Silvers, blues, greens and yellows can catch, as can fluorescent colors. I have a few bunker spoons dressed with a scale pattern reflective tape that are killers, along with Crippled Alewive spoons in unusual color combinations.

## Surgical Tube Lures

Charter captains who specialize in stripers have been using surgical tubing for lures for decades and they use these big lures to catch a lot of bass. Tube lures, called hose in the Chesapeake, are offered in a variety of styles, sizes and rigging methods for different conditions. Long, slim tubes in 14 to 18-inch lengths with a single 6/0 hook are trolled in spring and summer for school bass with a sandworm on the back in New England waters. These famous "Tube and Worm" lures can catch bass on wire line when nothing else seems to work and are particularly effective on school size fish. Just what a bass sees in a piece of surgical tubing with a worm hanging off the hook is beyond me, but if it works, fish it!

Jumbo tubes in 16 and 18-inch lengths made from thin-wall, wide-diameter tubing with two 9/0 or larger single hooks in them are trolled for jumbo bass in the late fall months. They account for more than a few 50s each year. These lures must be stored so they retain a natural bend in the tubing so they will swim invitingly when trolled at slow speeds. Store them in a small, round bucket or wrapped around a coffee can or similar object to preserve a natural bend in the rubber tubing.

Tube lures that incorporate swimming heads and split bodies with bead chain in the middle are another potent type of surgical tube lure. Some have tin squid heads that impart a side-to-side wobble, while the rear section of tubing in the two-piece body spins enticingly. This style of tube lure works exceedingly well on wire line, downriggers or as a dropper down the middle of an umbrella rig. There are even small versions that beach fishermen can cast and retrieve quite successfully.

As with other trolling lures, get to know what speed generates the best action with a specific tube lure. Pull them alongside the boat at various speeds and watch how speed changes alter the lure's action. A properly running big tube should spin slowly. A split-body tube lure is working right when the tail is turning over at a moderate pace, not spinning wildly. Swimming-head tubes should wobble enticingly from side to side as the tail spins.

# Umbrella and Spreader Rigs

You either hate 'em or love 'em, there's little middle ground when it comes to umbrella rigs for trolling. Most fishermen tolerate them only because they catch fish so well. Others consider them unfair with their multiple hooks and wire frames while many experienced trollers and charter captains wouldn't go bass fishing without them.

An umbrella rig is a unique concept that allows a troller to imitate a school of baitfish with a single lure. It consists of a stainless steel wire frame, joined on a central axis where the line to the reel is attached. From each arm of the wire frame, a short tube with a hook is mounted, and a larger tube is run down the center of the rig on a 3 to 5-foot leader. Umbrella rigs are available in two arm, usually called a spreader rig, four arm, and six-arm configurations. Some have smaller tubes on each arm hung from rings halfway between the center axis and the end of the arm, but these teaser tubes are not armed with hooks.

The effect they have in the water is to simulate a small school of baitfish, with a single larger baitfish or small predator fish swimming behind the school. Whatever your feelings on the use of umbrella rigs might be, rest assured that they do catch fish and often times, when nothing else in the boat is working.

For ease of use, I avoid six-arm rigs and stick with four-arm rigs in which the arms are not longer than 12 inches from the axis. They are easier to control and still present the same enticing appearance in the water. The hook carrying tubes at the end of each arm work best when they are made using bead chain rather than a regular swivel. Bead chain allows the tubes to swim better at slower speeds and we know how important correct lure action and trolling slow for bass is.

The drop back lure, usually the lure that will receive the greatest amount of attention and strikes from bass, is of particular importance. Tube lures like J & J's Tee Jay Squid and Smilin' Tee Jays, Ultimus

**A double header of school-sized striped bass caught on an umbrella rig trolled on wire line.**

Tackle's Swimming Tubes and Banana type tubes produce well, but on occasion, a Bomber or Gibbs trolling swimmer plug will work wonders down the middle of an umbrella. It pays to experiment with the dropper lures on an umbrella, as well as the color of the tubes.

Bass fishermen tend to use more subdued tube colors rather than the hot colors used when trolling umbrellas for bluefish. Wine, red, dark green, purple, black, amber and even blue are preferred. At times, bright colored tubes work also. We've had times when bass would jump all over hot yellow tubes on umbrellas when the old-timers said you had to be using dark colors. You can mix up the colors on a rig, also, but most often, try running three tubes of the same color and one contrasting. See if the fish are showing a preference for that day and then switch your rigs to emphasize that color.

When using umbrellas or spreaders for bass, the key to attracting stripers rather than bluefish is, you guessed it, trolling speed. I've caught stripers on umbrella rigs at 2 knots. An added benefit of pulling rigs slowly is that they will run deeper at the slower speeds. Here's a trick we've used with rigs when bass are holding deep, say over 50 feet. When the fish are marked on the depthfinder, the boat is bumped out of gear and allowed to coast momentarily. As the speed slows, the rigs sink deeper. When the boat is put back in gear and the rigs begin to rise, the fish will attack. How long to keep the boat out of gear, letting the rigs sink, is a judgment call on the skipper's part. If you let them sink a little too long, you can hang them up on the bottom and each umbrella and the dropper lure you lose can cost you $20.

I've recently found some mini-umbrella rigs with four arms that can be used with downriggers. These mini-rigs are only about 14 inches across, from the tip of one arm to the tip of the other, and their reduced size means that the drag they create in the water is light enough to be able to keep your line in the release clip of the downrigger weight.

## Bucktails and Doodlebugs

The old reliable bucktail, called a doodlebug by old-timers, still accounts for many stripers in lakes, rivers, bays and around structure in the ocean. They are not to be underestimated as a bucktail will often save the day when nothing else produces.

I can remember a trip to Virginia's Lake Anna to fish for the lake-bound stripers that are stocked there. The month was February and the bass were holding on deep drop-offs around creek channels and on some steeper points. After trying a variety of lures and live baits, the guide handed me a 1/4-ounce white bucktail with a chartreuse split tail plastic trailer and asked if I knew how to fish one. "No problem" was my reply, and he instructed me to let it sink to get down to the fish we'd seen on the graph recorder holding at 30 feet.

It took two casts before our first striper of the morning hit the bucktail with all the finesse of a brook trout taking a nymph. I set the hook and it was off to the races as a 20 pounder did its level best to take all the 8-pound test line off the reel. We caught another ten bass from that school before they turned off, but it took a simple white bucktail to get the job done.

Bucktails are still the lure of choice among Long Island's bridge fishermen and for nighttime rock jumpers around New England's many breachways. They catch fish from jetty rocks and larger bucktails are deadly when jigged and trolled on wire line from the Chesapeake Bay to New England's Elizabeth Island Chain.

For many years, when fishing the Hudson River near Croton Bay for early spring stripers, the first artificials to attract any attention from the bass was a white or yellow Upperman, flat bucktail, which we would sweeten with a tiny piece of sandworm. The same proved true during an April outing in the Salt Pond in Wakefield, Rhode Island. Fishing some deep channels for school fish with light tackle, the only lures that caught fish were bucktails.

No matter where you fish for striped bass, bucktails can be productive lures, especially early in the seasons when waters are cold and fish are moving slowly. At those times, you can crawl a bucktail along the bottom and catch fish. Learning to use them well can benefit your efforts greatly.

Bucktails consist of a lead or tin head with hair, feathers or nylon "fishair" and some have added flash generated by strips of mylar tied in. A bucktail is simple and effective. These lures have no action of their own, so it is up to the angler to make them come alive in the water. At times they can catch by simply casting and reeling them back with a slow, straight retrieve. At other times, bouncing them around and off rocks or along a sand bottom with lifts of the rod tip during the retrieve gets more attention. Most times, bucktails work better with the addition of a pork rind trailer or some type of bait to "sweeten" them and add additional action to the lure.

There are even bucktails made specifically for trolling. Large versions, usually weighing at least three ounces and as much as five ounces are trolled on mono or wire line using either a straight unhampered action, but more often, jigged by an angler holding the rod to enhance the action of the lure being pulled through the water by the boat. This jigging/trolling technique was called "rowing the boat" years ago because the angler working the rod would hold the tip close to the water and sweep the rod tip forward in a motion similar to paddling a canoe.

A special bucktail that is used for jigging by trollers is the parachute

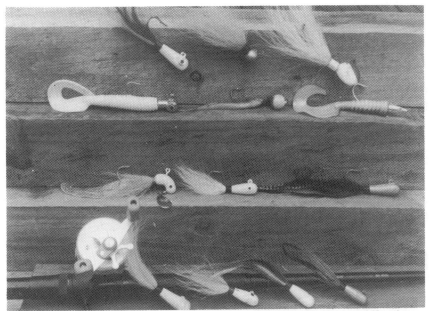

**An old-time lure that still works today. Bucktails are simple, but effective. Add a strip of pork rind or a plastic tail for added motion.**

jig. It is tied using nylon fishair with some facing the rear of the lure and some facing forward, over the lead head. When the lure is jigged, the hair flares and billows enticingly. Trolling bucktails are usually used in conjunction with a large, trolling strip of pork rind to provide the most appealing action. This method of trolling is done exclusively with wire line and is a lot of work and effort to do correctly. But, one thing is for sure, if you jig bucktails on wire for any length of time, it will certainly build up some serious arm muscles quickly. Look out Arnold Schwarzenegger!

## *Teasers*

Beach fishermen have discovered the effectiveness of using a second lure in front of a plug, rigged eel or even a tin squid. Called a teaser, the smaller lure can illicit strikes when single lures will not. Even when game fish aren't actively feeding, the teaser, also called a dropper, will often strike at a bait that is being chased by another fish. Biologists call this a competitive feeding response and it is ingrained into a game fish's brain by nature.

It works because predator fish are naturally competitive when feeding. If they see another fish, especially a smaller fish, chasing something to eat, the natural reaction is to eat it first. Sometimes, the reaction is to eat the fish chasing the forage, so even when a fish hits your main lure instead of the teaser, it was the teaser that triggered the response.

Teasers can be handsomely-tied streamer flies, soft-plastic fish imitations or small plastic eels. They all work, but the key is to have them on a leader just ahead of a larger lure. The teaser rig is usually tied to a 30 to 40-pound test leader on a dropper loop about 18 to 24 inches ahead of the main lure. The teaser is attached to the dropper loop and will appear to be a small baitfish being chased by the larger lure.

Teasers are particularly effective from summer through the fall when fish are feeding heavily and the competition is great. Under these circumstances, you will find yourself hooking two bass at once from time to time.

# Pork Rind

While not a lure in itself, pork rind can often mean the difference between strikes and striking out. Pork rind trailers are offered by Uncle Josh, the originator and still the largest supplier of these products to the fishing community.

Pork rind is used as a trailer on lures like bucktails, spoons, trolling jigs and tin squids. They are made in a wide variety of sizes and shapes from 7-inch long offshore strips used on trolling bucktails to small strips with forked tails and hooks attached to use behind bucktails and tins. Do not overlook the effectiveness of pork rind as an addition to a variety of lures used for striped bass.

# Lures for Flyrodding

If chasing striped bass with a fly rod strikes your fancy, a few simple fly patterns and popping bugs are recommended, but there is plenty of room for experimentation. Most large streamer-style flies, like the venerable Lefty's Deceiver, will do nicely for bass when they are feeding on smaller baitfish. Colors should be selected to resemble the available bait. On occasion, I've found nicely tied teasers (meant for surf fishing) on tackle shop walls that made excellent streamer flies for stripers.

Many flies are weighted to help get them down and when bass are holding near the bottom in 20 feet or more, intermediate or fast sinking lines are a must to get your lures to them. Some flyrodders fishing from boats are using only fast sinking shooting heads with Dacron backing to get their offerings deep enough and this method has proven to work quite well.

The action you impart to your flies will make them come alive in the water. It is a good idea to spend some time in quite waters or around a local pool working flies to learn how to make them look enticing. Some bass fishermen use a very short section of bead chain in front of their flies to generate a rising and falling with each striping action they impart to the fly.

A local fly fishing legend in my area ties some rather unique flies for bass. One of his all time favorites is tied from deer hide with the hair trimmed and shaped to look like a baby flounder. He claims it is deadly when fished around inlets and channel edges in sheltered waters in the spring. Other sharpies tie flies that resemble crabs, and there's an entire new generation of epoxy-coated creations that defy the traditional streamer fly look, but they sure catch fish.

Bass found on bay flats in the spring will often fall for small popper and slider surface patterns which come in a variety of shapes and sizes. For schoolies, try to use bugs that are not much bigger than 2½ inches in length and work them at a moderate retrieve pace for the best results.

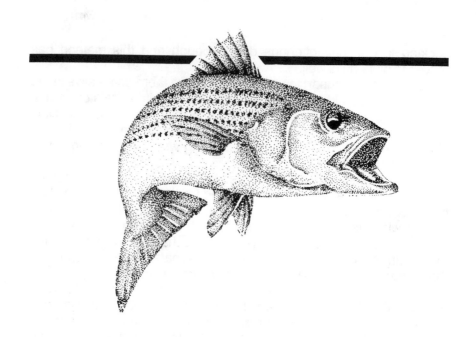

## Chapter Seven

# LOCATING STRIPED BASS

Locating stripers is not the easiest part of becoming a successful bass fisherman, but it doesn't take a magician to find them either. Many fishermen overestimate how difficult it is to find and tempt these great game fish, which is part of the lore and legend that surrounds the striper. Striped bass fishing is only as difficult as you allow it to be through lack of effort to learn their habits.

Granted, stripers have been in shorter supply over the past two decades after years of exploitation by both commercial and recreational fishermen. Loss of spawning and nursery grounds, and the ravages of pollution added to the decline. For over 50 years, striped bass were the target of increasing numbers of commercial fishermen who netted them in the ocean, along the beaches and even in their spawning rivers. For too long, a New England rod and reeler's prowess as a fisherman was judged not by his sportsmanship, but by how many pounds of bass he sold at the co-op in a given week. Long Island's infamous beach haul seiners were credited with killing hundreds of tons of bass each fall run, while leaving the beaches littered with dead bluefish, and under-sized bass, because their market value was too low to bother keeping. Ocean seiners and trawlers off North Carolina targeted wintering fish with great success. Netters decimated bass populations in fish nets set across the mouths of spawning rivers and in estuaries from the Hudson to North Carolina. The recreational fishermen of the day rarely, if ever, saw fit to release a striped bass once it was on the beach or in the boat. It's really no surprise that the striped bass population fell into a down cycle that approached complete collapse of the Atlantic stock by the decade of the 80s.

While the sins of the past are being addressed by state and federal government bodies, and a growing number of sport fishermen are trying hard to put the sport back in fishing by promoting and practicing catch and release, or even better, tag and release, the final jury on the striped bass recovery is still out. The initial signs look promising and recreational striped bass fishing has seen several consecutive years of healthy improvement.

Today, along most of the Atlantic range of the striped bass, you can actually fish for stripers and expect to catch a few, sometimes even a great many. The key to increasing the chances of catching bass on a more consistent basis will be your willingness to devote time to learn about the fish and the patterns it follows. Part of the key to the future of the striped bass will depend upon your willingness to abide by size and catch limits and the care you take in releasing fish that are not to be consumed.

# Spawning and Migrational Patterns

Stripers, like most game fish, follow certain behavioral patterns. Much of where striped bass go and what they do once they get there is in response to, or directly effected by, environmental factors. There are three major influences that we need to understand; annual migration patterns, feeding patterns and daily activity patterns.

Migration patterns include the annual spawning run into freshwater to reproduce and, in the case of the Chesapeake Bay and Albemarle Sound races, their northward migration during the late spring and southward migration in the fall to return to their wintering areas to spawn again in the spring.

While the Chesapeake and Albemarle Sound races migrate great distances, other races, like those of the Hudson River and the St. Lawrence River, will migrate out of their estuary habitat into the open oceans to feed during the abundance of summer, although their migrations will not be as distant. By understanding these migrational patterns, you will have a better idea of when striper concentrations will be heaviest in your home waters, in addition to unlocking the secrets of where local stripers from your area can be found at the different seasons of the year.

The major influences on migrational patterns are time of year and water temperatures. Striped bass spawn when they do because the coming of spring usually provides adequate freshwater flow in spawning rivers, a necessity of successful reproduction, and an increase in water temperature. Additional factors influencing the migrations of certain races of striped bass also include a phototropic response to the changing length of daylight hours and available forage. The Chesapeake race will travel as far north as Canadian waters, while Hudson, Connecticut River and bass spawned in smaller rivers in New Jersey will make less dramatic regional migrations.

## Feeding and Daily Activity Patterns

While spawning and migrational patterns effect the seasonal movements of large concentrations of bass, daily activity and feeding patterns will influence where you might be likely to find stripers on any given day during the season. Factors that influence daily activity patterns may change rapidly and will cause the movement of striped bass within a local area. These can include tides, currents, moon phases, sunlight, available food and water temperature.

Over the years, I've caught stripers in salt and freshwater in water temperatures as low as 46 degrees to as high as 79 degrees. The theory that striped bass get lethargic when water temperatures rise into the mid to upper 70s just doesn't hold true. The summer of 1991 is a prime example, with night bass action proving excellent for big fish even when beach temperatures soared to 80 degrees. The fish we were catching, and breaking off rather regularly, were certainly not down on fighting power. More than a few were totally uncontrollable on 20-pound test spinning tackle despite the warm water.

Striped bass are more tolerant of a wide range of water temperatures than most game fish. Long before bluefish appear because of cold water temperatures in the spring, stripers are already on the scene. In the fall, bluefish will be gone before the water reaches the low 50s, but stripers will still be there when the water dips into the 40s.

Let's look at a few scenarios and how patterns can play a part. First, let's go to the Delaware River during late April or early May. Bass are being caught on cut herring baits and worms in the lower river, south of the Commodore Barry Bridge. As May approaches and the water warms into the low to mid 50s, a large body of bass moves further upriver and proceeds north to spawn. The river has become stable as spring floods have dissipated and large schools of blueback herring are also making their spawning run providing the bass with a readily available food source. Smaller, immature bass will follow the spawners upriver simply to feed on the abundant baitfish.

Here a variety of factors are operating in concert and a fisherman who stays in tune with the river can use these factors as a barometer

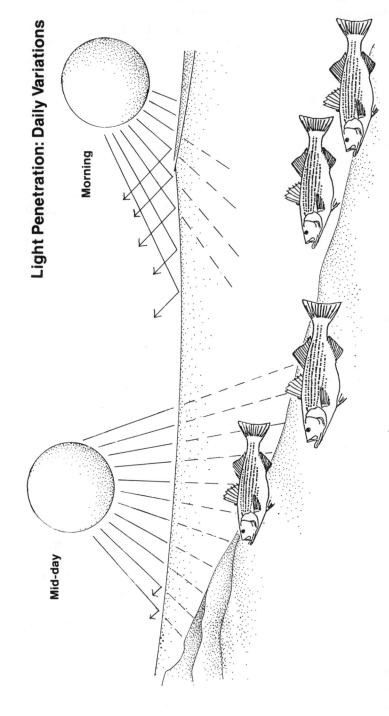

# Light Penetration: Daily Variations

Morning

Mid-day

High sun penetrates deep into the water, limiting the movements of striped bass. Bass are more active at low sun angles.

# Light Penetration: Seasonal Variations

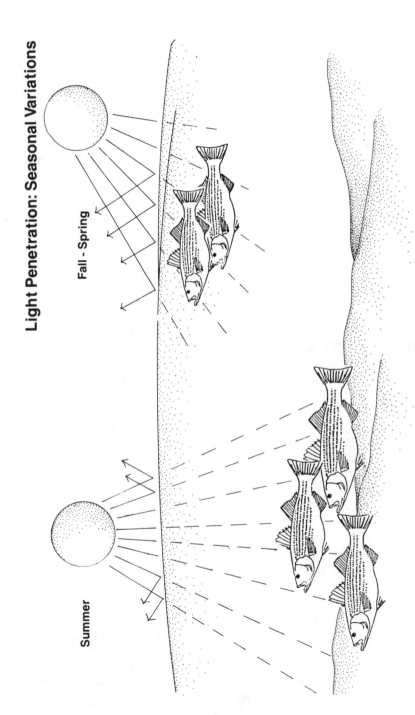

Fall - Spring

Summer

Bass feed mostly at night during the summer when sun is at high angle. Daytime activites are greatest in spring and fall.

for knowing when and where the bass are going to be. The water temperature is critical to the spawners, the river's flow is strong, but not flooding as it can be in February and March and an abundant food source is readily available.

The next factor effecting this seasonal pattern, especially below Trenton, is the tides, because bass will move and feed more readily on specific tides. We go fishing in a small shallow draft aluminum boat, working it up into the shallows of the Trenton Falls area with the incoming tide, just as the feeding bass will. The bass will target the herring, so your terminal tackle must match the appearance of herring. The water is moving fast and the bass are actively feeding, so a fast moving artificial like a popper or a shallow running swimming plug in silver or white should do the trick. Understanding the conditions affecting the fish on a daily, monthly or seasonal basis will put you in a position to score with these bass more consistently. Using this formula for the past several seasons, we've been able to catch upwards of 50 bass on a tide, when conditions are perfect, ranging in size from a few pounds up to 20 pounds.

Here's another example. The month is late May or very early June and migrating Chesapeake bass are moving up the coast headed for the waters north of Montauk and up into New England. Since these fish have already spawned in their home waters in March and April, they are usually hungry and are quick to react to the last of the spring run of herring or the first schools of bunker to arrive in the area. The place is Barnegat Inlet, a wide, fast-flowing inlet that carries huge quantities of tidal water in and out of Barnegat Bay, along with schools of blueback herring and bunker.

We have a supply of blueback herring in the bait pen that is quickly transferred to the boat's baitwell. We load the tackle on board and head for the inlet for some serious livelining. My fishing partner and I are pretty sure there will be larger fish at the inlet; migrating fish heading north. The locals call these migrating bass "fresh fish" because they are slim from not feeding regularly on their northward run, and they have a clean, shiny appearance.

The next consideration is tides. The inlet can really be ripping during the middle stages of both the incoming and outgoing, so our planned arrival is early evening, about halfway through the incoming. We set up the boat just off the north jetty, using the engine to hold our position, and place two live herring in the rip formed over a sunken east section of the rock pile. It doesn't take long and we both hook into keeper-size bass. As the tide stage continues, the fishing gets hotter. The important factors are knowing that the bass will be in an area as part of their seasonal migration, knowing the right bait that would attract them, understanding the tide stages which the fish would most likely be feeding on and having the right bait to interest the fish.

No matter where you fish for striped bass, the more you learn about the seasonal and local movements of these fish, the greater your chances of being in the right place with the right lures or bait at just the right time. Let's look at some other factors that can play a part in finding striped bass.

# Sunlight

Stripers move to and from shallow water feeding areas depending upon available light. Like many fish, they react to bright light because they have no eyelids to protect the eye's retina, only the narrow focusing adjustments that can be made by the contraction and expansion of the pupil.

The dark of night is often a good time to catch school bass, like this fish which is about to be released.

During the height of the summer months, when the sun is high over head and penetrating more deeply into the water column, bass will become almost exclusively nocturnal feeders. They will move into shallow feeding areas under the cover of darkness and let their excellent low-light vision and sense of smell guide them on their feeding forays. Their highly developed lateral line receives impulses and vibrations as bait and water flow near the fish. As the sun rises, they will move into deeper waters and stop feeding until the following night.

As the season passes into fall, bass will become more acclimated to feeding during the daylight hours, since the sun is lower on the horizon and not penetrating the water column nearly as deeply, and because large schools of migrating baitfish will become easy prey during this time. As the influencing factors change, so does the striper's daily activity pattern. Now, let's add one last important factor to the equation, structure!

# Structure Fishing

Striped bass are, most often, structure oriented feeders. Fishing structure was popularized by the explosion of interest in freshwater bass fishing that erupted in the 1970s. Largemouth bass fishing pros found that freshwater bass had specific preferences for different types of bottom contours associated with water depth, vegetation, natural and man-made objects in the water. They loosely termed them "structure" and in doing so founded a whole new approach to fishing. Knowledgeable anglers were structure fishing in both fresh and saltwater for decades, but they just didn't know it had a name.

For stripers, structure can consist of a wide variety of bottom configuration. Along open sand beaches, bars are the most prevalent form of structure, but beach structure can also include rocks, points of land that create rips, jetties, wrecks, breachways or inlets.

For boat fishermen, structure can be areas of changing bottom contour like lumps, ridges, rock piles, hard bottom, wrecks and areas of constricted water flow between two land masses like passes between islands or around shore points or peninsulas.

For river or inshore fishermen, structure can be where streams enter the river creating mixing currents, rock piles, channels, bridge abutments, piers, pilings or drop-offs. For bay fishermen, examples of structure include channels, flats and grass beds.

Obviously, structure is a very loosely defined term, but locating structure is often the key factor influencing a striper's daily activity patterns. Why? Because structure attracts baitfish, eels, clams, crabs or other sources of food for the striper. With its physiological adapta-

**This bass was caught a few yards from the rocky jetty at Barnegat Inlet. Most coastal inlets are good attractors of striped bass.**

tions, stripers are highly adept at using structure along with the currents and rips that structure generates, to feed successfully. At certain times of the year, bass will become bait oriented more than structure oriented. This occurs most frequently during the fall migrations southward, when huge schools of baitfish will congregate on the inshore grounds. These massive schools of bait will often be intercepted by feeding bass with little or no structure orientation, but it won't keep stripers from chowing down when the opportunity presents itself. At times like these, the presence of a massive school of bait will be the magnet that draws fish, not necessarily the bottom structure.

## *Inshore Structure*

In New England, rocky shorelines are the structure that attract the bait and the bass. From Long Island's south shore to Cape Hatteras, the sandy beaches are more open with few obstructions except man-made jetties. On open beaches, sand bars become the structure fishermen seek out. Finding productive sand bars that will attract and hold bass is an interesting job in itself, requiring scouting time. Low tide is the best time to find beach structure, although it is usually the worst time to fish it.

The most important tool for finding sand bars is the fisherman's eyes and his ability to understand what they are looking at. The need to record where prime sand bars are, so they can be returned to during optimum tide stages to catch fish, is critical. It requires the time to get to know a stretch of beach and its hidden features and some type of recording or marking code is needed to help you find your way back to these places once they are located. Some surf anglers make mental maps of the beach structure. Do your beach scouting at dead low tide, when bars are either exposed or waves can easily be seen breaking on them.

Once you've located a prominent bar, look for areas where the bar has breaks in it, creating small underwater inlets that allow bait to move into the trough between the outer bar and the beach. When you find a break or irregularity in the outer bar, find a way to mark it with a piece of driftwood up the beach from the bar. The best markers are inconspicuous so other fishermen don't have too easy a time locating your hard-earned spots. In hard-fished areas that see a lot of competition among surf fishermen for prime fishing real estate, anglers will play games with each others markers, so this isn't always the best way to go.

A more modern way to mark locations of prime beach structure is with a hand-held LORAN. These inexpensive navigational devises are excellent for this purpose and more and more beach fishermen are employing them to save the "waypoints" of hot structure breaks without having to mark them physically. Once you try one, you'll be hard pressed to go back to the old ways. The pairs of numbers, called TDs, can be kept in a small notebook.

Beach structure can also be important to boat fishermen who troll along the ocean side of the outer bar or cast into it with artificials or natural baits. Just remember when working beach structure of this nature from a boat, you're in shallow water and an unexpected wave can literally pick you up and deposit you on the bar or, even worse, capsize your boat. Careful attention must be paid to sea conditions when fishing this tight to bars from a boat, because ocean conditions and waves can be quite unpredictable.

In areas where beach structure is in the form of rocks, like around jetties or groins, the rock piles are the structure attracting bait and stripers. From Long Island's north shore through southern Canada, many beaches are literally strewn with naturally occurring rocks that form excellent, bass attracting structure. Scouting these rocks is a job that is also done at low tide. Learning where they are when the tide rises is again a matter of keeping good notes, marking the beach physically or punching the numbers into your LORAN.

# Sheltered Waters

When fishing sheltered waters like those inside an inlet, a bay or river, structure again can be different. Bridges are excellent bass attracting structure, especially when the ocean waters are rough and dirty from a storm. We often fish inside our home rivers after a strong northeaster has left the ocean too rough to fish comfortably and the water is dirty with sand stirred up by the large waves. We'll anchor uptide of a bridge and chum with clams or bunker chunks to attract bass, many times with considerable success. In areas of Long Island, this is common practice even when the weather is good and the ocean relatively calm. A small group of stout-hearted fishermen fish the many south shore bridges from their spans, working bucktails around the abutments and in and out of the shadows created by the lights above and they catch quite a few bass.

Besides bridges, fishing for bass inside can be effective when done around channels, especially in back water channels that attract large baitfish, eels or soft crabs. Many sharpies who claim to catch their fish on the surf side are actually catching their fish in quiet waters like these on lonely nights.

# Offshore Structure

Offshore is a relative term and in the case of the striped bass, offshore can be anything out of casting range of the beach. Boat fishermen look for bottom contours and the currents, rips and sanctuary they provide. Navigational charts help locate areas likely to hold bait and bass. When checked out with a depthfinder, you can customize the chart with notations and added markings.

The boat fisherman is looking for ledges, banks, deep holes, inshore wrecks and areas of hard bottom, be it underwater rock formations, clam beds, oyster bars or sandy shoals. Just finding this structure isn't always good enough, because not all offshore structure will hold bass all the time. Other factors will influence a location's productivity including current flow, tides, time of day and presence of bait. It is necessary to understand how these factors will affect the daily activity patterns of bass in your area if you are going to score from the boat. Luckily, trolling allows an angler to cover a wide expanse of water in search of feeding bass.

Once you've found fish, mark the location on your chart and save the locations "numbers" in your LORAN for the next trip. The more time you spend on the water, the easier it will become to recognize patterns for specific fish movements and feeding behavior.

## Fishing Log

**Date** NOV. 26, 1991

**Species** STRIPED BASS

**Weather** AIR TEMP 46; WATER TEMP 54; LIGHT RAIN; CLOUDY

**Wind** W 5 to 10 KNOTS

**Tide** HIGH AT BARNEGAT INLET 7:36 AM

**Moon** 3 DAYS BEFORE FULL MOON

**Location** OFF ISLAND BEACH STATE PARK

**Comments** JOE NUNZ & CHUCK SCHROEDER ABOARD. TROLLED WIRE WITH BUNKER SPOONS, TUBES & RIGS, DOWNRIGGERS WITH HERRING TYPE PLUGS. WHITE RELIABLE BUNKER SPOONS HOT IN 60+ FEET. MOST HITS CAME USING 250 FT OF WIRE + 6 OZ. DRAIL, WORKING SPOONS AT 3 MPH. BEST DAY TROLLING ALL SEASON. ONE FISH CAUGHT ON DOWNRIGGER WITH WHITE STORM MAC PLUG.

**Catch** 11 BASS FROM 25 TO 46 lbs. 2 OVER 40, 3 OVER 30, REST IN 20'S. TAGGED ALL BUT THE 46, 48 AND 28 lb FISH.

# The Log Book

It would be nearly impossible to remember all the factors that were affecting fishing each time you ventured out during a season, much less on a year in and year out basis. But the ability to tap this past fishing information and use it to gain a better understanding of striper patterns in your area, can make you an increasingly more productive fisherman each year. For that reason, most serious striper fishermen keep a detailed log book which they fill out in detail after each trip. They refer to it regularly to see where they caught last year or the year before, on what lure or bait, and under what conditions.

A log can be simply a pocket notebook or, in the case of some fishermen I know, can even be a personal computer. It should contain entries for each trip including date, weather conditions, ocean conditions, moon phases, tide phases, areas fished, presence of bait, types of bait or lures used and the fish caught. While each fishing trip's information might seem unimportant, as the entries become more numerous, the log will become a wealth of knowledge that will affect fishing habits and fishing success for years to come.

I also make entries about fishing lore that I pick up from other knowledgeable fishermen, especially the old-timers. A few years ago, a fisherman with over 40 years of experience mentioned that around the Fourth of July, the jetties in a certain town along my stretch of the striper coast always produced big fish. It sounded rather vague and he added that he hadn't really fished these jetties at the right time for some years. But when I found myself planning an evening's fishing with rigged eels the day after the Fourth in 1991, the notes came to light and my fishing buddy and I decided to try those jetties.

We scored on two bass in the 20s that smashed our rigged eels right off the bat. But surely those weren't the big fish the old-timer was talking about. And they weren't! Between midnight and 2 o'clock we hooked four bass that screamed our drags and pulled our lines right back into the jetty rocks with impunity. They were savage fish that literally pounded themselves into the jetty rocks to break loose. We couldn't even turn these fish with 8-foot spinning sticks and reels loaded with 20-pound test. When the tide hit low and the action stopped, we were left shaking in our boots from the experience.

During the next few evenings we boated several fish in the 30s and had a couple more run-ins with huge fish, one that broke 30-pound test after smashing a live eel. After an experience like that, you can bet I never turn a deaf ear to an experienced fisherman who lets loose with a pearl of wisdom, however far fetched it might sound at the time.

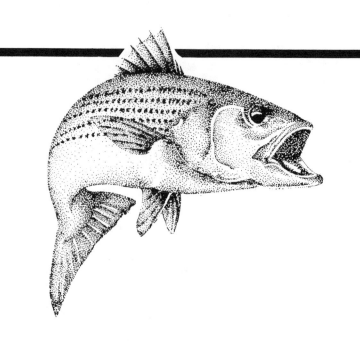

## Chapter Eight

# DRIFT FISHING TECHNIQUES

Fishing from a drifting boat is one of the most rewarding and enjoyable ways to catch striped bass. Running an open boat from jetty to jetty, killing the engine and drifting as you make pinpoint casts around the rockpile in hopes of tempting a strike is just one of the many techniques used to fool striped bass from a drifting boat.

Working diamond jigs while drifting over a tightly packed school of southward migrating bass in the fall is another proven method. Also popular with drift anglers is fishing inlets or canals with bucktails or live bait as the boat drifts with the current, while others like to cast towards bridge pilings at slack tide. Drifting baits in rips has also accounted for many trophy fish. All these techniques produce bass while working from the deck of a drifting boat.

In this chapter we'll take a look at these techniques and get a feel for the times and places to use them. You'll be quick to agree that these methods can be great fun and very productive.

They all have one common requirement to be effective and that is boat control. How you position the boat and your ability to keep it where the fish are most likely to be feeding under existing current and wind conditions will be important to your fishing success. If wind and current are mild, maintaining proper boat position can be a pretty simple matter. When wind and current are more severe, greater skill and more time at the helm of the boat will be necessary.

Some of these techniques require you to work a boat close to rocks, pilings, jetties and in areas which can generate rips, eddies and sometimes standing waves of considerable proportions. Fishermen with limited boating experience can easily find themselves in a dangerous situation. Always pay careful attention to the water around you and keep a watchful eye on changing tide, wind and water conditions. Always play it safe when you are unsure of yourself and your boat's ability to perform adequately under any circumstances.

# Drifting Inlets and Canals

The prime ingredient when drifting inlets and canals with baits or artificials is water movement, or current. A tidal current strong enough to move the boat and allow the angler to cover water, keeping the baits in areas that have the greatest potential for holding fish is essential. Tidal influence is critical to fish activity in these areas, so keep close watch on the tides for your area.

Determining tide for inlets is easy, since most inlets are listed on local tide charts. Canals pose a different problem since their tide schedule is often very different from surrounding ocean waters. For example, the Point Pleasant Canal in Ocean County, New Jersey has been producing striped bass since it was built in the 1930s. This unique body of water is influenced by tidal action from the Manasquan River on its northern side and upper Barnegat Bay on its southern side. The difference in high tide can be as much as three hours from the Manasquan Inlet, only two miles away and it is extremely important to be in the canal at the right tide stage to experience fishable conditions.

The best fishing in this canal revolves around slack high tide, from the end of the incoming through the first hour of the outgoing. Feeding activity might continue later into the tide, but the water will be ripping through the canal so quickly that boat control becomes extremely difficult and getting your lures or baits to perform well is almost impossible.

Inlets are unique areas of structure and they can be productive for most of the fishing season. They serve as the entrance to tidal rivers and bays for game fish and bait, in addition to eels, crabs and small baitfish that smaller stripers prefer. They can offer excellent fishing, even at times when surrounding ocean waters are not producing well.

When large baitfish such as herring or bunker are using inlets as expressways from the ocean into sheltered waters, livelining becomes a deadly technique. For the best results, use a simple livelining rig without weight as described in Chapter Four. Live eels and a variety of artificials can also be used successfully in inlets, but know-

# Drifting An Inlet

**Live bait**

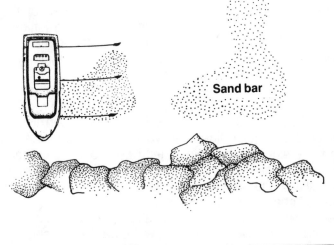

Sand bar

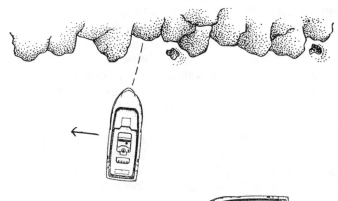

**Casting**

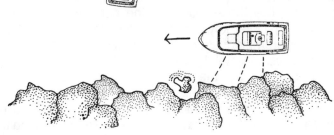

ing where to fish them in the inlet will make the difference between success and failure.

In inlets or canals, bass will most often be found around areas of rip currents and turbulence. When fishing in inlets, the most productive areas lie along the rocks or bulkheads that make up the sides or retaining walls. The water flowing along the sides of the inlet is disturbed by the uneven surfaces of the retaining jetties and they create areas of turbulence that disorient baitfish and make them easy prey for a fish like the striped bass which can stay in control of its movement, even in heavy currents.

Therefore, the basic strategy for fishing inlets and canals from a drifting boat is to keep your baits or lures close to the rocky sides. For example, if you're fishing the inside of an inlet with live herring or bunker on an outgoing tide, start your drift at the inside of the inlet, close to one side of the retaining jetty. Lob your live bait close to the wall and drift it along with the tide. If the bait swims away from the rocks, reel it in and then re-cast it towards the rocks where you have the greatest chance of attracting a hit.

When fishing live baits in areas of strong current, be sure to give the bass a chance to mouth and swallow the bait before setting the hook. Bass will hit a big baitfish, crush and scale it in its gullet and then swallow it. While there is no rule of thumb for how long to wait before the hook set, give the fish a chance to run a little with the reel in free spool. Be sure to set the hook hard and only after you let the line come tight between you and the fish, since strong currents can put a belly in the line that will act as a shock absorber when you set the hook. Trying to set a hook with a belly in the line most often leads to a poor hook-up and lost fish. Once you get the hook in a fish, don't hesitate to strike it a second or third time if you are unsure of how solid the hook-up might be.

When livelining eels, the same considerations apply. Keep the eels close to the rocks along the side of the inlet. Pay particular attention to areas that generate large, noticeable rips. If there are areas of sunken rocks, like those found on the north jetty of New Jersey's famous Barnegat Inlet, key in on that area and fish it hard. Concentrating on rips or prominent structure features will increase your chances of catching bass. Most inlets will have significant rips at the end of the jetties on both sides of the inlet and these rips will often hold fish, especially on the outgoing tide.

Inlets that are extremely wide or have bars built up from years of siltation can offer additional structure. These sand bars and the resulting holes around them can hold bass and can be drifted using the same techniques. A few of the inlets along Long Island's south shore have deep holes where bass will often hold waiting for the tide to wash a free dinner to them.

Local anglers drift these inlets using a three-way-swivel rig and drop sinker, using a whole, fresh squid for bait. The larger the squid, the better. As the sinker bounces bottom, the angler must stay aware of changing bottom depth and make adjustments in the line to be sure the bait drops into holes as the boat drifts over them. The sinker weight will vary with current flow. This simple technique can also work with other baits such as live eels, small blackfish or cunners and is applicable to many inlets along the coast, not just those on Long Island.

Bucktails are an effective lure that can be fished in inlets. The required weight of the bucktail will vary with the speed of the drift, so use a lure that is heavy enough to stay deep and near the bottom. Too light a lure will be overpowered by the tidal flow. Use a strip of pork rind or a plastic worm (the new scented worms like Berkley's Power Worm, work extremely well on bucktails) to add some flavor and a larger profile in the water. Jig it slowly or let it sink and simply swim the bucktail back on a slow retrieve. You can also just let the bucktail out behind the boat and bounce it up and down on the bottom as the boat drifts with the current.

When tidal flow is calm or very light, you can fish a variety of lures around inlet rocks and in the less forceful rips. Rigged eels, bucktails and plugs can be fished in these areas too, but once the tide flow picks up, they will loose their effectiveness and you have to switch back to bucktails or live baits.

Inlets can offer action on both incoming and outgoing tides, although incoming tide usually doesn't produce well until the last half of the tide stage. When fishing inlets, try to plan your fishing for the last half of the incoming and fish through slack and work as much of the outgoing as possible with drift techniques.

## *Drifting Tidal Rivers and Bays*

The areas inside inlets such as tidal rivers or nearby bay waters present additional opportunities to catch stripers from a drifting boat. At times when conditions are not fishable at the inlets, the sheltered waters nearby can often save the day, or night, as the case might be. One example that comes to mind revolves around fluctuating ocean water temperatures. When winds in my area of the striper coast come out of the south for any period of time in late spring or summer, beach temperatures plummet. Two days of south winds in late June can produce a drop of more than 10 degrees in water temperature along the beach and as that water flows into inlets on the incoming tide, fish will often hightail it for a warmer locale.

That warmer water can be found a mile or more off the beach or inside the tidal river or bay that feeds the inlet. Sometimes a short ride to structure that can be only a few hundred yards from the back of the inlet can put you in water dramatically warmer than the water in the inlet and on the surrounding beaches. At times like this, fishing inside can often produce nice catches of bass.

Try fishing around bridge abutments, pilings, bulkheads and boat docks. When the tide is moving lightly, you can fish these areas without the aid of an anchor. Canals, as previously mentioned, can also harbor more fish when water in the ocean or inlet are cold and driven inside to find relief. In nearby bay waters, look for areas of sedge banks, shallow coves with deep water holes, channels or areas where small streams enter the bay.

**The structure found near and around bridges frequently holds striped bass.**

# Drifting Cuts and Rips

The Race, Plum Gut, Montauk Point, Sandy Hook, the Cape May Rips, the Elizabeth Island of New England, the Chesapeake Bay Bridge-Tunnel and hundreds of less famous locations where tidal flow and underwater structure generate significant currents are places where striped bass gather to feed. They all present ideal locations where you can fish for bass from a drifting boat with a variety of baits or artificials. They all have severe changes in bottom depth or contour, plus strong current flow, which causes rips and upwellings of ocean water. Since striped bass are such successful hunters in areas where strong currents give them the upper hand in the survival game, you can be sure bass will be there. Some locations produce throughout the season while others will hold large numbers of bass only at certain times of the year. Regardless of when you fish them, there are several techniques to fool fish.

In deep-water locations, like the Race, where currents can reach upwards of ten knots, deep-water tactics become necessary. Popular methods include drifting live eels on heavy boat rods with enough weight to get them deep. Some fishermen use as much as a pound of lead to get the eels down to the feeding fish. Jigging with a heavy diamond jig can also produce, but is most effective early or late in the tide stage when currents subside a bit. This type of technique can also be productive when employed in offshore rips of shallower depth like those found in Cape May, New Jersey. The weight necessary to get the eel down to the feeding level of the bass is considerably less, and at times no weight is required at all.

Maneuvering is pretty simple. Scope out the area with a depthfinder and LORAN, and write down the TDs of those areas that hold fish. Then run the boat upcurrent of those areas and drift back over them. If a specific spot is producing the majority of your bites, short drift it, rather than wasting time making long drifts over unproductive bottom.

Shoreline rips like those at Sandy Hook or Montauk Point can be fished by drifting and casting live baits, plugs or bucktails when the tide is early or late in the stage and water movement less intense. When the current is ripping, bucktails or live baits drifted behind the boat will often do the trick, while lures lose their effectiveness due to the fast moving water and the speed of the drift.

# Drifting Shoreline Structure

Fishing shoreline structure from a boat is a productive method for catching stripers from late spring through the end of the season.

# Trolling Sand Bars And Beach Fronts

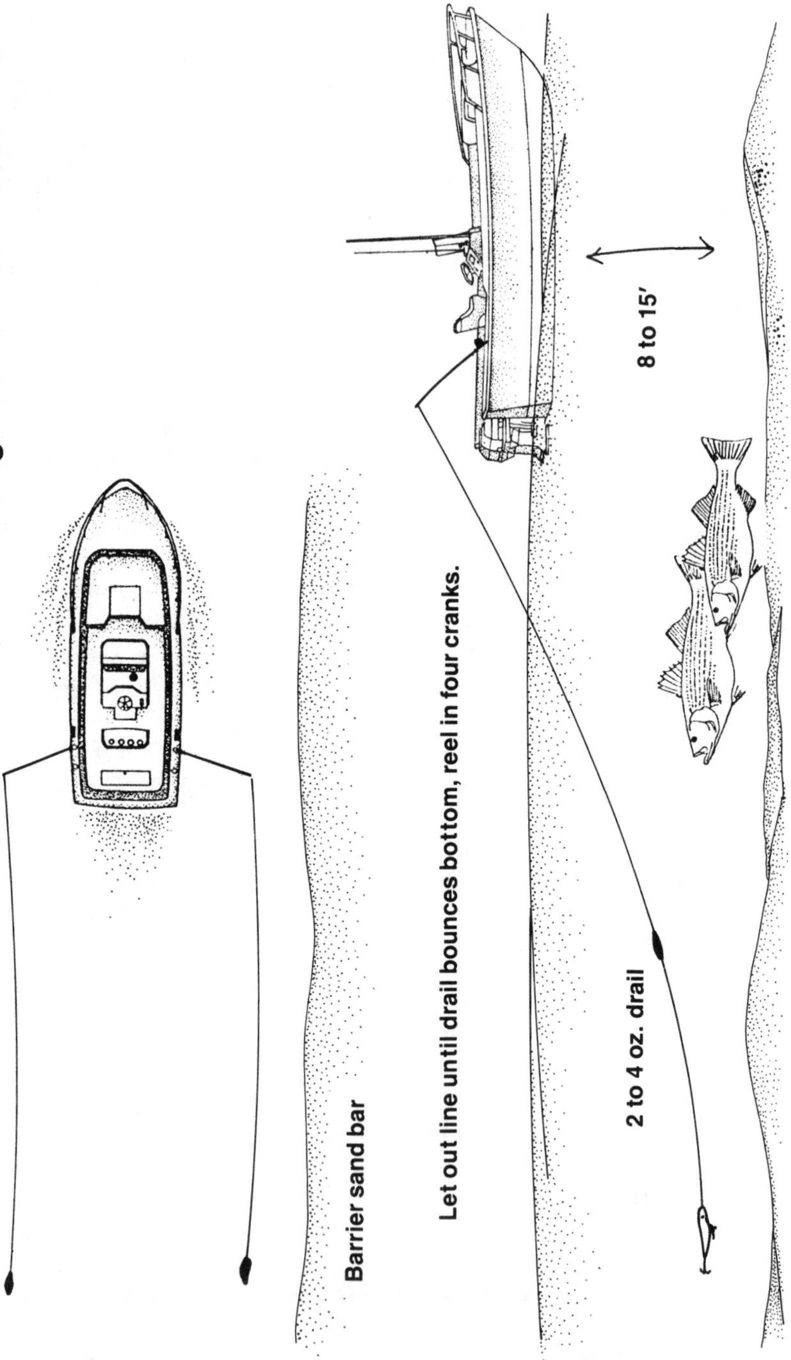

8 to 15'

Barrier sand bar

Let out line until drail bounces bottom, reel in four cranks.

2 to 4 oz. drail

Beach jetties, inlet jetties, sand bars, inshore wrecks and rock piles can hold bass and working from the decks of an open boat lets you cover a lot of water in search of fish. This type of fishing is one of my favorites, since my boat-fishing preferences reflect my earlier background as a beach and jetty fisherman. Many of the techniques used from a boat will mirror the techniques used by beach fishermen, and they can be even more effective when casting towards shore from a boat rather than from the shore outward. At times, wind and tide conditions will require you to control your boat position with the engine running at idle and by shifting in and out of gear as required to maintain or alter position.

Beach jetties abound along much of the striper coast and they are productive places to fish for bass. The baits used may vary with the time of year and the primary forage present, but cast and retrieve is the name of the game for much of the year. It is as important to learn the characteristics of each jetty for the boat fisherman as it is for the shore angler. The advantage of fishing jetties from a boat is the added mobility. If one jetty doesn't hold fish, simply crank up the engine and move to the next jetty, or the next.

This fishing is best done from a small to midsize center console boat, but aluminum skiffs can also get in tight and offer a viable option when sea conditions are favorable for their use. Just remember that tin boats are small craft and you should use your judgment whenever using them in the ocean.

The selection of productive baits and fishing around shoreline structure is varied and include live eels, herring, bunker and the venerable rigged eel. Swimming plugs of varying styles and sizes, poppers, bucktails, tin squids and teaser rigs are right at home being tossed at shoreline structure and each has its time and place.

When using swimming plugs or rigged eels, let the action of the waves work to your advantage by letting each incoming wave add additional action to the lure. You will feel the pull of the lure increase when a wave flows around it. Stop cranking momentarily and let the lure swim in place in the current the wave creates. Bass will often hit the lure when it is swimming in place in a wave.

When you approach a jetty, make your initial casts from a short distance away from the visible rocks at the jetty end. Many jetties have long skirts of fallen rocks around the front and sides. These rocks have been knocked down by storms and waves, and are usually called the fan of the jetty. In some cases, these underwater rocks offer the best fish-holding structure and bass will often be found on them. That's why it is important to learn the composition and layout of each jetty as you fish. That information will help you when approaching the jetty and can also be a safety factor as underwater rocks can do quite a bit of damage to the boat hull.

# Casting To Shore Structure

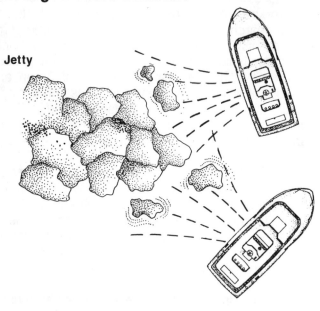

Jetty

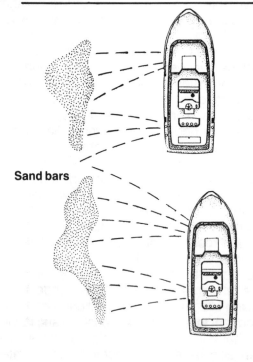

Sand bars

Watch how the waves strike the jetty front and take notice of any prominent rips that are being generated on one side or the other. Fish those rips with care as you work your way in closer to the jetty. Bass will sometimes congregate around the area of strongest rip current as they search for baitfish that become disoriented by the wave action.

While some fishermen swear by specific tide stages when fishing jetty structure, I've caught stripers around jetties on every tide stage. One interesting evening's fishing comes to mind. It was a very warm summer night in August, 1990 and a friend who rarely fishes with me at night decided to come along. The game plan was to toss rigged eels at the jetties, but conditions were not good for this fishing. By midnight, we were looking at dead low water, hardly a breath of moving air and no water movement around the jetty rocks. To make matters worse, there was one of the worse cases of "fire in the water (phosphorescence)" I'd ever seen.

After trying one jetty after another only because my friend didn't want to give up early, we pulled up on one particularly quiet jetty that had hardly a hint of movement around the base. I cast a rigged eel at the jetty front where there was barely three feet of water. As soon as it landed, the water looked like someone flushed a toilet right under the eel from the swirl of a striking bass. The fish mounted a powerful run and left a trail of phosphorescence six feet long behind it, making the whole scene that much more eerie. After a brisk fight, we boated a 30-pound bass that the old-timers would have told you had no business being where it was and feeding under the prevailing conditions. So, regardless of the tide stage or conditions, don't count out the fish-attracting ability of jetties. Fish them whenever you can get out and, as I do, forget about lackluster conditions because you never know.

When using large baitfish around jetties, if the wind and wave conditions are mild, it is rarely necessary to anchor. You can lay off a jetty and swim your baits into the rocks using one of the several hooking methods described in Chapter Four. Large baitfish are deadly around jetties or outfall pipes from shoreline ponds or lakes from the beginning of the herring run in the spring until the last of the bunker have migrated south and out of your territory in the fall. If these baitfish are available to you, never pass up the opportunity to fish them around jetty structure.

Sand bars are also productive when fished from a drifting boat casting into them. In fact, it can be more productive because boat fishermen can often get closer to the structure and can move with the action, should the fish move up or down the beach, moving with the bait. You can follow schools of bait or bass with a boat easier than walking the beach, even with a beach buggy at your disposal. Plugs, bucktails, tins or rigged eels can be effective here, but in the fall, needlefish and small swimmers produce best. This is an excellent place to employ a teaser rig. In the fall, metals like jigs, tins squids or nordic eel type lures bounced along the sand bottom like a sand eel, can be particularly effective.

# *Jigging Bass From A Drifting Boat*

When the fall run is in full swing, boat anglers have an advantage when large schools of medium-size bass school tightly and migrate southward along the coast in deeper water off the beaches. They can be found in the shallow 15 or 20-foot water to as deep as 70 feet, and they present the ideal opportunity for jigging.

Locating these fish can be aided by bird activity, but more often you will have to rely heavily on your depthfinder, searching out areas of underwater structure like hard bottom, mussel beds or areas of bottom irregularities. Sometimes you will locate schools of bass just working their way along open water keying in on schools of baitfish that are abundant in the fall months in inshore waters. When you find them, jigging with relatively light tackle is great fun and can be extremely fast fishing. It isn't uncommon to catch dozens of nice fish using this method, if you can find and hold the boat over schooled bass.

**This bass, caught by the author, hit a diamond jig worked just off the bottom.**

Using your depthfinder, you can distinguish between schools of stripers and bluefish or bait, because the bass will almost always be just off the bottom, while blues will be marked higher in the water column. When you find a school of bass like this, diamond jigs and other similar metal lures like Crippled Herring jigs, Tin Minnows, Dungenous Stingers and Wobble Eels can be deadly in the hands of a skilled fisherman. Your choice of jig style should be tempered with a knowledge of what the prevalent baitfish in the area might be. While diamond jigs work well on bass when sand eels are in residence, they do not work well when the primary baitfish is sea herring, peanut bunker or butterfish. A switch to a deeper-bodied jig like the Crippled Herring or Tin Minnow will put you into fish when the diamond jiggers are cranking away and catching nothing.

There has been almost a total absence of sand eels in my local waters for the past two years and, consequently, diamond jigs have not caught bass well in the fall. But when we discovered deep bodied jigs like the Crippled Herring made by Luhr Jensen and the Tin Minnow made by J & J Tackle, we started "matching the hatch" and catching fish on these jigs with consistent results. We had days when we would catch upwards of 30 bass on these jigs, while fishermen using diamond jigs nearby were only catching an occasional fish, or mostly bluefish.

Obviously, the first key to jigging migrating bass is to locate the schools and then try to determine the direction they are moving and the speed so you can stay with the school for a period of time. It is critical to keep the boat directly over the school to be truly effective with jigs. When the boat is in position, drop a 2 to 4-ounce jig to the bottom and work it slowly. Working a jig fast will produce bluefish, not striped bass. It also pays to keep the jig near the bottom, so don't reel it all the way to the surface before free-spooling it back to the bottom.

Two basic jigging techniques will usually work. If the bass are holding very tight to the bottom, drop the jig until it hits bottom, then lift the rod tip four or five feet and then drop the tip so the lure flutters back down again slowly. Most hits will come on the drop down.

If the bass are aggressive, you can often catch them on a s-l-o-w, straight retrieve. Sometimes a bass will follow the jig right up to the boat before striking, but the slow retrieve is what gets their attention. Pick up the retrieve speed and it will be bluefish city.

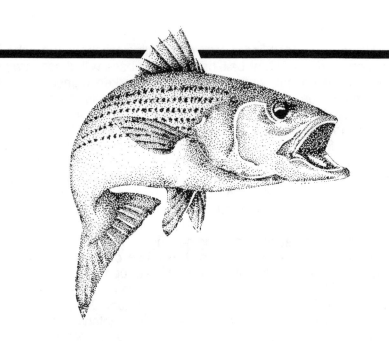

## Chapter Nine

# TROLLING STRATEGIES

Trolling offers the advantage of allowing the boat fisherman to cover large areas, or many areas, where striped bass are likely to be found. The three most popular ways to troll are with monofilament or Dacron line, wire line rigs and, the newest arrival on the saltwater trolling scene, the downrigger. When deep trolling, I often combine two types of gear, running two outfits from downriggers and two additional wire line outfits from horizontal rod holders to cover a wider range of the water column and to present a greater variety of lures. This system has been responsible for catching fish on days when using only one trolling method might not have put fish in the boat.

Trolling with monofilament or Dacron is effective in shallow water, but stripers often feed deep down in the water column, so deep trolling with wire line or downriggers is usually even more productive.

Stripers migrating in the open ocean or in the deeper areas of large bays like the Chesapeake, especially in the spring and fall are searching for baitfish concentrations as much as structure. At these times, you can score well trolling, but only if you can control the depth of the lures you are using, being sure to get them down to where the bass are holding and feeding.

Fishing along the beaches in the late fall, large bass can be found feeding on sea herring deep in the water column. The baitfish are in water from 40 to 90 feet deep and exhibit a tendency to hug the bottom in large schools. Bass will respond to lures that imitate the herring, but only if they are trolled deep. The use of wire line or downriggers, depending upon the lures being used, are the best methods of getting your offerings where they need to be. Trying to troll this deep is difficult with mono or Dacron outfits, since extremely heavy drails are needed. Planers offer an alternative, but most fishermen dislike using them for stripers and they are not compatible with many lures. Mono/Dacron rigs can be used for shallow water fishing and are preferred by many anglers who troll in water from 15 to 30 feet deep.

# Trolling Speed

One of the most important factors to keep in mind when trolling for stripers regardless of the method you are using, or the tackle being employed, is trolling speed. Striped bass prefer slow moving lures and baits, unlike many other game fish more readily attracted to fast moving lures. When it comes to preferred trolling speeds, the rule of thumb is "the slower, the better!"

In fact, many would-be striper fishermen find they have a problem with their ability to troll bass effectively, simply because they can't get their boat to troll slow enough. How slow is slow? Trolling speeds of 1½ to 4 knots will cover most conditions and lure types. If the boat is unable to attain these slow speeds without having to bump the engine in and out of gear, then you will need some form of specialized equipment to help alleviate the problem. For inboard boats, a special device called a trolling valve, designed to reduce speeds, can be added to the transmission. For outboard and sterndrive boats, an item called a "Whale's Tail" that attaches to the cavitation plate of the engine and is lowered behind the propeller when trolling to reduce thrust can be the answer. Or, if these items are too expensive or too much trouble to install, you can always fall back on the simplest, most inexpensive device, a sea anchor.

A sea anchor is like a small parachute that is deployed alongside the boat on a rope tied to a spring line cleat. It billows open and slows the forward momentum of the boat. The only problem you face with a sea anchor is that it can get in the way of trolling lures or fish being fought to the boat, and occasionally must be removed when a fish is brought to the boat and then redeployed after the fish is boated. A charter captain friend, Billy Brower, who runs a 36-foot Runaway, "Brokers", uses two 5-gallon buckets tied to six feet of 3/8-inch nylon line to reduce the trolling speed of his big boat. He ties one to the spring line cleat on each side of his boat and keeps the lines long enough to get them in the water creating drag, but short enough to prevent them from extending beyond the transom of the boat, so they stay out of the way of trolling rods and fish being played. Take your pick of speed reduction techniques, but getting the boat to troll slow is your first and foremost consideration when trolling bass.

My 23-foot Mako, powered with a single 225 horsepower Yamaha, idles down to 600 rpms in gear. It will troll at speeds as slow as 1 knot, without a sputter or pop from the big motor. Twin outboard boats usually need only shut one engine off to troll down to striper speeds. Sterndrive boats often experience more of a problem in attaining slow trolling speeds. A friend's 23-Seacraft, powered by a single, V8 I/O will not idle slow enough to troll bass without the aid of a sea anchor, probably because I/O's utilize a considerably larger diameter propeller, since they have more torque and do not turn the high rpms that outboards are capable of attaining. If you have a V8 powered I/O in a midsize boat, a sea anchor is probably in your future, too.

Not all striper lures require slow speeds. Some spoons troll better at speed between 3 and 4 knots, depending upon the size and style, but the rule of thumb applies here too. The slower you can troll a bass lure, even a spoon, and still maintain the proper action, the better your chances of catching bass.

To control boat speed more accurately, I recommend installing a trolling speed indicator. Many of today's modern sonar units have optional trolling speed indicators that plug right into the unit and read out in a small information box directly on the screen. If your unit does not have this capability, invest in a separate speed indicator, the type that uses a small paddle wheel probe mounted on the transom of the boat. Once you have the ability to accurately determine boat speed, you can establish the speed at which specific lures work best and maintain it on a consistent basis.

# Lure Selection

There is a wide variety of lures that will catch stripers when trolling. Not all of these lures are compatible with each of the three methods of trolling that have been mentioned. Refer back to Chapter Five for detailed information on specific trolling lure types, but keep in mind that some lures are limited to a specific type of tackle to attain satisfactory results.

Take the bunker spoon. These large lures work best when trolled with wire line on a soft action rod. They are almost impossible to run on downriggers, since the amount of pull they exert on the line makes it difficult to keep the line in the release clip. Attaining the desired action of a bunker spoon, critical to their ability to catch bass, depends on using them with a rod that is soft and flexible, which aids their action dramatically. When I first started fishing bunker spoons, I tried them on mono trolling rigs with very stiff 7-foot trolling rods. While I thought they were swimming well, even though I had no experience for use in making a comparison, I just didn't catch bass on them. Then a striper-wise charter skipper took mercy on me and showed me why they weren't working.

He showed me a pair of long, 9-foot, soft-action custom rods mounted with Penn Senator reels loaded with 40-pound test monel trolling wire. He explained that much of the wide, side-to-side action of a bunker spoon, when it is working correctly, is the result of the spoon working in concert with the soft, pumping action of the rod. He added that the wire line was critical because it has absolutely no stretch to inhibit the interplay between the spoon and the rod.

He had me watch as he put out the biggest of the Montauk Bunker Spoons made by Joe Julian of Atlantic Highlands, New Jersey. After he laid out 150 feet of wire (he had the line marked at 50-foot intervals) and brought the boat to the proper rpms, he stepped back to the transom and pointed to the rod, telling me, "You see how the rod pumps in long, soft arches and then pulls back on the spoon? The two are working together to give the spoon the action that bass love so much, those wide swings it takes from side to side. They can swing as much as six feet from side to side when they dig in and the rod pulls back on them. That's the ticket!"

While the wire line, soft-rod theory holds true today, we've found that the extra long rods are not absolutely necessary to do the job. A soft-action rod of 6½ to 7 feet will swim a bunker spoon just fine when a horizontal rod holder, one that places the rod out to the side of the boat and out over the water, is employed. The key is the no stretch wire line, which gives you the benefit of positive depth control, and the interplay of the rod and the spoon to create the action that drives big bass to strike these hubcap size lures. The extra long specialty spoon rods do add some extra kick to big spoons. I recently fished a pair of 10 footers custom-made by Julian's and they were quite impressive.

Other types of lures work well with specific tackle. Umbrella rigs have been catching stripers, sometimes two or three at a time, for decades and they are still one of the most effective lures you can use today. Their shear bulk and the water resistance of a full-size umbrella rig makes using them on downriggers less than desirable. Umbrellas work best on mono/Dacron rigs or, even better, on wire line. A new generation of mini-umbrellas, with four shorter six-inch arms, will work on downriggers, but they have not proven to be as effective as their big brothers.

Small swimming plugs like the Bomber Long A and the Storm Mac lures can be very effective trolling, but they are small and do not troll well on wire line. But combine them with a downrigger in deep water or a mono outfit with a light drail for trolling shallow around sand bars and they become a deadly bait. Single tube lures like a J & J Smilin'

Tee Jay or Tee Jay Squid are highly versatile and can be effective when trolled on mono, wire or downriggers. Matching the lure to the correct trolling method is mostly common sense, recognizing what makes specific lures work and what might inhibit their action. The more thought you put into lure selection and understanding each type of lure's characteristics, the more effective you will be trolling.

A word on trolling natural baits is in order. Live baitfish, specifically menhaden, can be slow trolled for bass. They are most effective when used in conjunction with downriggers to easily control depth. They cannot be used with wire, as the wire will drag the fish down in an unnatural manner, but they can be used with mono and a light drail. To get results trolling live bunker, a special rig that employs a stinger hook at the fish's tail is necessary, since the bass will not have any time to mouth and swallow the bait. Speed for trolling live baits is painstakingly slow, as slow as you can possibly move the boat. It is also possible to troll live eels, in a similar manner, but this is best accomplished with the rod in hand, so you can free spool the reel when a fish strikes, providing some time for the bass to eat the bait.

# Trolling Patterns

Bass trolling patterns are usually set up with a smaller number of lures than offshore trolling, which often requires getting as many lures in the water as you possibly can using outriggers to spread the lure pattern wide. I know some offshore captains running boats of 36-feet and larger that can run 9 to 11 rods simultaneously. This is overkill for bass and you will rarely find even the biggest boat using more than five outfits at once. More often than not, two to four outfits are used.

I utilize two to four outfits on my boat; two wire line outfits and two downriggers. If I am trolling shallow water of 10 to 25 feet, like along the outsides of sand bars, I will usually only run two, occasionally three, mono outfits with light drails to gain the depth needed to keep the lures close to the bottom.

Most captains try to match lure types within the spread of the lures. When using two wire line outfits, a pair of spoons, tubes or umbrella rigs are usually employed. Similarly, with downriggers or mono rigs, two similar type lures are used, but there is no rule that demands you match lures. There are days when searching for a combination that will catch fish, we will use completely different lures on each trolling outfit, such as a spoon on the starboard rod and an umbrella or a big plug on the port rod. One of the things I like about running down-riggers and wire line at the same time is I can run two umbrellas or spoons on the wire and a pair of plugs or single-tube lures on the downriggers all at the same time. Since the downrigger mounted lures are usually dropped back 50 to 75 feet behind the trolling ball

## Trolling Patterns

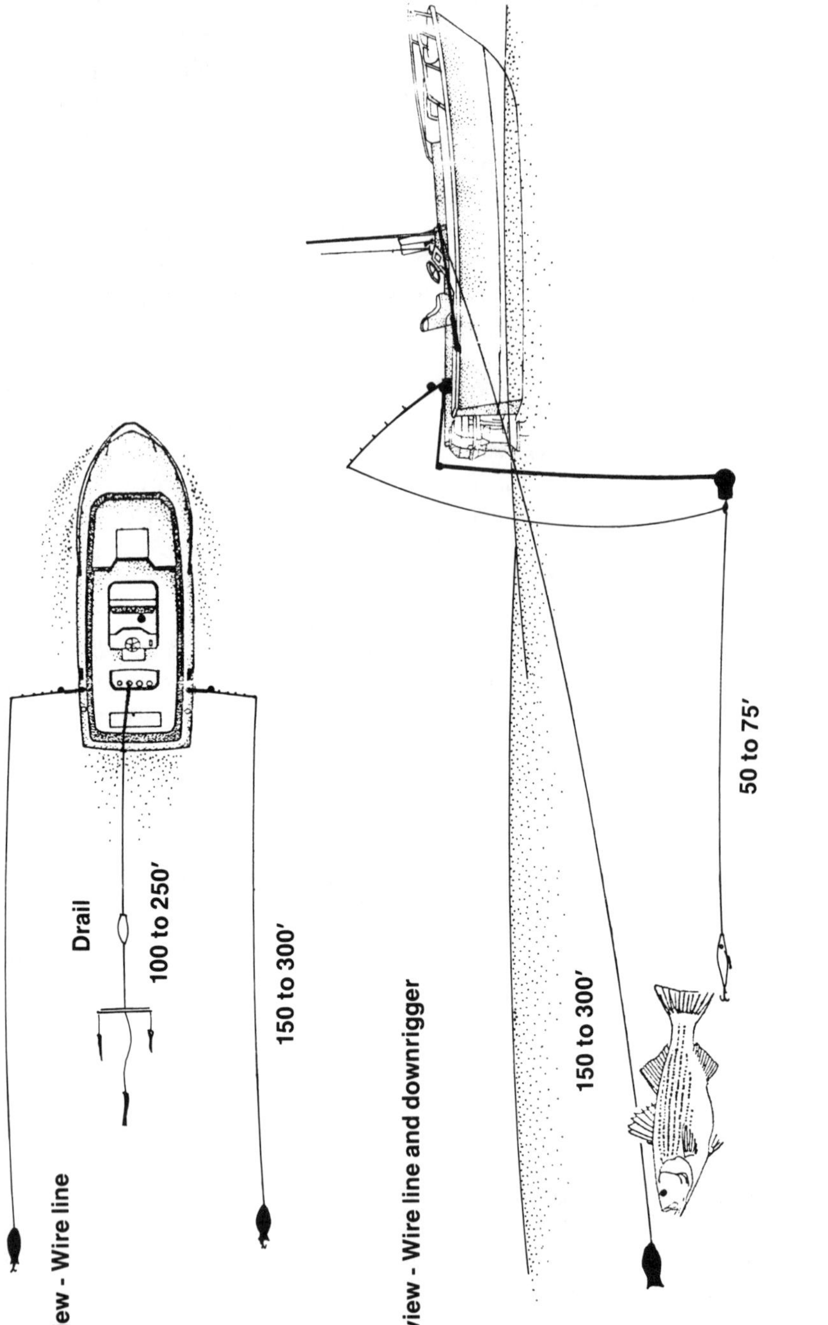

### Top view - Wire line

Drail

100 to 250'

150 to 300'

### Side view - Wire line and downrigger

150 to 300'

50 to 75'

and set at a specific depth, they don't come into contact with the wire line lures, which are set back 150 to 250 feet behind the boat. It is an ideal combination for trying a variety of lures in a short period of time and the boat can be maneuvered in relatively tight turns to work over small structure.

## *Trolling with Mono Rigs*

What constitutes shallow water for stripers? Trolling done in water less than 25 to 30 feet deep. Most trolling done in bays and on inshore ocean structure like sand bars fall into this category. This is where mono/Dacron outfits have a place and I always keep a pair on board my boat in the fall for just these circumstances. Since I like to troll shallow water with relatively light line, rarely over 20-pound test, I often use the same outfits I employ with downriggers as mono trolling rigs. Trolling drails are all you need to get lures or baits down. For trolling around sand bars, a two to five-ounce drail is usually sufficient to keep your lures near the bottom. A 10 to 20-foot, 40-pound test leader running from the drail to a single snap completes this simple rig. Big or small swimmers, swimming tube lures, bucktails with a strip of pork rind, artificial or natural rigged eels, umbrella rigs, spreader bars or even live baitfish can be used effectively here. Trolling sand bars is most effective early in the day, from a couple hours before daybreak to a couple of hours after first light and again late in the day.

When trolling bars with small plugs, tubes or rigged eels, establish trolling speed by setting the lure out alongside the boat and visually check its action. Then drop it back behind the boat until you feel the drail hit bottom once, then drop back until the drail hits a second time and put the reel in gear. This method will assure you that the lure is near the bottom, where it will get the most attention from feeding bass. If the drail doesn't hit bottom in this manner, you will probably have to switch to a slightly heavier trolling drail.

This same, simple mono trolling technique can be used in rivers, lakes and bays effectively and will catch stripers of all sizes, depending upon the size of the lures you use. It has its depth limitations, so when more depth is needed, larger drail weights will have to be employed.

Chesapeake and San Francisco Bay trollers use a different type of trolling weight arrangement to attain depths of 25 to 30 feet with mono/Dacron rigs. This rig is used around structure in heavy, running currents with a variety of lures. Crippled Alewives, Drone Spoons, big bucktails or daisy chains of Hoochie skirted lures are a few lures that are used in this manner. The rig incorporates a three-way swivel with a large bank or ball sinker dropped down from the swivel about two

# Trolling A Rip

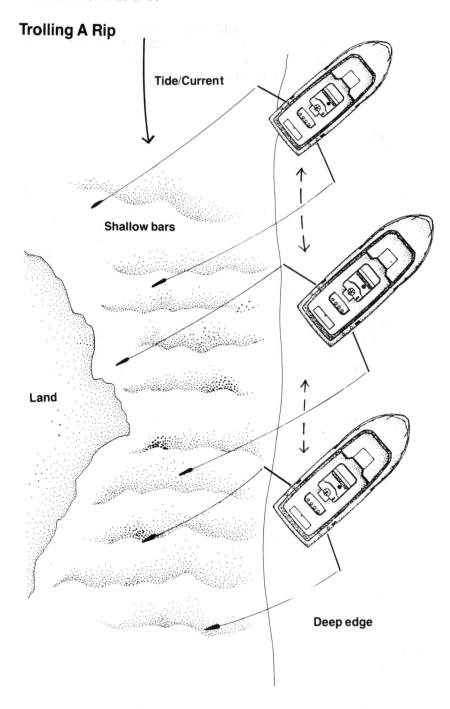

Tide/Current

Shallow bars

Land

Deep edge

feet on a length of leader. The weight can actually be bounced along the bottom, while the lure rides just above it on a leader 10 to 20 feet long, or longer. This method is effective when used by an experienced skipper, but with other deep water trolling alternatives available, like wire line or downriggers, this method seems cumbersome, at best.

A technique we call the "bump and go" is highly effective with mono trolling outfits when employed around shallow rips and can be used with plugs or even live baits. In my home waters, the rips at Sandy Hook offer a prime location for using this technique, but similar rips can be found along many areas such as Cape May, Montauk or in Chesapeake Bay. If you're not familiar with Sandy Hook, it is the tip of a long spit of sand that extends several miles out from the mainland, acting as a barrier between the ocean and Sandy Hook Bay. A powerful rip builds at the tip of the Hook on a running tide that washes over sand bars and attracts stripers to feed on the disoriented baitfish that get caught up in its currents.

The key to catching bass in the rips is to position the boat uptide of prime locations and drop big plugs, or live bunker or eels, back into the churning currents. The boat's position is maintained by bumping the engine in and out of gear, letting the lures or baits work in the current, rather than using the forward motion of the boat to generate action. By working the steering wheel and the throttle, a practiced skipper can move his boat from side to side, moving his plugs across the rip.

This technique can also be used with weighted lures around prominent structure like bridge abutments, navigational markers or rock out croppings. Boat position is controlled in a similar manner, allowing the strong rip currents to generate lure action. In the Chesapeake, the same method will catch stripers around the abutments of the Chesapeake Bay Bridge Tunnel.

# *Wire Line*

Wire line trolling has been around for decades and is widely recognized as a highly effective trolling technique for catching fish in saltwater. It is used to catch stripers and bluefish, but in southern waters, wire line trollers catch tuna, wahoo and king mackerel with the same basic techniques using different lures. The reason for using wire line is not because wire doesn't break (it does) because it is inherently stronger than mono (it isn't). The most widely used trolling wire is 40-pound test, or about the same test as used on most monofilament trolling outfits. Wire is used because of the characteristics it exhibits when trolling, which allow the angler to attain greater depth control. Wire's weight and its ability to cut through the water with less resistance than other types

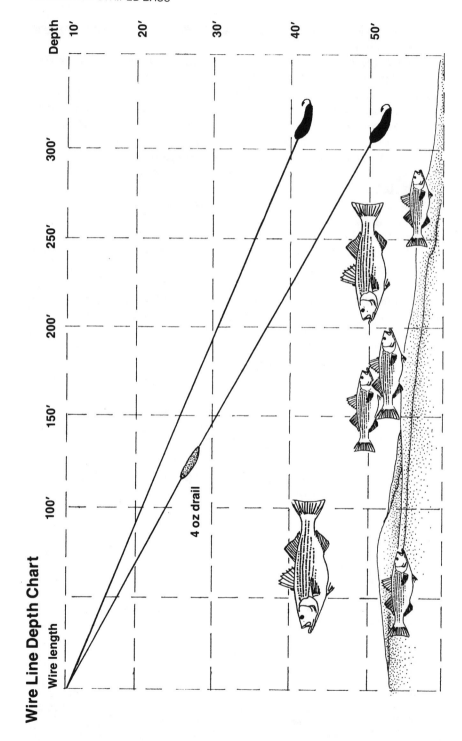

**Wire Line Depth Chart**

Wire length

4 oz drail

Depth
10'
20'
30'
40'
50'

100'
150'
200'
250'
300'

of line are the key to its popularity and its ability to get lures deeper than mono or Dacron.

Some anglers look down their nose at wire line calling it unsporting and the International Game Fish Association leads the way in promoting this snobbery. They do not recognize potential record fish when caught on wire, but many striped bass fishermen don't go out of their way to recognize the IGFA for similar reasons. If you've ever thrilled to the strike of a trophy bass smashing a big spoon trolled on wire, you will certainly disagree with the assessment that wire is unsporting. Since wire has no stretch, it becomes a direct connection to the fish. The angler can feel every shake of the fish's head, every pulse of the tail, every arm-wearying rush a bass makes when played on this tackle. As are most of the serious striped bass trollers I know, I am a proponent of wire line as one of the most consistent methods of catching trophy bass, especially during the fall run. Any method that lets you go out and catch fish in the 30 to 50-pound class regularly, can't be all bad in anyone's book, and wire does just that.

Wire line allows a great degree of depth control. The general rule of thumb for establishing lure depth is one foot of depth for every 10 feet of wire (in the water). If you have 150 feet of wire in the water, your lures will be about 15 feet below the surface, 200 feet of wire provides 20 feet of depth, 300 feet gets the lures down to about 30 feet. The use of more than 300 feet of wire begins to have a reverse effect on lure depth as the wire itself will begin to plane back up, generating less depth penetration. If the fish are deeper than 30 feet, add a drail weight at the end of the wire before the monofilament leader to gain more depth. Rule of thumb here is a gain of 5 additional feet for each four ounces of drail weight. Putting it all together, it is possible to attain trolling depths of 40 or more feet with wire line and 8-ounce drails.

This rule of thumb is based on average trolling speeds of about 3 knots, but slower trolling speeds will allow your lures to sink to even greater depths. A perfect example occurs each fall when we use large tube lures or umbrella rigs. During daylight hours, bass can be found in water of 50 feet or more. We can often reach them without resorting to the use of additional drail weights by cutting the trolling speed in half. If the fish won't rise up to rigs or tubes trolled at 3 knots, try slowing the trolling speed to 1½ knots. The lures will be carried deeper by the weight of the line. You can often bounce bottom in 40 feet using this technique, without using drails.

Here's a wire line trick that works with umbrellas, tubes and big plugs that will help you get deeper. It is a variation of the "bump and go" technique used with mono outfits and it comes into play when bass are holding deep. It is particularly effective when your trolling lures are being plagued by bluefish. As is often the case during the fall run, big bluefish will be found on the same grounds as bass. The

**This happy angler trolled this hefty bass on an umbrella rig fished deep on wire line.**

bluefish will usually establish their feeding station at mid-water depths and the bass will be found under them. Bass will hit tubes or umbrella rigs trolled at slower speeds than will interest the bluefish and the bass are deeper than the blues. Here's how to get them.

With all the wire deployed, keep the trolling speed in the 2½ knot range. When fish are marked on the depthfinder, even if they are only bluefish at mid-water, bump the engine out of gear and let the boat speed diminish to almost a standstill, allowing the lures to settle to a deeper level. Bump the engine back in gear and bring the trolling speed back up to 2½ knots. This carries the lures below the blues into the feeding zone of the bass. If bass are there, they will strike on the descent or shortly after you re-engage the engine as the rigs begin to ascend from the lower depth. Often the strike will come when the boat is close to dead in the water, and since the wire has no stretch, the fish will usually be hooked. This technique is recommended for fishing over open sand or mud bottom. Try this on hard bottom or around areas with excessive bottom structure and you can hang up and loose some expensive terminal tackle.

Big spoons and wire line are a match made in heaven. Most big spoon designs have been with us for decades and they have never lost their popularity. They have a reputation for catching bass, especially big bass, and the reputation is much deserved. Some of the most famous spoons include the bunker spoon, the Crippled Alewive, the Drone and the Tony Accetta Pet. Combined with a wire line outfit, they are deadly during the spring and fall months. Bunker Spoons in their large and small sizes and the 11/0 and 13/0 versions of the Crippled Alewive are absolutely deadly during the fall run when bass are smashing schools of bunker or sea herring. Wire line is the best delivery system to get the most action from these oversized offerings.

When trolling spoons, be sure to match the trolling speed to the action of the spoon. Not all spoons work at the same speeds, so watch them work alongside the boat before dropping them back. Spoons are worked at consistent speeds, "bump and go" techniques don't work with them. Be sure you have a rod that works in harmony with the spoons and be ready for some of the most savage strikes you'll ever see from a striped bass. They hit big spoons so hard it inspires awe in most anglers.

Here's a tip you will find helpful when playing a fish with wire line. Remember that wire has no stretch, so any slack you allow to form between the rod tip and the hook will provide an opportunity for the fish to get off. The fish can use the leverage generated by the weight of the wire and the weight of the large lures to help pry the hook loose from its mouth, adding to the necessity of keeping the slack out.

When playing a bass on wire, try to pump the rod as little as possible. Use the reel more and the rod less. When the fish is fighting deep and you have to pump to bring him up, make your lifts short and keep the line tight as you reel down at the top of each stroke. I've seen many big bass lost on wire by inexperienced anglers who pump the rod widely, lifting the tip high in the air and then dropping the tip more quickly than they can pick up the line with the reel. Keep your strokes smooth and short and you'll get your fish to the boat. It also pays to keep bumping the boat's engine(s) in and out of gear to maintain slight headway and to keep slack from getting between you and the fish.

# *Downriggers*

Imported from the salmon fisheries of the West Coast and Great Lakes, downriggers fit striped bass fishing perfectly. Downriggers are best able to provide depth control at trolling speeds of 1 to 4 knots, prime striper trolling speeds. They loose their effectiveness when speeds get beyond 4 knots due to the problem of blow back, caused by water pressure pushing the large trolling weight, or ball, back and up behind the boat. The faster the trolling speed, the less the depth penetration. At 6 knots, blow back can eat up more than 50% of the depth you think you are gaining with the downrigger, pushing the ball far behind the boat and high up in the water column.

Blow back can be averted to some extent by the use of heavier and more streamlined downrigger weights. For saltwater fishing, I've found a "water slicer" style weight of 12 pounds keeps my lures down with the least amount of blow back at typical striper trolling speeds. A second advantage to this style of weight is the large fin section of bendable metal. Since I run a pair of downriggers off the transom corners of my boat, bending the fin so that each ball runs slightly to the outside of the boat helps give my lures a wider spread and keeps them from tangling in tight turns. It takes a little experimentation with the fins to get just the right amount of spread since a slight bend can generate a lot of push out to the side. Once you get it right, the balls track away from each other.

Since downriggers are still somewhat new to saltwater, there isn't much reference material to be found on the subject. When I installed them on my boat, it took two seasons of experimentation before I hit on some combinations that worked consistently for bass.

A wide variety of lures and live baits can be fished with downriggers and they can be placed at depths unattainable with wire line. Plugs, smaller spoons, natural or artificial rigged eels, spreader bars, tube lures, nylons, hoochies, and live herring or bunker can be trolled with downriggers. Spreader bars armed with light-weight salmon trolling spoons on short drop backs have caught school fish impressively well and nothing we've found to date makes single swimming style tube lures more effective than the precise depth control offered by downriggers.

Stripers don't seem shy about having the downrigger weight pulled through their feeding grounds, which means that an excessive drop back from the release clip at the ball to the lure trailing behind is not necessary. For most bass fishing situations, a 50-foot drop back is adequate. At times, you might find the fish a little skittish, and you can increase the drop back to 75 feet or even 100 feet, but we've found these instances rare. Keep in mind that the shorter the drop back to the lure, the better the hook set when a bass hits your offering.

Using downriggers is a team effort. It requires frequent communication between the man at the helm watching the depthfinder and the crew working the downriggers, to match the bottom contour. If you're using them over relatively even bottom, little change in depth settings is necessary, except to find the feeding zone the bass prefer on a given day. Even bottom is not necessarily where downriggers offer the most benefit. Our best results have come using riggers over hard bottom areas with sharp changes in depth, areas where bass are at home seeking baitfish close to the bottom. It's places like these that nothing matches a downrigger's performance and almost instant response to radical changes in depth.

When fishing areas of this nature, the procedure is for the man at

# Mono, Wire Downrigger Depth Comparisons

**Mono**

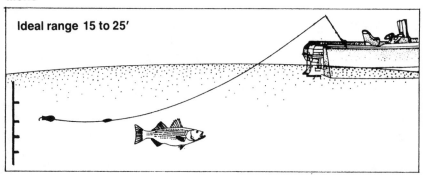

Ideal range 15 to 25'

**Wire**

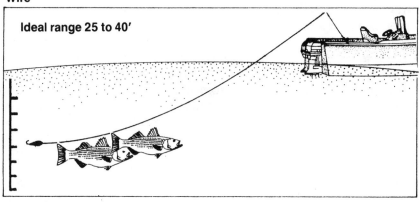

Ideal range 25 to 40'

**Downrigger**

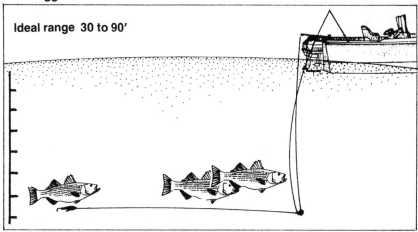

Ideal range 30 to 90'

the helm to relay information about changes in depth to the man at the riggers. When a drop-off is reached, it is voiced loud and clear so the downrigger ball can be lowered to the new depth rapidly. This makes your lures follow the contour of the drop-off and actually descend down the face of the drop-off, often triggering strikes from fish on the descent. The same goes for rises in the bottom. When the boat passes over a rise and the ball is raised, your lures will gradually rise up, giving the natural appearance of baitfish working their way from deep water to the shallow. No other trolling technique is capable of this instant and natural appearing rise and fall when trolling without drastic changes in trolling speed.

As you become familiar with downriggers, you will find that you can control the depth of your lures to within a couple of feet of the bottom, a real bonus when bass are not actively feeding and unwilling to rise to lures. On days when bass hug the bottom and do not respond to other trolling techniques, we've been able to coax them into striking lures pulled right in front of their noses on a downrigger.

When sand eels are the primary food, a simple technique we hit upon catches bass exceedingly well. Sand eels get their name because they dive into and out of the sand, often in an effort to avoid predators. When they pop up from the bottom they leave a puff of

**When trolling with wire and a downrigger, use side rod holders to spread the wire line and fish the downrigger line in the center of the pattern.**

sand, which attracts predators looking for an easy meal. The puff of sand can be artificially created by working the downrigger weight so close to the bottom that it occasionally touches, creating the puff. By keeping your lure on a tight drop back from the ball, 35 to 50 feet, it will pass through the puff only seconds after the ball makes it and into the sight of an already interested bass. This is a technique for clean, sandy bottom areas and not for use around hard bottom or structure.

Downriggers are at home fishing relatively shallow waters, as well as deep. Some of the shallow water techniques described earlier in the chapter can easily be accomplished with a downrigger, instead of using a mono/Dacron outfit with cumbersome, heavy drail weights. We've had success using downriggers on bass in waters as shallow as 15 feet, but when used in extremely shallow water, an increase in the length of the drop back from the ball to the lure is in order to avoid having the lures running too close to the boat's engine noise.

# *Downriggers with Live Bait*

Live baits can be used with downriggers. King mackerel fishermen in more southern waters have been trolling menhaden with down-riggers for some time and become quite proficient at it. They use a double hook rig, with a single hook through the bunker's nose and a treble stinger hook near the tail, since a king mackerel (or bass) striking a trolled live bait must be hooked almost immediately. It will not have the time to mouth and swallow the bait before the line comes tight to set the hook.

One thing to recognize when trolling live bait is that speeds should be kept agonizingly slow. You can even work them by bumping the engine(s) in and out of gear just enough to keep the drop back from the bait to the ball tight.

Since downriggers are such a recent addition to the saltwater trollers arsenal, don't feel limited to the techniques we've covered. Let your imagination run wild. Don't hesitate to try something new and unusual in the way you use them and the lures you pull with them. Innovate and you could come up with a technique capable of putting bass in the boat when all else fails.

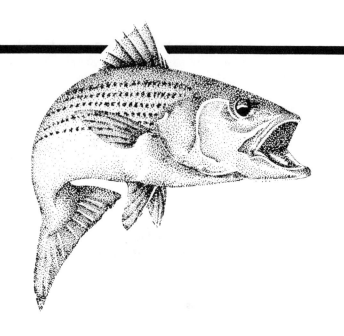

Chapter Ten

# FISHING AT ANCHOR

An anchored boat offers a platform for a variety of effective striped bass fishing techniques. Chumming with clams, cut herring or chunks of menhaden; bottom fishing with worms or other soft baits, casting to bridges, fishing live or dead baits in strong running currents or holding off jetties or beach structure under adverse wind or tide conditions are all easily accomplished from an anchored boat. Let's look at these techniques and when to use them.

An anchor system must be capable of holding bottom in strong currents or winds, but the size and weight of the anchor is not the only factor that determines holding power. You've probably seen an inexperienced boater trying in vain to get a hold on the bottom with the rope attached directly to the anchor and no chain. It can be a comical scene, but also unsafe. For fishing purposes we're going to toss out the "boating manual" anchoring rules that says multiply the water depth by five to seven times to get the length of anchor line required. We'll use a more efficient system designed just for fishing.

Anchor chain is used to protect the bitter end of the rope that attaches at the anchor end from chafing, but more importantly, it helps the anchor get a solid bite in the bottom. It's the weight of the chain that keeps the anchor down and allows it to grab and hold bottom quickly. The more chain used, the less rope necessary to hold bottom and the faster the anchor will lock up. For the average small boat of 18 to 25 feet, a Danforth style anchor from 8 to 13 pounds is sufficient when combined with an 8-foot length of heavy chain.

Many experienced boaters will use even more chain, up to 12 feet, to increase the anchor's bite. On board my boat, I keep a back-up anchor and an additional length of chain, so if conditions warrant, I can double up on the 8-foot length that is already attached to the anchor in the locker. When anchoring on soft sand or mud bottom, especially in strong currents or high winds, I can always get a good bite and lock up with a minimum of line deployed.

Because of the heavier anchor and chain, the amount of line let out between the anchor and the boat should be two to three times the depth of the water. If you are in 20 feet of water, 60 feet of rope will be necessary. If you're anchoring in 80 feet of water, it may be necessary to deploy 240 feet of anchor line or more to hold bottom securely. Keep in mind that it is extremely important to have a properly rigged anchor system when fishing around structure in strong currents, like around bridges or off the end of jetties or rock piles. These are not the places you want to have your anchor slip or fail to grab because you can be too close to the structure to regain control of the boat before hitting it or being tossed onto the rocks by wave action. Whenever anchoring close to structure or near other boats, extreme caution should be exercised.

# *Boat Position*

The most important part of anchoring is positioning the boat and it's not always as easy as it might seem. Whether anchoring in a river, bay area with strong currents or in the ocean where winds and tides will effect the lay of the boat, some practice and common sense is necessary. After determining where you want to position your boat, run upcurrent or upwind of the position, whichever seems to be exerting the greatest influence on the boat, and take the boat out of gear. When the boat's forward momentum stops, see which direction the boat drifts. Note any interaction between wind and current. The direction the boat drifts will usually determine how the boat will lay at anchor.

Then determine how much anchor line will be required to hold the boat in position. Estimate how far away that will place your anchor from the position you wish the boat to be in at rest. These calculations will determine where you will have to drop the anchor to bring the boat where you want it to lay. Keep in mind that while the safe minimum of anchor rode is three times the depth the anchor was dropped in, that doesn't mean you can't drop back further on the line, so when you estimate where the anchor drops, always err on the side of too much rode, rather than not enough.

If the boat does not come to rest where you want it to be on the first

# Anchoring Techniques

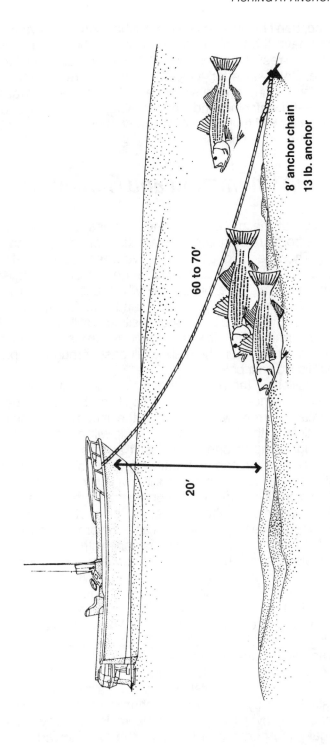

20'

60 to 70'

8' anchor chain

13 lb. anchor

drop, don't hesitate to pull the anchor and adjust your drop point until you have the boat positioned exactly where you want it. Once you come to rest at anchor, you will usually be fishing in that spot for some time. Don't settle for "close enough." There have been nights when fishing around bridge structure that boat position was the difference between catching and not catching, and we have often spent as much as half an hour putting the boat in the right spot before starting to chum or cast our lures.

# Clam Chumming and Bunker Chunking

Two of the more popular techniques for attracting and catching bass from an anchored boat are clam chumming and bunker chunking. These techniques are effective when used in tidal rivers and bays around bridges, over channel edges or on the edge of a drop-off. They can also be productive when used around inlets and near pronounced beach structure or sand bars. Since chumming is used to bring the fish to the baits, boat position is still important. It is necessary to determine the structure you want to fish and position the boat upcurrent, so your chum slick will pass through the prime areas and pull fish to your baits.

Positioning the boat so that a slick works its way through a bridge is simple since the structure is easily visible above the water and the primary current will be that of the incoming or outgoing tide. But positioning the boat so that a slick will pass over a set of bars or through a rip in open water isn't always that easy, since your anchored position can be greatly affected not only by water current, but also by the wind. The chum slick will only be affected by the current. Therefore, it is extremely important to determine the prominent current flow over an area when positioning the boat to begin a slick, not letting the wind force you to anchor in an unfavorable location.

Most chumming for stripers is done with clams. Serious chummers will also place a bunch of crushed clams in a chum pot suspended from the boat to sweeten the slick. When selecting hook baits, squeeze the whole clam over the transom of the boat before placing it on the hook so that the juices will further sweeten the slick. Toss only small pieces of clam into the slick. You want to attract the bass to the slick, not feed them. Distribute just enough to keep them interested so when your hook bait drops back into the slick on a slack line, they won't hesitate to gobble it down.

Chunking with cut fish is done in a similar manner, but the slick is established by tossing small chunks of oily fish, like menhaden or mackerel, over the boat's transom in carefully metered amounts. Again, the purpose is to attract the bass toward the source of the

# Clam Chumming Techniques

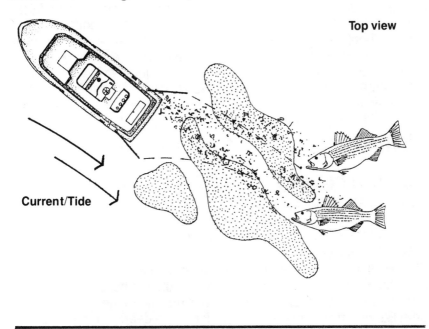

**Top view**

**Current/Tide**

---

**Side view**

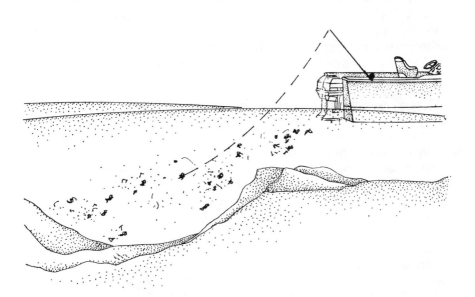

**Clam chum disperses behind boat in current and draw striped bass towards baited hooks.**

chunks, not to feed them. You need just enough bait in the water to create a slick and substantial scent trail. Hook baits should be larger than the chunks tossed into the chum slick. With both clams or chunks, hook baits should be fed back into the slick so they move naturally with the current. If you drop them back on a tight line, you will decrease the number of fish that will show an interest in your offering. If the current is strong and the baits won't sink down in the slick, small or rubber core sinkers can be added to get them down. Don't overload the line with weight, usually no more than a 1/4 to 1/2 ounce is needed to do the trick.

## Bottom Fishing with Bait

It is as easy to fish soft or dead baits on the bottom from an anchored boat as it is to fish them from the beach, and a boat fisherman can often do it more effectively than a beach fisherman. Pick the location you feel will hold fish, or find an area that will funnel fish past your position. Anchor up and put out the baited lines. If using worms, a simple Carolina or fish-finder rig will do the job. For chunk baits like menhaden or mackerel, or for whole dead finger mullet, sand eels or other baitfish, go with a fish-finder or surf bass rig with a cork float to keep the baits off the bottom. When using whole surf clams or crabs, use the fish-finder rig.

In areas of Virginia and New England, head boat fishermen will fish dead eels on a single hook, drop sinker rig and catch bass from deep water holes or offshore rips. There's no finesse here, just locate the fish and try to tempt them into hitting your baited hook.

## Casting and Livelining Structure

When winds or currents are too strong to allow fishing structure from a drifting boat, it is possible to do the job by simply anchoring close enough to make your casts or get your live baits to swim in tight to it. This technique is used regularly in rivers and bays to get close enough to bridges or shoreline structure that hold fish and to work that location for a long period of time. Night fishing in rivers around bridges is a prime example. Stripers will usually pass through the structure offered by the bridge abutments at some stage of the tide and if you know which abutments have the most pronounced holes or rubble around them, that's where you most likely want to spend your time fishing. Concentrate casts around the rigs that form on the downtide side of the abuntments.

By anchoring the boat uptide and dropping back into casting position, you can concentrate your efforts on these areas. Your lure
selection can vary, including everything from plugs to rigged eels, but
we've found that a properly presented bucktail can be most deadly
fished in these locations. Even when I chum or chunk in these
locations, I keep a rod handy with a bucktail and plastic worm, pork
rind or squid strip. When things are slow, I work the bucktail near the
structure, often with nothing more than a straight, slow retrieve, and it
catches fish regularly. Bucktails are at their best when fished in strong
currents because their action is not adversely affected by the fast
moving water like most other lures.

## Anchoring At A Bridge

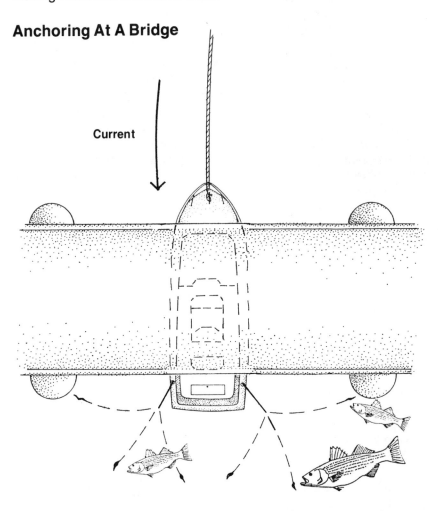

Current

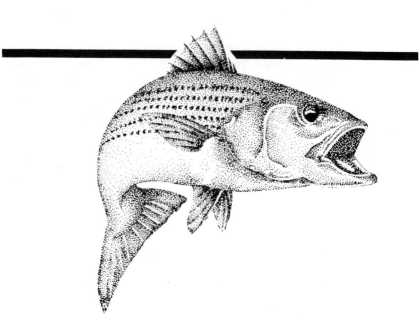

**Chapter Eleven**

# SURF AND JETTY TACTICS

You don't have to have a boat to catch striped bass. From school fish to trophies, beach fishermen account for a large portion of the annual catch of striped bass and many of them are among the most knowledgeable fishermen you will ever meet. They must learn their fishing environment well, because they lack the mobility of a boat and are forced to concentrate their efforts within the confines of the wash, extending outward only as far as their casting ability permits. Fortunately, striped bass spend much of their feeding time in the shallow water close to shore, hunting for the wide variety of food sources that are found there, using their physical dexterity and acute senses to feed in the skinny water.

At certain times of the year, beach fishermen will outscore boaters. Long before boat fishermen are on the water in early spring, hearty bank fishermen are catching stripers in tidal rivers on seaworms. During mid to late spring, when bass are scarce on offshore ridges and lumps, beach and jetty fishermen dunking clams can reap a harvest of school-size fish. In the summer months when trollers are hard pressed to cull a bass from the schools of voracious bluefish, surfcasters leisurely working beach structure with shedder or calico crabs, live or rigged eels can catch bass regularly. In the fall, when bass are available for all, the number of surf anglers pounding the prime stretches of beach in search of a trophy linesider can be akin to rush hour on a subway platform in midtown Manhattan.

Serious surf fishermen feel their sport is far more challenging than catching bass from a boat because it is more difficult. It requires diligence and great physical effort, casting for hours with oversized rods, reels and lures, trudging from one location to another through sand or over treacherous, slippery rocks. Beach anglers learn through trial and error, after investing many hours on beach or jetty, those locations that hold fish at different times of the year or at different stages of the tide.

Shore fishing is challenging and highly rewarding and it usually instills a great respect for the ocean and the fish by those who fish it well. While I now do more of my fishing from boats, I first grew to love the striped bass while jumping rock piles and walking sand beaches with the long rod in my hand, a bag of lures over my shoulder and with leaky waders chilling my feet. I still revel at the times when I don my beach fisherman's garb and fish for bass with my feet firmly planted on the end of a rock pile or as the waves swirl around me, hip deep in water, standing on a bar casting into the darkness waiting for the strike that will signal the fight is on again.

If you've never tried surf fishing for bass, it is different from anything you've ever done from a boat. It is fishing at its most basic. There's no water-bound chariot to whisk you to the offshore grounds. When you luck into your first real blitz on the beach, with birds swarming over your head and diving at the frantic baitfish that feeding stripers have driven to the surface, you feel much more a part of the action as the drama of life in the sea that is played out around your feet. It is indescribable, something that must be experienced, that must be felt, to be understood.

Even on evenings when bass are not found, the solitude of casting into the inky blackness of the ocean on a lonely stretch of beach at night, instills a feeling different than any I've ever experienced while fishing. It's at those times that a fisherman realizes that the sea is a living, moving entity unto itself. It is then that you understand what it is that beckons so many people to its shores to cast for the bounty that is found within its waters. Fishing from the beach is a very special endeavor, one that I find hard to label as a "sport" because the word simply doesn't do it enough justice.

## *Fishing Sand Beaches*

Open beaches are the most difficult terrain to understand for the novice striper fishermen. When faced with a beach that stretches to either side of you for miles, what is it that makes one place hold fish and another, often just a few hundred feet away be barren. The answer is in your ability to learn to "read the beach." The more proficient you become at finding the signs that suggest where to fish, the more effective you will be at catching stripers, or any fish in the surf for that matter.

Few sand beaches are barren of structure. It is there, just under the breaking waves. The structure is in the form of sand bars, those shifting hills, ridges and gullies that are formed by the continuous action of the waves against the shore. Waves will cause sand to be washed into the sea or pushed up onto the beach, forming ridges that would look very much like the wind blown sand dunes found well above the water line. If only you could move the water away for a closer look, but alas, mother nature does that twice a day and we call it low tide. Bars act like any other form of structure, attracting baitfish and predators alike. But they also cover and expose crabs, clams or sand bugs, welcome additions to a striper's diet. When you locate a break in a bar that parallels the beach, with the resulting hole and mini-inlet it creates, you've struck pay dirt in your effort to locate good shoreline structure.

The time to learn a beach is not at night when you're out fishing, but during the daylight hours and at low tide. It's then that the ocean will give you a chance to see what's out there. Some prominent bars will actually become partially exposed, but more often, you will see the bars by the pattern of the waves breaking on them when the tide is out.

Search for waves that curl and break some distance off the beach. If the waves break several times before hitting the shore, it indicates a series of parallel bars. If the waves have sections that don't break until they are almost on shore, then you've located an opening or break in the bar. Note these locations well, with the deeper water holes they usually create and the natural inlets they form, where one section or bar ends and another begins. These are spots surf fishermen covet, because when the tide is on the rise and the bass move in, they become traps for milling baitfish and prime hunting grounds for able-bodied predators. As the tide drops, the action that can be had around such openings in the bar can be the stuff tales are made of.

Tides are probably more important for surf fishermen than for boat fishermen. Bass will move onto beach structure with an incoming tide and will desert it when the water drops too low for their liking. Some beach areas will produce best on incoming water and others on outgoing water, there is no hard and fast rule. But moving water is usually important and action will usually drop off dramatically when either dead high or low water is reached.

Not all beaches form bars in the same manner. Prevailing winds, tides and man-made inlets will cause bars to form in dramatically

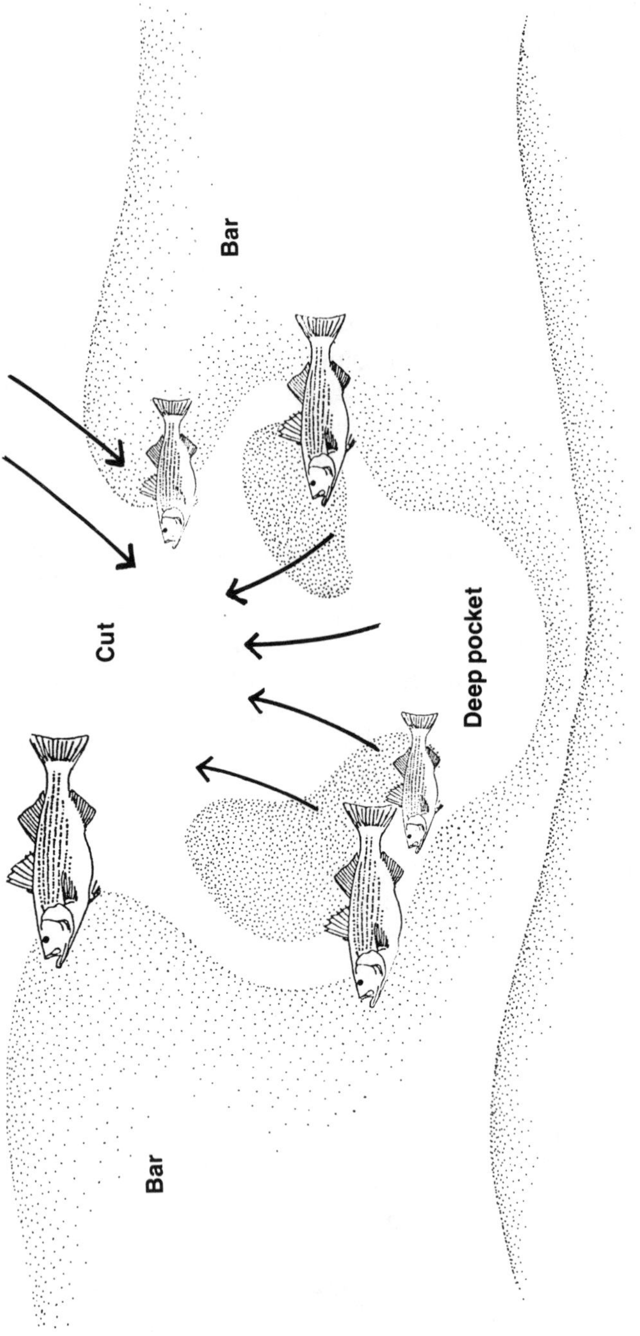

# Beach Structure - Deep Hole

Bar

Bar

Cut

Deep pocket

Beach

# Beach Structure - Sand Bar

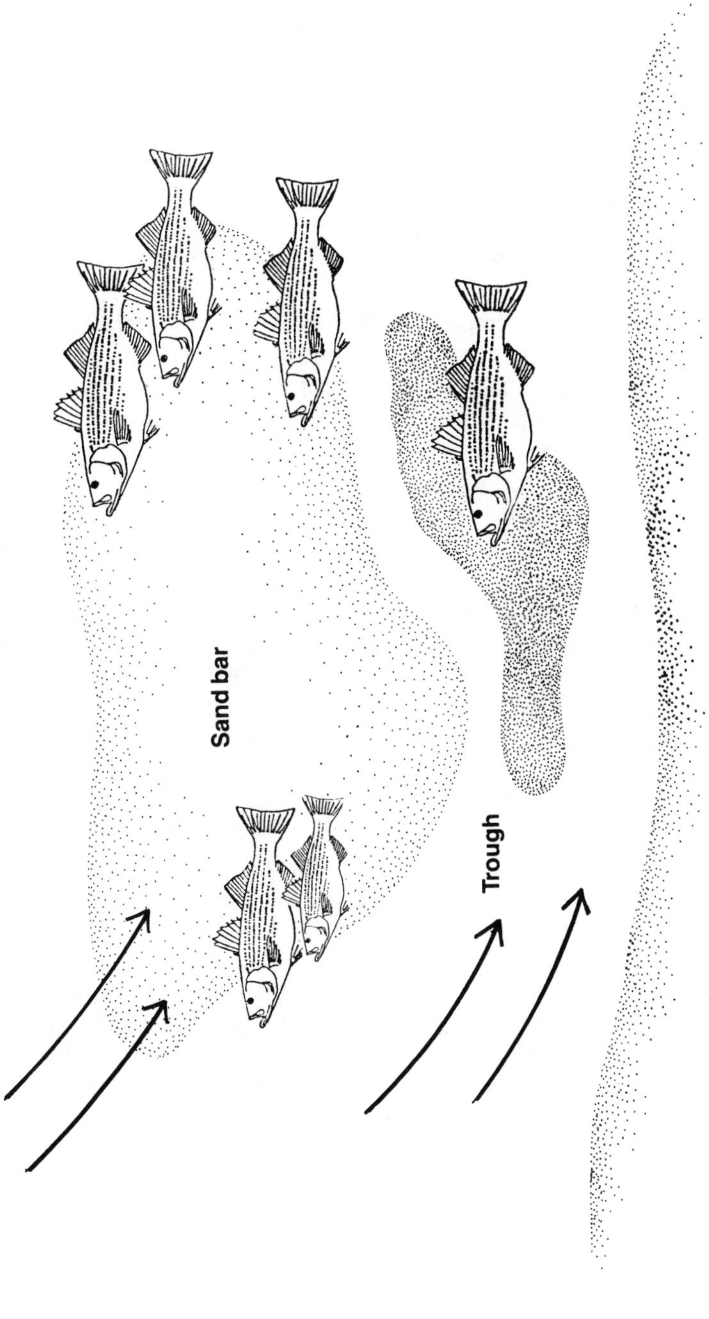

Sand bar

Trough

Beach

different ways. The bars I fish in the center portion of New Jersey are quite different from the way bars form along the south shore of Long Island. The main reason is that the prevailing winds effect beaches that run in a north to south direction, like those in New Jersey, differently than they do beaches that run in an east to west direction, like those found on the south shore of Long Island. New Jersey's open beaches build bars that run parallel to the shoreline, sometimes with series of parallel bars, one slightly further out than the next. Long Island's south shore finds bars that can form at angles to the shoreline, or even perpendicular and extending outward into the ocean for hundreds of feet.

Bars are more confused in their pattern when located near strong running inlets. Here, the ocean has a tendency to build bars and shallow sand-filled flats around inlets that shift with the seasons and years. Many inlets, if left to the forces of nature, will fill in or shift southward rather than stay stationary. Inlets have come and gone in most states along the Atlantic coastline.

The trick is to use these bars to your fishing advantage by learning their present patterns, re-evaluating them with each new season because they do change, and keeping a record of their ability to produce fish. The knowledgeable surf fisherman not only casts to bars, but walks onto them at optimum tide stages, using them as a platform to fish further out into the open ocean waters. This practice can be risky business when tried by a newcomer and is not recommended unless you have someone to teach you the ropes. It's a good idea to have a fishing buddy along just in case an emergency arises. Finding yourself on the end of a bar too far into an incoming tide as the trough behind you gets deeper and deeper, preventing your safe return to the beach, is a scary and dangerous situation. I've seen surf fishermen dragged onto the beach by friends, very frightened and totally exhausted, after getting themselves into just such a bind. Learn your beaches well and don't be fool-hardy.

When you've located prime beach structure, fishing it effectively is your next concern. Being there at the right time is as important as being in the right place. Most beach structure is not productive at low tide, although low tide is the best time to find structure. The rule of thumb is to fish beach structure during the last half of the incoming, as bait and game fish work their way into the shallows, and again during the outgoing tide as long as fishing action continues. Keep in mind that "rules of thumb" are often broken. Some particularly deep holes or spots around inlets will produce, even on a low tide, but places like this are the exception.

Work each area of structure carefully with fan casts so that you cover it well with each lure or bait you decide to try on a given tide. Work the prime areas of structure the hardest, but don't ignore the area surrounding the structure as fish will sometimes lie away from the structure proper, waiting for the opportune moment to move in on unsuspecting prey. If, after you've worked an area hard, there is no action, move along to the next spot you've noted from your daylight inspection of the beach. While a good spot might hold bass at one time or another, they don't always hold fish every day or night. The fish could be just down the beach a few hundred yards away.

## *Fishing Rocky Beaches*

For bass fishermen who pound the surf line from the north shore of Long Island to the coasts of Maine and northward into Nova Scotia and New Brunswick, beaches strewn with rocks are a common occurrence. Some will have sand bars, but they are of such gravelly consistency or rimmed and filled with so many large boulders that they are no longer prominent enough to be a major consideration. The rocks themselves are the structure that attracts bass and they demand attention by striper fishermen.

Certain rocky areas hold bass under specific tide and wind conditions. Watching the wind and tide and how they generate rip currents and pockets of white water around their bases will help you key in on when to fish them. One place that comes to mind is Narragansett Bay in Rhode Island, a rock-strewn section of coast where casting is done while standing on large shoreline boulders. The beaches around Pt. Judith, where Long Island Sound and Narragansett meet, are a bass fisherman's dream. Large glacial rocks abound near shore and on the beach and they can hold large bass through much of the fishing season. They are ideal places to fish big plugs and live baits, and many a trophy fish is taken from the boulder's bases.

This type of terrain is more self explanatory than sand beach structure and it remains in place from year to year, unlike shifting bars. It should be treated like any hard structure and fished carefully. At different times of the year, bass will be found prowling the rocks in search of the wide variety of food they attract, from worms to clams, baitfish to crabs.

Jetty fishing is somewhat different from fishing open beaches or even beaches with rock structure, because the angler is standing on the structure that is attracting bait and the bass, rather than casting out to it. Jetties provide an excellent platform for fishing a wide variety of artificials as well as live baits, with eels and large baitfish deadly offerings. Working them around the base of the rocks, usually not more than 50 feet from where you are standing, is often the key. Most of the strikes you will experience when fishing a jetty will come close in, rather than at the end of a long cast, because the bass feed right close to the rocks. Keep in mind that in most areas where jetties are numerous, like the beaches of northern New Jersey, sand bars are almost non-existent because the jetties were built to preclude their formation and stop beach erosion. However, short bars with nearby deep holes are common.

During the many years that casting from jetties comprised the bulk of my striper fishing, I can think of only a few times when bass were caught far out from the rocks. Those were almost always times when bass were off the jetty fronts chasing schools of baitfish, rather than concentrating on feeding opportunities around the jetty itself. When baitfish are scarce, jetties present feeding opportunities because they attract crabs, seaworms, sandbugs and other tasty morsels bass enjoy.

When fishing along the open beaches is all but at a standstill, jetties can produce stripers throughout the season, especially during the doldrums of the summer months. Carefully concentrating fishing effort around these man-made striped bass feeding stations accounts for a great number of fish caught throughout the year. A variety of baits and lures work, varying with the season. Live baits, plugs or tins with teasers, rigged eels (probably the most deadly offering you can use around jetty rocks) and bucktails all have their time and place.

Jetties are prime night fishing spots. Most serious bass anglers

**Jetties are favorite places to fish along much of the East Coast because they are accessible and hold good numbers of fish.**

rarely fish jetties during the daylight hours, with the possible exception of the late fall when bass will remain more active and have a tendency to continue to feed shallow after sunrise. Daylight feedings can be successful with a variety of fresh baits like crabs or clams. Both are particularly effective when used following a storm or blow that riles up the surf line exposing and often crushing these creatures. Sandbugs can also be effective fished around jetties, either from the rocks or the sandy stretches between the jetties proper.

Eels and jetties go together like late fall fishing and a big thermos of coffee. There is probably no more deadly combination than rockpiles and eels, either live or rigged. Each summer, more bass fall to eels than most baits or lures combined and this is especially true around rockpiles like jetties. A close second to the eel would be swimming minnow plugs like the Bomber, Redfin, Mambo Minnow and Nils Master Invincible, which seem to imitate a wide range of small baitfish that will congregate around the rocks at different times of the year. Color preference may differ from place to place or with the seasons, but the action suits striped bass quite frequently. Add a teaser to the plug and you've got two bases covered in one cast.

# Inlets and Breachways

Jetties found around inlets are unique structures and often differ in the techniques that work around them and the ways they are fished. Not only do they offer the rocks that attract fish to beach jetties, but they have the added bonus (or at times, hindrance) of strong tidal currents. While fishing the outside walls of inlet jetties can be very similar to fishing a beach jetty, fishing the inside portions differ greatly with the stages of the tide.

The tides become a prime consideration when fishing inside and around the mouth of inlets and they will effect the times and baits you can fish effectively. Trying to work a rigged eel in a roaring outgoing tide in an inlet is a near impossibility. It is equally difficult to work plugs and other swimming lures when the tide is running hard, regardless of direction. To work the inside of an inlet with a live bait on a running tide, it becomes necessary to walk the bait along with the current, trying to keep it close to the rocks that will attract the bass.

One of the most effective lures to use in an inlet during a running tide is a large bucktail, sweetened with a large strip of pork rind. It can be bounced along the bottom with the current, getting down into the feeding zone of the bass, or kept close to the rocks where bass will be searching for bait being thrown about in the confusing currents they generate.

Your options become greater when tidal currents are not so strong, near the end of the tide or during the beginning of the tide. Big plugs, swimming plugs and a variety of other lures and baits can be fished during these stages quite effectivity, but once the tide swings into full force, you must choose your offerings accordingly.

# Fishing Inside

Not all shoreline fishing is done from jetties or beaches. In fact, many excellent areas of structure are often overlooked by shore-bound fishermen. Maybe they are just too obvious or in such populated or built-up areas that they don't register with striper fishermen, but they can produce some excellent bass fishing, nonetheless. Areas found inside inlets, lower areas of tidal rivers and canals can offer fine bass fishing to the dedicated fishermen who takes the time to learn their secrets.

Pay particular attention to major structures found inside inlets. Bridges are probably the most overlooked bass attracting structure for shoreline fishermen. There has always been a small, clandestine contingent of striper fanatics that walk the structures of the bridges found along Long Island's south shore. They know the bridges intimately and work their current and shadow lines with conventional tackle and big bucktails in much the same way a stream trout fisherman works the riffles of a stream. They score regularly with big bass that move into these areas on specific moon phases and after strong blows from particular wind directions.

But you don't have to live on Long Island to fish bridges and you don't always have to do it from the span, itself. The Connecticut River and some of the bridges that cross its waters close to the Sound are excellent places to fish using a variety of techniques. The Merrimack River in New Hampshire will often hold bass around its bridges for many miles upstream from its mouth. A good friend tells me about his exploits on this great tidal river and how lonely much of the fishing is, with hardly anyone else fishing for these stripers.

In my local waters, bass can often be found inside inlets and around bridge structure after a strong northeast blow. Fishing the bases of the bridges with many of the same lures and baits used outside will often produce. Bucktails are particularly effective lures and swimming plugs and rigged eels will produce when the tide wanes.

The tidal rivers of the Chesapeake offer incredible striper fishing almost year-round. During the spawning run, many are literally choked with cow bass and the smaller males that are there to reproduce. Well after the spawning run and the departure of the big fish, the rivers will hold great bodies of schoolies, providing a prolific catch-and-release fishery.

The fish become even more river oriented the further north and south one goes in the striped bass' range. The St. Johns River in Florida is the home of this race of striped bass year-round. Fishing in its waters is a year-round proposition and structure can often play a key role in where you find these bass. Nova Scotia and New Brunswick, the base of the Canadian striper population, finds most of the best action around the mouths and inside tidal rivers. In Maine, many of the biggest bass are caught inside tidal rivers during the season, both migratory bass from the southern races and the nonmigratory fish of the race that makes its home near these rivers year-round.

Canals offer another interesting environment to fish for striped bass. While bass use canals as passageways, they will sometimes linger in them when bait is present. Baitfish might differ from their normal prey in the confines of canals, since open ocean baits like herring and bunker are not usually found there, but blackfish and flounder are, and bass are not shy about feeding on these species. Although menhaden aren't found in canals regularly, a live menhaden fished around the walls of the canal will catch stripers there.

Old-timers tell stories of 30 and 40-pound bass being caught from the Point Pleasant Canal, a 2½ mile long, man-made connection between the Manasquan River and the northernmost reaches of Barnegat Bay. They would use a live flounder, herring, bunker or even seaworm, and walk the banks of the canal following their bait as it was carried on the tide. I've seen pictures of bass caught this way. Few anglers bothered fishing the canal for years, but more recently, as the striper population began to blossom again, the canal sees ever increasing pressure from fishermen on foot along its edges as well as anglers drifting it at night from boats.

The key to fishing many canals, especially narrow ones like the Point Pleasant Canal, is to keep your baits or lures close in to the bulkhead or down in the deeper holes. Most canals are best fished during the end stages of either the incoming or outgoing tide when the rush of water current isn't too strong to make bait presentation close to impossible. Bass will usually feed along the sides of the canal, rather than in the middle, so they can take advantage of the turbulence of the water there. The exceptions arise when bass lie in deep holes or around bridge abutments and pilings in the canal. Any areas of severe turbulence generated by structure is a good place to concentrate your efforts.

In bay and estuary environments, fishing eroded banks in unpopulated areas is another place often overlooked by shore-bound fishermen. Many bays have areas of sedge banks that hold interesting morsels of food for school bass. Worms, crabs and immature fish that spend their first few months or years of life in places like this will attract young stripers to feed on them. They seem to share a common attraction for most immature fish species, but to the striper they all spell dinner.

Fishing these banks with bucktails, worms or similar soft baits can be a highly productive way to catch school bass, not only early in the season when wintering bass will be found, but also during the spring, summer and into the fall, when many young bass will stay within the confines of the estuary environment for the bountiful food it offers and the relative safety, when compared with the open ocean. Shore anglers can take advantage of this environment to enjoy some excellent light tackle fishing opportunities for schoolies.

**Big bass, light line. This striper was over 40 pounds, yet was taken in the surf on 8-pound test line.**

# Tides, Moon Phases, Currents and Wind

Being in the right place is not your only consideration when striper fishing. Being there at the right time is also very important. The right time of day, time of year and right phases of the moon, favorable current and wind direction will all combine to affect fish activity along beaches, in bays and tidal rivers and on jetty fronts. Most striped bass feeding activity will take place early in the morning, late in the afternoon as the sun sinks in the sky or under the cover of darkness. As the sun rises high in the sky, bass will usually slip out of the shallows into the sanctuary of deeper water away from the bright sunlight. During the early months of spring and again in the wanning months of fall, this becomes less prevalent because the sun is at a lower angle in the southern sky and much of the direct sunlight reflects off the surface of the water rather than penetrating it, but it is still a factor to take into consideration.

When fishing the inside bays, the cover of darkness is even more important, since light penetration and daytime boat traffic create a commotion that drives fish into deeper water or puts them off the feed. The more heavily trafficked an area is, the more important it is to fish it when it is quite and calm, which is almost always at night.

For many serious striped bass fishermen, their fishing is limited almost exclusively to nighttime. It makes bass fishing a good choice for people who work hard during the day, but don't mind losing a few hours sleep to enjoy their sport. Many of my friends hold down regular day jobs and do their fishing under the cover of darkness. Depending on tides and feeding patterns, they will either fish after work or dinner to catch a prime tide or they will get up early and fish the tide until sun up, when they will run home and get cleaned up for work. It helps to be something of an insomniac, or at least a person that is capable of getting by on a limited amount of sleep, but most serious striper fishermen seem to have that ability in common.

Moon phases affect feeding activity. Most avid striper fishermen tell tales that revolve around the action on the October or November full moon. There is much validity to these stories because the moon generates exaggerated tide stages that trigger heavy feeding binges among many predatory fish and also precipitates migratory movements, especially in striped bass.

Of particular interest are the extended flood tides that accompany full moon periods. Moon tides will be far higher than neap tides, flooding areas of sand and marshes in sheltered waters, carrying heavy volumes of organic matter back into the bays and oceans when the tide turns to outgoing. This triggers voracious feeding among baitfish and striped bass alike, not just on the day of the full

**Fishing the right moon phase helps bring more striped bass in the landing net.**

moon, but during the preceding days and for several days after. This is also true of new moon phases, but to a lesser degree. Either way, these moon phases present ideal times to be on the water or beach chasing bass.

## The Right Combination

It becomes obvious that when two or three of the above mentioned factors happen to coincide, the chances of catching stripers are greatly increased. Night tides on the days preceding and following a full moon are optimum times to fish for bass. Add to this a benevolent wind, one that either helps drive bait into the beach, but that is mild enough not to make casting into it an impossibility and the fishing conditions become ideal. A wind at your back can also be a help, especially when fishing from the beach, because it can extend your casting range considerable.

When night fishing, a second consideration comes into play with regard to moon phases and that's the amount of ambient light the moon casts on the water. While extremely bright, moonlit nights don't always produce great fishing, those nights when there is enough light to silhouette moving objects easily in the water will often bring bone-jarring strikes from feeding bass. Just keep in mind that a bass most often targets a bait or lure from below when feeding on baitfish. That means that your offering should be easy for the fish to silhouette from below, against the brightness of the sky and a dark color, especially black, silhouettes best against a light background. On nights when there is little natural light, better results are often had by using a white plug, which stands out better against a dark sky. Rules of thumb are made to be broken, so don't let this keep you from experimenting. It may sound strange, but I've seen nights when the bass would only hit a strange, mustard yellow plug with black spots and others when bright yellow was the ticket, so color can be a factor to consider.

Tim Coleman, editor of the New England edition of The Fisherman, and an expert bass fisherman with more hours logged in the dark than most people spend at work during half a lifetime, fishes with only two colors at night, white and black. He occasionally varies from this color scheme, but only to don a plug that is half black and half white. He has caught many big bass from the surf following this simple strategy, including two 50s in one night and a 67 the following fall.

Another quick word about tides stages, moon phases, currents and wind and their effect on bass feeding habits. Sometimes, no matter what the experts tell you, you will catch bass at totally the wrong time and under the absolute worst conditions. If you fish for bass long enough, it will happen to you, take my word for it.

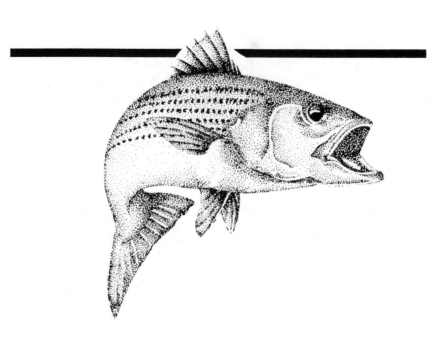

## Chapter Twelve

# THE END GAME

Before you start fishing, it is wise to check the things that can easily cost you a trophy striper. Your tackle has to be up to the challenge as much as your spirit. Start with the line. If it's used, pull some off the reel and see if it lays in tight coils when slack. If the line has taken a set, it usually means the outer sheath is getting hard from exposure to water and light. Replace it. More fish are lost to worn and old line than to any other link in the tackle chain. If the line feels okay, it is wise to strip off a five or ten foot section and retie your terminal gear or leader system before each trip. If the fishing is hot and the terminal end of the line is getting worked pretty hard, don't hesitate to strip off a few feet on the water and retie your gear. Just remember to discard used line in a receptacle and not into the water!

If you are using trolling gear, check the line in the same manner, check all knots and if any look weak or worn, retie them. I usually replace leaders on trolling outfits regularly, sometimes before each trip and keep a leader bag handy with prettied replacements in case fishing is good and the leaders are taking a beating. With wire line, be sure that there are no kinks in the wire to cause weak spots and that your haywire twists are sound.

Closely examine your rods regularly. Check the guides for signs of grooving, corrosion or wear. In the case of Fuji style ceramic or aluminum oxide guides, check them for damage because they can chip or crack from a sharp impact. If one is damaged, or if metal guides are grooved or worn, they must be replaced or they will wear your line and cost you fish. Most tackle shops can handle the job.

If your guides are showing corrosion around the bases, you can clean them with some soda, cola works best, and a tiny, soft wire brush. Check the reel seats, too. Before finishing, apply a light spray of WD40 or similar lubricant to help prevent a reoccurrence of the problem. I even spray the rod blanks to keep them looking new and shiny.

Your reels should be in good working order. Give them a going over and pay special attention to the drags. If the drags are not up to par, especially if you are fishing with relatively light tackle, then have them serviced and the drag washers replaced. After you've hooked a 30-pound bass on 12-pound test is no time to find out the drag isn't up to the challenge. Service your spinning reel drags yourself. Most can be smoothed by adding a few drops of light reel oil or WD40, but check the owner's manual before you do this to be sure it is compatible with the manufacturers instructions and the drag material used in the reel. While servicing conventional reels is beyond the capabilities of most fishermen, local tackle shops can handle the job if you can't.

Setting the drags on your reel should be accomplished with a scale. Rule of thumb is to set the drag to slip at approximately 1/3 the rated strength of the line. If you've got a reel loaded with 12-pound test, the drag should be set at about 4 pounds. That may not sound like much, but it generates a lot of pressure on a running fish. You can tire a large fish out with only 4 pounds of drag, but it might take some time. When fishing heavier line, you can exert greater drag pressure, tiring a fish all the faster.

The drag should be set with the line running through the rod's guides and the scale reading taken with the rod bent as if fighting a fish. To do this, attach the terminal end of the line to the scale leaving at least 6 feet of line between the rod tip and the scale, and pull back on the rod until the drag slips. Check the pounds of pull reading on the scale at the moment the drag slips and that will indicate your actual drag setting. The lighter the line used, the more critical the drag setting becomes since the allowable margin of error decreases with the pound test.

Use only the best terminal gear like swivels, snap, hooks and rigs, selected to match the line rating of the outfit you are using. Cheap terminal tackle is just asking for trouble. Then do a final check on the rest of the gear you'll need that day. Are the points on the gaffs sharp? Is there a good selection of lures and rigs in your jetty bag or tackle box for this time of year? Is your bait fresh and do you have an ample supply for the day's or evening's fishing? Run a complete mental check list and when everything checks out, you're ready to go. Now comes the end game, because you are going to catch bass.

## Playing the Fish

You're on the water, beach or jetty using the information you've acquired to find and tempt bass and success is sure to come. When you hook that first fish, playing it correctly presents the next great hurdle. Playing a bass differs with the style of fishing and the tackle you used to hook it. Here are a few tips that will help you get that fish in the boat or on the beach.

When employing spinning or plugging tackle, especially when you hook a sizable fish, keep as calm as possible. If the fish makes a hard charge up the beach, don't stand there with your feet planted like stone. Stay loose and mobile. Move, if necessary, to follow the fish past other anglers or to avoid being cut off on jetty rocks or obstructions. Mobility also holds true when fishing from a boat. If the boat is not at anchor, a wise skipper can use it to maneuver the angler into a position of advantage during the fight, but moving the boat should be done only when absolutely necessary and with an experienced hand at the wheel. An incorrect move by the man at the helm can cost you a fish as easily as it can help you win the battle.

When a fish makes a run, keep the rod tip high, so your line has a greater chance of clearing obstructions like shallow sand bars, rocks or mussel beds. Don't reel when the fish is taking line because you'll only twist the line and won't gain any back. During the run, hold on and let the fish go, adjusting your position if need be. You've got a lot of line on the reel, so don't sweat it. Use your tackle to advantage. Don't let the fish force you to make mistakes in haste or during the excitement of the moment, something that is easily said but hard for a newcomer to accomplish. Staying in control becomes much easier with experience.

Use the rod to work the fish, not the reel. Bring the fish to you by firmly lifting the rod and then dropping the rod tip as you reel in the line gained by the procedure. Don't drop the rod too quickly, creating slack in the line between the rod tip and the fish. Slack line gives the fish an opportunity to throw the hook.

Never tighten up on the drag as you work a fish closer to you near the end of the fight. If anything, slightly loosen the drag so the fish can't break it if it makes a final, strong lunge when it sees the boat or approaches the wash. If some extra drag is needed during the fight to coax a large fish up from below the boat or to bring it back over a bar, you can do this by cupping a spinning reel's spool with the hand that you use to turn the reel handle. If the fish lunges while you're cupping the spool, release the pressure immediately and let the fish run again.

Extra drag and lifting pressure can be exerted on a conventional reel by pressing the line to the foregrip of the rod with the thumb of your left hand (the hand holding the foregrip) when lifting, or, by laying the thumb of your right hand (the hand operating the reel handle) on the reel's spool and lifting with the rod. Again, if the fish lunges, release the line immediately and let the fish take line under normal drag pressure.

When playing fish with wire line, a different lift and drop procedure is necessary because it is much easier to generate slack in wire since it has no stretch acting like a shock absorber as is the case with monofilament. When playing a fish back to the boat with this tackle, use shorter, greatly abbreviated lifts and drops and be sure to reel in the slack as you drop the rod tip so no slack is created. Many charter captains will tell novice anglers who are unfamiliar with wire not to lift the rod at all, but to simply winch the fish in with the reel. This is hard work, a real strain on the arms and wrists. If the fish is big or if you have multiple fish on an umbrella rig, it can be painful and will tire even the strongest angler out in no time. Some people say charter skippers do this on purpose, to get the party tired so an early return to the dock is accomplished. The truth is, the skipper wants you to winch the fish in because you will lose fewer fish. If you're an inexperienced angler trying to pump and reel with wire, you'll probably lose more than you catch. It requires practice and even experienced anglers will lose an occasional fish when they become too exuberant with the pumping action.

# Getting Them Out of the Water

How you bring a bass into the boat or onto the beach will depend first on what your intentions are for the fish. If it is to be kept for the dinner table, the most effective manner of finishing the fight is with a gaff. A quick sweep with a sharp gaff, planted into the belly or near the head, will put an end to the fight and bring the fish into the boat or onto the beach or jetty. But gaffs are a final solution and offer no chance to change your mind should you decide to release the bass. Be sure the fish is of legal size and that this is the fish you want to keep before you stick it. Once the gaff penetrates the fish, it's a dead fish.

Gaffing a bass is simple enough when your gaffs are kept sharp and readily at hand. For boat fishermen, a 4 to 6-foot gaff with a 3 or 4-inch hook will serve well. Beach fishermen use short gaffs, usually less than 2 feet in length and jetty anglers use a variety of gaffs, some with fiberglass handles 7 to 10 feet in length to reach the water. Gaffing style differs from one angler to the next, but try to gaff the fish in an area away from the prime fillet meat. Don't gaff the fish in the shoulders or sides, if it can be avoided.

For boat fishermen, gaffing is easily accomplished by bringing the fish alongside the gunwale parallel to the boat's side. The gaff should be positioned under the fish with it outstretched enough so solid purchase can be made by the gaffer as he pulls it towards himself with a strong, hard yank. Try to gaff your fish from underneath, near the forward portion of the body, just behind the gills. Don't play around when it's time to sink the gaff. A single swift pull on the gaff handle should be all it takes to plant the hook and swing the fish in the boat.

But what if the fish is to be released, a situation that arises more often than keeping them in this day and age? Obviously, gaffing is out of the question. So alternative measures for boating and unhooking the fish become necessary and there are a few ways you can go. A beach fisherman can simply work a fish into the wash and let a wave deposit it on the sand. Don't kick the fish onto the beach, simply lead it into the shallows with your rod or by holding the shock leader in hand. If the fish shakes off before you beach it, it's no big deal because he was going back anyway.

Both boat or beach fishermen can employ a tailer, a device we discussed earlier. By snaring the bass' tail with this gaff replacement, you gain control of the fish and can bring it aboard or onto the beach for unhooking, and tagging, if you choice to do so. A net is used by many head boats that jig bass so the mate can bring fish aboard from the high decks and then release short fish, or fish caught by patrons who already have their limit.

If you are fishing from the surf or a private boat that allows you to reach down to the water, you can lip a striper in the same manner freshwater fishermen lip a largemouth bass. Stripers have no real teeth, just a sandpaper-like roughness which allows an angler to get a good grip on the fish's lower jaw. Lipping is not recommended if the bass has a mouth full of plug with multiple treble hooks, since a shake of its head can put one in your hand. But when fishing with single hook

**School are safely handled by "lipping" the lower jaw to immobilize the fish for easy hook removal.**

lures like diamond jigs, bucktails or trolling tubes, or if you are using bait rigs with single hooks, by all means lip the fish and lift it into the boat. It's easy on you and the fish.

Lipping is also not recommended if the fish are much over 20 pounds. While holding a bass by the lower jaw will usually quell any tendency to thrash about, this is not necessarily the case with bigger bass and trying to lift a big fish with a lip lock can be difficult, if not impossible.

Unlike the hunter who tracks his quarry with rifle or bow, a fisherman has the unprecedented ability to release his game after the fight is over, alive and free, back into its natural habitat. This is powerful, heady stuff and something that more and more fishermen that pursue and catch striped bass participate in. Try it and you will surely like catch and release. Don't get dragged into the trap of showing off dead fish to impress your friends to stroke your own ego. Nor is it your responsibility to feed the neighborhood with your catch when release is a much more fitting finale to a successful battle with such a magnificent creature. Keep a trophy or what fish you intend to consume, but never waste a striped bass.

Which brings you to a decision. You've got a bass that's an obvious keeper alongside the boat or in the wash at your feet. What are you going to do with it? Is it going to be allowed to swim free again, or is it coming home for dinner? Please understand that I have no problem with eating striped bass. I've enjoyed them for years and am thrilled to have a bass grace the dinner table from time to time. If eating the fish is your desire, by all means, keep the fish.

But, if the fish is short (undersized) legal size limit, or if you already have a limit in the box, then you must release it. Some of the most serious striper fishermen I know rarely kill any fish preferring to release them all regardless of bag or size limits. You do have another choice when release is the path and that is to tag the fish before releasing it.

Tagging is an interesting bonus when fishing for stripers under today's regulations and growing conservation ethic. Pete Barrett, of The Fisherman Magazine, calls tagging "adopting a fish," an analogy that I rather like. Unfortunately, you don't get to hear from your adopted offspring on a regular basis since recaptures of fish that have been tagged run about 5% on average. But it is of great interest to learn about the roamings of fish you have caught through tagging. When a recapture occurs, both the tagger and the angler reporting the recapture receive detailed reports from the tagging program managers.

The library of information gathered as a result of tagging efforts by state and federal government agencies that operate large scale programs, combined with the statistics gathered by independent organizations like the American Littoral Society, (ALS) whose members

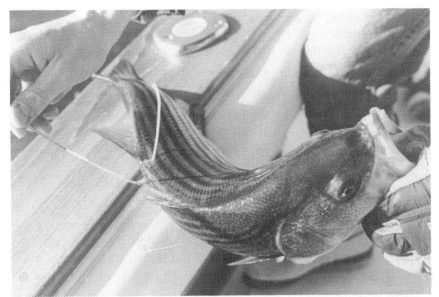

**Yellow spaghetti tag is placed in meaty portion on the back of the bass and does no harm to the fish. Scientific data gathered from tagging studies is essential to good management.**

operate their own, private and self-supported tagging programs, has helped increase the knowledge and understanding we have about the often confusing lifestyle of the striped bass. Becoming part of the study increases your appreciation and makes you part of the solution, rather than part of the problem.

What is tagging all about and how can a sport angler like you participate? Start out by becoming a member of an organization like the (ALS), which is headquartered in Sandy Hook Marine Labs, Highlands, NJ 07732 (908-291-0055). An individual membership costs $20 per year ($10 for students, $25 for an entire fishing club) and comes with a subscription to the society's quarterly magazine, "The Underwater Naturalist." Besides administering a comprehensive in-shore species tagging program boasting over a 150,000 member tagged fish in the past twenty-five years, the Society offers interesting naturalist weekends and extended study field trips. They are a unique organization and one worth joining.

The word littoral means "related to, situated or growing on or near a shore of the sea." The Society studies the littoral zone, or the areas where ocean and estuary waters meet the land, and the animals and plants that inhabit this strange and special place. For that reason, the goal of the tagging program is to study fish species that inhabit the littoral zone. Since striped bass are one of the predators at the top of the food chain and because they inhabit all regions of the littoral zone along most of the eastern seaboard of the United States, they are of prime interest to the study. In fact, member taggers are such fanatical striped bass fishermen that the vast majority of fish tagged under this program are stripers.

In addition to the ALS, some fishing clubs operate their own tagging programs, which can be laudable, but if the information doesn't go any further than the club, it is of little scientific value on the whole. For that reason, the ALS program is superior, because the information gathered by member taggers is shared through computer link with other major studies and with the National Marine Fisheries Service mainframe at Woodshole Oceanographic Institute in Woodshole, Massachusetts.

Members purchase tags from the ALS at a cost of $5 per package of ten with a tag needle used to insert them and instructions on their use. The Society charges for tags to keep the program self-supporting and program directors are proud of the fact that they have never needed government funding to run the tagging program since its inception in 1965.

The ALS uses "spaghetti tags", which are nothing more than a thin tube of bright yellow vinyl with a number and a return address to report the capture of fish sporting the tag. It is inserted into the fish with a special hollow needle. The tag slides into the needle and the needle is then passed through the flesh of the fish between the dorsal and tail fins, about 1 inch down from the top of the back. When tagging a bass, first use the tip of the needle to lift a scale at the correct location and then insert the needle into the flesh and push it through and out the other side. Pull the needle completely through and then slide it off the tag, which leaves the tag in place. Tie an overhand knot in the tag leaving plenty of slack so the fish can grow into it without it becoming too tight as the fish grows. Be sure not to tie the address or identification number into the knot or in the small wound created by the needle. Finish up clipping off any excess tag protruding from the knot.

The fish should then be measured from the tip of the nose to the fork of the tail, recording the measurements on the information card that accompanies each tag. Note the place of capture and the general condition of the fish. If you carry a hand scale, quickly weigh the fish and then gently return it to the water. This procedure can be streamlined if you take the time to set up a tagging station on the boat or beach before you begin fishing. Buggy fishermen can use the tailgate of their truck or the top of the cooler in the cooler rack. As an example, I use the seat cushion on the front of the center console of my boat. It is prepared by laying out a wet towel, a needle with tag in place is secured behind the cushion ready for use, and its matching numbered card and a pencil kept in the electronics box behind the steering wheel. A small, tape measure is also at the ready as well as a Chatillon scale to check the fish's weight.

When a fish is caught, it is promptly unhooked. During this procedure avoid putting your hands in the fish's gill plate for a grip. Try carrying bass by gripping the lower jaw and supporting the body weight by placing your other hand under its belly or grabbing it near the tail.

Lay the fish on the wet towel and drape the end over its head and eyes. This will have a calming effect on the fish, usually keeping it from thrashing about while the tagging procedure is carried out. Insert the tag, tie it off and clip the excess. Then take the fish's vital statistics and gently release it. Note the measurements on the card, the location of the catch and fill out the rest of the card when you get home. The entire procedure should take no more than a minute with just a little practice.

When tagging during the spring or summer when water temperatures are cool, bass can be handled and released easily without stressing them. When tagging during the summer months when water temperatures are high, bass should be handled quickly because they can suffer shock from the procedure more easily. Therefore, how you release your fish becomes more critical, so extra care is advised. After tagging, place the fish back in the water keeping a grip on the lower jaw and supporting its body weight with a hand under its belly or near its tail. If the fish begins to roll onto its side as you remove your supporting hand from under its body, then it will have to be revived. This is accomplished by holding the fish and moving it back and forth in the water, keeping its mouth open with the hand grasping its lower jaw. This movement will force water over its gills and increase the oxygen making its way into the fish's blood stream.

This procedure can take from a few seconds on some fish, to as long as five minutes or more on others. Larger fish seem to succumb to stress easier than smaller specimens in hot water, so give them time to revive and become reacclimated so survival is more probable. While actual figures are still being debated, it is believed that release mortality (the number of fish that die after being caught and released) is under 10% for stripers, not a bad figure when you consider how poorly many anglers handle and release fish.

Should you catch a tagged striped bass follow these steps: If it is under legal size or if you are going to release it anyway, measure the fish from the tip of the nose to the fork of the tail, then record the measurement, tag number and address on a piece of paper and release the fish. Then notify the tagging agency, whether it's the ALS or another program. If the fish is to be kept, you can do your measuring when you return home before cleaning it, but this time return the tag by mail to the tagging agency.

Some tagging programs offer rewards, like the one run by the Hudson River Foundation. They hold an annual drawing for people who return tag information and you can win from $5 to $5,000 for your efforts.

# Caring for Your Catch

When you keep a bass for the table, taking care of it is as simple as putting it on ice. Bass are a white-meat fish that do not benefit from being bled like tuna or bluefish. It is not necessary to head or gut them quickly, either. But, it is always a good idea to ice your catch as soon as you can, especially if you are fishing during the warmer months of the year. Any fish being kept for consumption will taste better if it is put on ice immediately, and bass are no exception.

If your boat does not have an insulated fish box built in, you should plan to have a cooler with ice on board. Even if it does, you should carry ample ice to chill your catch. Beach fishermen should keep a cooler with ice in their buggy or car trunk to handle this chore once a keeper is beached. Cleaning can be done at a later time, but it is recommended that the fish be filleted within 12 hours of the catch for the best eating quality. When we night fish and decide to keep a fish to eat, it is iced down at once, but often not filleted until after we get home and get some sleep. On occasion, that might be 8 or 10 hours or more after the fish was caught, but it doesn't seem to make a difference in the eating quality, as long as the fish is kept chilled and out of any water created by the melting ice.

You will also find that a fish that has been iced down is easier to fillet cleanly than one that is fresh from the water or one that has been allowed to lay about and get warm. The flesh lifts off the rack with less tearing and is far more firm to handle when chilled.

# Cleaning Your Catch

Most fishermen who eat bass, fillet them for cooking rather than gutting and scaling them, but certain recipes call for stuffing or baking a whole bass. To prepare a whole bass for stuffing or baking, the fish will have to be eviscerated or gutted. Before you gut the fish, scale it with the back of a stiff knife, by scraping the fish from the tail forward, toward the head. A bass' scales are large and hard, and the job can be made easier by using a scaling tool, available at most tackle and bait shops.

Once the fish is scaled, use a sharp, stiff bladed knife to gut the fish.

**Make a slit behind the gills from top of fish to belly.**

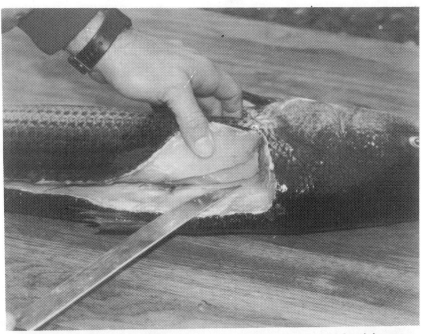

**Make cut along back top of fish, working the knife over the back bone.**

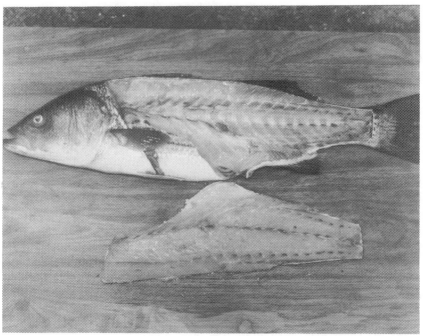

**Continue to cut down to the belly until fillet is cut free from the fish.**

**Lay skin side down, slide knife along skin to remove skin from fillet.**

**Cut fillet lengthwise into two parts.**

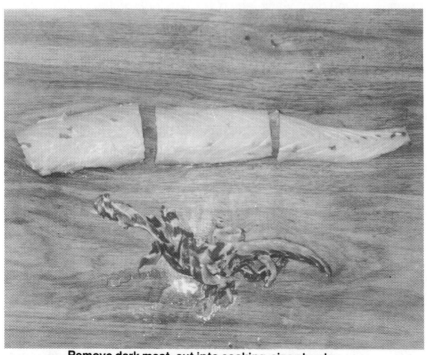

**Remove dark meat, cut into cooking-size chunks.**

Insert the tip of the blade into the fish's anal vent and cut forward to the gills, but try not to insert the knife too deeply into the body cavity or you will cut the internal organs and make a messy job all the more messy. Try to make your belly cut shallow, by only using the tip of the knifes blade, and when complete, open the body cavity and pull out all of the internal organs.

After cleaning a bass, it is a good idea to check the stomach contents to see what it has been chowing down on for future reference.

Moving forward, remove the gills by cutting their anchoring points at the top and bottom. Using the tip of the knife blade, run it down the spine, inside the body cavity, to remove the blood line that is found there. Once this cut is made, a spoon or your fingernail will make scraping out the blood line easier. Wash the fish thoroughly with fresh water and it's ready for baking or stuffing.

Filleting a bass is even easier, since no gutting or scaling is necessary and most of the best striper recipes use fillets. Since the average bass kept for consumption is usually close to 3 feet long, a large fillet knife with a relatively stiff blade is a must. Save the little 6-inch, flexible bladed knives for flounder. Get a 9-inch blade. Some of the better serrated edged knives will also work well for filleting stripers.

Start by making an incision just behind the gills angled slightly forward, so you don't waste any of the fine meat just behind the head. Cut down to the rib cage. Make another cut from top to bottom just forward of the tail fin, slicing down to the bone. Then, using the tip portion of the blade, make a cut from the head to the tail, down the back, alongside of the dorsal fin. Use this incision to begin the filleting process, by carefully slicing from the back down with the knife blade angled to remove the meat from the bones.

Work the knife over and around the rib cage and upon reaching the bottom of the fish's side, cut through the skin as pictured. Repeat this procedure on the other side and you will have two fillets, with the skin on. Next step is to remove the skin by laying the fillet on a flat surface, skin side down, and starting at the tail, lay the knife between the skin and the flesh. Angle the knife slightly downward, so it peels the meat off the skin as you work it from back to front.

Once the fillet is skinned, flip it over and you will see the blood line. Remove the blood line by cutting the fillet in two pieces as shown and then carefully slicing the red meat away from the white. When completed, you will have two clean, white meat pieces from each fillet, which can be sectioned into serving size portions, if desired.

If you are cleaning a particularly large bass, here's a trick I use to make striped bass fillet mignon's. The meat of the upper back, located just behind the head, will be very thick. On a bass of 40 pounds, it can be four inches thick or more, which makes cooking a time consuming procedure. Try this simple technique for some interesting eating.

After filleting and skinning a large bass, cut off thickest section of fillet, which is the portion that was located above the rib cage. Then, using a sharp knife, cut that portion of fillet into steaks about 1½ inches thick. The resulting pieces will look like white fillet mignon and are amazingly tasty when broiled or grilled with just a little butter or oil.

You now have the final reward from your fishing experience; a dinner fit for a king, provided courtesy of the king of the surf.

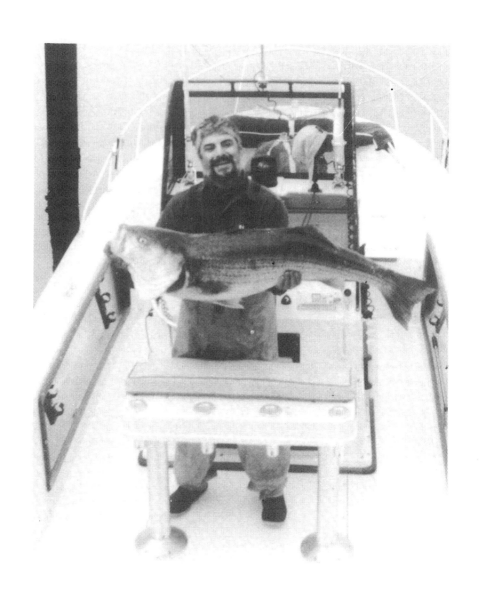

# ABOUT THE AUTHOR

Sport fishing is Gary Caputi's life and livelihood. At age 8, after saving money from odd jobs, his mother drove him to the headquarters of the Garcia Corporation a few miles from the family home in New Jersey where he proudly purchased his first spinning outfit, a venerable Mitchell 300 and a matching Conolon rod. He insisted on buying it at the Garcia company's home office, and the service manager, after much coaxing from mom, was kind enough to comply with the little boy's dream by accommodating the sale.

In 1972, as a business and marketing graduate of Fairleigh Dickinson University, his first job would take him back to Garcia, where he worked in the public relations department under well-known fisherman and writer, Dick Wolff. It was there he met Pete Barrett, who introduced him to striped bass fishing in the Hudson River, which began a life-long obsession with this great game fish.

He left Garcia to join the New Jersey Edition of The Fisherman magazine where he began his writing career with a comical story about the opening day of trout season. Since then he has published numerous feature-length stories in many local, regional and national fishing magazines.

Gary spent ten years as an independent sales representative for several fishing tackle companies, returned to ad sales for The Fisherman and then Fishing World. Throughout his career, he has maintained a deep love and a boundless affection for sport fishing and the marine environment.

His experience with striped bass ranges from the rivers of Maine to the beaches of North Carolina. He has chased stripers in ocean waters, estuaries and freshwater impoundments from beaches, rockpiles and boats, never losing his admiration and respect for the species. Today, he resides at the New Jersey shore with his wife, Jeannette and their daughter, Samantha. He frequently fishes for bass from his center console docked in the Manasquan River, or from the beaches and jetties that abound along his section of the striper coast.